C0-AUT-904

DISCARDED

PUBLIC DECISION-MAKING PROCESSES AND ASYMMETRY OF INFORMATION

PUBLIC DECISION-MAKING PROCESSES AND ASYMMETRY OF INFORMATION

edited by

Massimo Marrelli
University of Naples, Italy

and

Giacomo Pignataro
University of Catania, Italy

KLUWER ACADEMIC PUBLISHERS
Boston / Dordrecht / London

FLORIDA GULF COAST
UNIVERSITY LIBRARY

Distributors for North, Central and South America:
Kluwer Academic Publishers
101 Philip Drive
Assinippi Park
Norwell, Massachusetts 02061 USA
Telephone (781) 871-6600
Fax (781) 871-6528
E-Mail <kluwer@wkap.com>

Distributors for all other countries:
Kluwer Academic Publishers Group
Distribution Centre
Post Office Box 322
3300 AH Dordrecht, THE NETHERLANDS
Telephone 31 78 6392 392
Fax 31 78 6546 474
E-Mail <orderdept@wkap.nl>

 Electronic Services <http://www.wkap.nl>

Library of Congress Cataloging-in-Publication Data

Marelli, M.
   Public decision-making processes and asymmetry of information
/ edited by Massimo Marrelli and Giacomo Pignataro.
        p. cm.
   Includes bibliographical references and index.
   ISBN 0-7923-7238-7 (alk. paper)
      1. Economic policy--Decision making. 2. Information theory in economics.
3. Pressure groups. 4. Trade regulations. I. Pignataro, Giacomo. II. Title.

HD87 .P825 2001
338.9'001'156--dc21

                                                                00-048689

Copyright © 2001 by Kluwer Academic Publishers.

All rights reserved. No part of this publication may be reproduced, stored in a
retrieval system or transmitted in any form or by any means, mechanical, photo-
copying, recording, or otherwise, without the prior written permission of the
publisher, Kluwer Academic Publishers, 101 Philip Drive, Assinippi Park, Norwell,
Massachusetts 02061

Printed on acid-free paper.

Printed in the United States of America

FLORIDA GULF COAST
UNIVERSITY LIBRARY

Contents

Preface

The problems arising from the existence of asymmetric information in public decision making have been widely explored by economists. Most of the traditional analysis of public sector activities has been reviewed to take account of the possible distortions arising from an asymmetric distribution of relevant information among the actors of the public decision-making process. A normative approach has been developed to design incentive schemes which tackle adverse selection and moral hazard problems within public organisations: our understanding of these problems is now much better, and some of the mechanisms designed have had important practical implications. While this analysis is still under way in many fields of public economics, as the papers by Jones and Zanola, and Trimarchi witness, a debate is ongoing on the possible theoretical limitations of this approach and on its actual relevance for public sector activities. This book encompasses different contributions to these issues, on both theoretical and practical areas, which were firstly presented at a conference in Catania.

The innermost problem in the current discussion arises from the fact that this normative analysis is firmly rooted in the complete contracting framework, with the consequence that, despite the analytical complexities of most models, their results rely on very simplified assumptions. Most complexities of the organisation of public sector, and more generally, of writing "contracts", are therefore swept away. Once the need for an incomplete contracting approach is recognised, the question becomes how to relax some of the assumptions characterising the complete contracting framework, without getting *ad hoc* results. This general theme is dealt with in the Introduction to this book, written by Jean Jacques Laffont, which sets the general grid to interpret the position of its papers in this debate. The starting point of Laffont's analysis is the set of inherent assumptions of the complete contracting paradigm. The relaxation of some of these assumption may contribute to focus on observed characteristics of public decision-making processes like: existence of constraints on commitment, favouritism, collusion in multi-agent structures, multiprincipal governing structures, incompleteness of constitutional control. He therefore recalls some contributions that can be organised along these different strands, looking at four basic policy questions, regulation of natural monopolies, procurement and auctions, provision of public goods, and economics of the environment. In his partial coverage of the incomplete contracting world, Laffont stresses the difficulties and the risk of a line of research which derives implications that may look *ad hoc*. In Laffont's words, "a useful guide but no panacea is to take as given the implications which are embodied in some realistic institutions (such as multiprincipal structure) rather than specifying too directly which variables are supposedly non contractible as the incomplete contract approach relying on non verifiability assumptions has been doing".

The four papers in Part 1 of the book are devoted to develop the analysis of some of the theoretical issues mentioned in the Introduction. The first two papers deal with one of the features characterising incomplete contracting, that is the multiprincipal nature of government and the complex nature of the political system. In their paper, Marrelli and Stroffolini, analyse how constitutional rules can be devised to reduce the inefficiencies of the political system due to the impossibility of discriminate consumers/voters through taxes. If the politician/regulator is not a benevolent one, do these inefficiencies inevitably lead to a retreat of public sector from intervention in the economy? Focusing on the case of regulation of firms, they study how the requirement of qualified majorities for granting discretionary power of regulation will reduce the expected welfare loss due to political inefficiency. They show that the introduction of qualified majorities can be seen as a constitutional devise to reduce the stake of capture and can also reduce the distortions caused by collusion between the regulatory agency and the firm.

Another important, but often neglected, issue concerns the characteristics of lobbying in a multistage organisation of policy-making. In principle, when the policy making process results from the interaction of different agents with some degree of authority, several opportunities for lobbying exist. Therefore, the overall influence of an interest group on the decision making process depends on the relative influence of that group at each tier of decision and on the hierarchical relationship linking those decisional levels. In his paper, Mazza presents some recent models of multi-tiered lobbying and highlights the novelties conveyed by this approach with respect to the traditional models of interest groups and regulatory capture. First, it is shown that interest groups play an important role in shaping the horizontal and vertical relationships within organisations. Second, the multi-tier approach to lobbying indicates that legislatorial oversight (delegation) can be endogenously induced by the influencing activities of lobbies. Third, competition for rents among interest groups extends across stages: a group with uneasy access to one stage of the organisation may prefer to shift lobbying investments to another, more favourable, stage.

The complex nature of public decision-making processes relies not only on its multiprincipal features, but also on the existence of multi-agent structures and in the consequent possibility of collusion. The remaining two papers of Part 1 deal with this problem. Lapecorella studies the incentive problem faced by a regulator who controls only one of two privately informed firms belonging to a monopolistic industry and relies on this firm for provision of correct incentives to the other. This issue is particularly relevant for those multi-product monopolistic industries, in which different firms are organised as hierarchies with one firm controlling the activity of the others, and has important policy implications. The paper presents the regulator's problem of designing effective incentives for the firm that is directly controlled, and the form of the optimal mechanism that prevents this firm from using strategically its private information as well as its contracting opportunities is derived. This incentive scheme is then compared with that designed to control each firm directly.

The multi-agent perspective is relevant not only to analyse those processes, which involve the control of different agent, but also when the internal organisation of each agent is considered. The theory of regulation has usually regarded firms as "black boxes", identifying them with their managers. In his paper, Pignataro looks at the existence of a workers' union within a firm, regulated in its output market, and considers the case of wage bargaining. The basic questions addressed in the paper are connected with the effects of regulation on wage bargaining and with the way the agreement between the firm and the union interferes with the firm's behaviour in the regulatory relationship. First, a specific control problem for the regulator is highlighted: even if the regulator is able to restrain the firm's monopoly power completely, union can extract other rents. Second, the existence of a union is a problem for the regulator for two reasons: it captures a share of the firm's informational rents and it also interferes with the strategic behaviour of the firm with respect to the regulatory scheme.

The complete contracting framework of the normative treatment of public decision-making processes with asymmetry of information raises not only some doubts on theoretical grounds but also on the practical implementability of its theoretical results. Part 2 of the book is therefore devoted to discuss the applications of the theory to different public sector activities. The first paper in the second part, by Waterson and Vagliasindi, is about the UK experience in the regulation of firms. They contrast the analytical sophistication in the design of regulatory schemes in theory, with the creation of *ad hoc* schemes in practice. Whilst the "simplicity requirement" explains the use of *ad hoc* frameworks, one can also note the dangers of the often observed absence of a clear conceptual base. This leads the authors to consider the main theoretical issues and the problems in their implementation. They first describe price regulation as practised in the UK, focusing on changes in the light of experience and interpretation in terms of simple models. Then they cover the structural issues in more details, including matters concerning the identification of natural monopoly and competitive issues. Finally, they move to some less-often aired questions of the nature of procedure and of type of agency in regulation.

Price regulation of firms, however, is not the only field for which theory claims its relevance: procurement is undoubtedly another one. In her paper, Rizzo reviews the relevance of most theoretical models on procurement and their recommendations on the importance of competition, in the light of the European Union experience. A widely debated issue is that, notwithstanding the extensive European legislation to open-up public markets, such an effort has not been successful. A common feature of EU member states' purchasing policies still seems to be that of favouring domestic suppliers. Theory and practice are compared in the paper, to argue that too much emphasis is put on competition, in theory, while, in practice, its role seems to be more controversial. The main argument emerging from the analysis is that heavy regulation in procurement, aimed at ensuring competition anyway, might not necessarily be effective in a domestic as well as European context.

As Laffont writes in the introduction to this book, "a systematic analysis of policy issues from [this] normative point of view which takes into account the decentralisation of information and the strategic behaviour of economic agents is under way and not quite achieved yet, even in the simplest frameworks, in areas such as health economics or environmental economics". We could also add cultural economics. The last two papers in Part 2 present the normative analysis of public sector activities in the area of health and cultural goods. Jones and Zanola survey different applications of agency models to health care provision. Possible agency relationships are identified and analysed, involving several economic actors: 1) the state, which encompasses politicians and administrators; 2) the general public in their role as both citizens and patients; 3) providers of insurance; purchasing agencies, such as GP fund holders and DHA in the UK; providers of health services. The introduction of third party payers, whether they be public or private insurers, brings about an agency relationship between insurers and insurees; consumers may not reveal their risk status and they do not have an incentive to minimise medical costs. In most systems the purchasing of health care is in the hands of third parties such as private insurers, sickness funds or DHA and GP fund holders. Here there is an agency problem when the government, as regulator, attempts to ensure that purchasers behave in the public interest. Another set of agency relationships involves the third party payer or purchaser as principal and the providers as agents. Agency relationships also occur within the internal organisation of hospitals and between government and citizens.

The paper by Trimarchi deals with the interaction between the public and the private sectors in financing producers selling goods with an informational content like education and the arts. Generally produced by non-profit institutions, such goods are characterised by different components, which often entail a trade-off. The non-profit institution producing information goods operates as the common agent of two principals, a public agency or department and a private firm, both uninformed about the agent's true type. If the principals do not act co-operatively, the agent is induced to misreport his own type and incentives fail. Principals find themselves in a dilemma, since each of them prefers the other to bear the wider proportion of the financial burden while he expects the agent to produce goods with a prevalence of his preferred characteristic. A solution is proposed in order to overcome adverse selection and it consists in principals separating the form of their support, with the public sector giving in-kind subsidies and the private sector giving monetary contributions to the non-profit.

The presentation of the papers in Catania was followed by a very lively discussion. Even if it is not possible to present this discussion within the boundaries of a book, the authors agreed to revise their papers in the light of the comments received.

Massimo Marrelli and Giacomo Pignataro

Acknowledgements

The editors wish to acknowledge with gratitude the contributions from the Italian Ministry for University and Scientific Research 40% for the research project "Asymmetries of Information and Public Decision-Making Processes", and from the Italian National Council of Research (grant No. AI95.00174.10).

Contributors

Andrew Jones: Professor of Economics, University of York.

Jean-Jacques Laffont: Professor of Economics, Gremaq and IDEI, Toulouse.

Fabrizia Lapecorella: Professor of Public Finance, University of Bari.

Massimo Marrelli: Professor of Public Finance, University of Napoli "Federico II".

Isidoro Mazza: Research Fellow in Public Finance, University of Catania.

Giacomo Pignataro: Professor of Public Finance, University of Catania.

Ilde Rizzo: Professor of Public Finance, University of Catania.

Francesca Stroffolini: Professor of Public Finance, University of Napoli "Federico II".

Michele Trimarchi: Professor of Public Finance, University of Catanzaro.

Maria Vagliasindi: European Bank for Reconstruction and Development, Chief Economist's Office.

Michael Waterson: Professor of Economics, University of Warwick.

Roberto Zanola: Research Fellow in Public Finance, University of Torino.

Introduction

THE ECONOMICS OF INFORMATION AND PUBLIC POLICY

Jean-Jacques Laffont
GREMAQ and IDEI, France.

1.   INTRODUCTION

Until recently public policy was designed by economists within the paradigm of an informed benevolent social maximiser. A lot of interesting insights have been derived from this approach, such as the role of Pigovian taxes to internalise externalities, the need for the Samuelson conditions to optimise the allocation of public goods, the insufficient power of linear taxes for dealing with the control of non convex technologies such as monopolies etc.

This approach led to a view of public policy which was clearly too optimistic. The need for taking into account the informational barriers to public intervention has revolutionised public economics in the last twenty years. The normative approach has been extended, through the mechanism design literature, to a world where the benevolent social optimiser is constrained by incentive compatibility conditions. Many new insights have been derived from this literature, around the nature of the distortions in the allocation of resources due to incentive constraints. Generally speaking, it appeared that private information is a source of private rents, which are costly to the social decision maker. The latter must then design rules which trade off the distribution of costly rents and inefficiencies in the allocation of resources.

A systematic analysis of policy issues from this normative point of view which takes into account the decentralisation of information and the strategic behaviour of economic agents is under way and not quite achieved yet, even in the simplest frameworks, in areas such as health economics or environmental economics.

This new normative approach has been carried out in a complete contracting framework which presumes in general no cost due to the complexity of contracts, no difficulty in committing to the indefinite future, no collusive behaviour of agents, available benevolent judges, no cost of communication etc. Once these irrealistic assumptions are relaxed, we enter the complex and still little explored world of public policy with incomplete contracts.

In this brief overview of the literature we will deal with four public policy questions, regulation of natural monopolies, procurement and auctions, provision of public goods and economics of the environment.

We will examine these four fields through the following filter in seven steps.

Step 1 will discuss the general normative mechanism design approach of the problem. Step 2 will inquire into the implementation of the optimal schemes and the comparison of institutions they permit. Then, we will cover partially the incomplete contract world by considering successively, in step 3 the commitment issue, in step 4 the favouritism question, in step 5 the problems of collusion, in step 6 the multiprincipal designs and in step 7 the political economy considerations. Finally, in a last section we will relate the papers of this conference to this grid of analysis.

2.   THE MECHANISM DESIGN APPROACH OF PUBLIC POLICY

With the work of Loeb and Magat (1979) and Baron and Myerson (1982), it was recognised that the essential problem of regulation for natural monopolies stems from the asymmetric information between the regulator and the monopoly, in particular with respect to the monopoly's cost function.

The problem was then formalised as a principal-agent problem, where the principal is the regulator and the agent is the firm. From the revelation principle we know that any type of regulation is equivalent to a revelation mechanism. This revelation mechanism is designed to elicit truthful revelation of the firm's private information by committing to a well defined use of this information, here a quantity of good to be produced and a monetary transfer from the regulator to the firm.

The first step of the analysis is to characterise the set of revelation mechanisms or the incentive constraints, which are additional constraints on the allocation of resources due to the decentralisation of information. In other words the set of incentive compatible feasible allocations is then defined. It characterises what is achievable when the incentives of actors are taken into account. In the Baron-Myerson model for example these constraints specify that production must be a non increasing function of the (unknown to the regulator) marginal cost and a transfer which, up to a constraint, is totally determined from the non increasing profile of production that one wishes to implement.

The second step of the normative analysis is then to optimise expected social welfare in the set of incentive compatible feasible allocations to determine the optimal revelation mechanism. Baron and Myerson (1982) shows that production must be decreased (or price must be increased) relatively to the full information level in order to decrease the informational rent captured by the firm. Pricing at marginal cost is not optimal any more. Alternatively, one must include now the informational cost in the cost of production. Laffont and Tirole (1986) generalises the model by assuming a double asymmetry of information (adverse selection cost parameter and moral hazard effort variable which decreases cost) and assuming also the (eventually noisy) observation of cost. This model is technically an adverse selection model, but is better adapted to regulation, which makes a heavy use of cost observability. A main conclusion of the work is that optimal mechanisms are somewhere between fixed price contracts and cost plus contracts, and pricing need not necessarily be distorted from marginal cost or Ramsey pricing.

It would be useful to extend the analysis to risk averse firms to take into account simultaneously risk sharing, moral hazard and adverse selection, but the optimisation of this problem is very complex and little is known (see McAfee and McMillan (1987) for the restriction to linear contracts and Laffont and Rochet (1998) for the case of non noisy cost observation).

Even though regulation can be also ex ante designed with auctions (Demsetz (1968)), it is rather in the domain of procurement that an extensive use of auctions is made. A procurement problem is a principal multi-agent problem, in which the principal attempts to use competition between agents to reduce the informational rent he must give up. Agents are assumed to behave in a Bayesian Nash non cooperative fashion.

Myerson (1981) characterised the optimal auctions for a seller of an indivisible commodity in the independent private value model of Vickrey. As soon as the agents' characteristics are correlated, the principal can generically design mechanisms which extract all the informational rents (Crémer and McLean (1988)). However, this result relies strongly on risk neutrality and the absence of limited liability constraints and of course on agents' Nash behaviour. Laffont and Tirole (1987) extend Myerson's analysis to the case of auctions of contracts. Recent work along these lines includes Branco (1995).

The provision of public goods has been a pioneered field for the development of a mechanism design approach to public policy. The first line of work (Groves (1973), Green and Laffont (1979a), Aspremont and Gérard-Varet (1979)) concentrated on the mechanisms implementing the first best Pareto optimal public good decision. Green and Laffont (1977) showed that such mechanisms could not be balanced and Aspremont and Gérard-Varet (1979) exhibited balanced mechanisms by weakening the incentive property from dominant strategy implementation to Bayesian Nash implementation. However, individual rationality was not obtained by these mechanisms.

Rob (1989) and Mailath and Postlewaite (1990) showed that little can be achieved under the individual rationality constraint when the number of agents becomes large. However, as argued in Green and Laffont (1979a) a weaker concept of ex ante individual rationality seems desirable here.

Laffont and Maskin (1979) (1980) have extended the characterisation of dominant strategy mechanisms and Bayesian Nash mechanisms without the restriction to a first best Pareto optimal choice of public goods, but no clear characterisation exists when individual rationality is taken into account, even if the optimisation problem shows that efficiency will have to be given up.

It was early recognised that the environmental policy problem is close to a public good problem (Dasgupta-Hammond-Maskin (1980)), but it is only recently that the mechanics of mechanism design has started being applied in this field (Baron (1985), Laffont (1995a), Laffont and Tirole (1996)). The problem is a combination of a regulation problem with a public good problem, since typically pollution is a public bad and a by-product of a production activity. The mechanism design approach will be useful to clarify the rather obscure debates on the choice of policy instruments that proliferate in this literature (see Boyer and Laffont (1999)).

3.   IMPLEMENTATION AND EVALUATION OF POLICIES

Once an optimal revelation mechanism has been obtained, the question of its implementation with particular institutions must be raised. It can also be compared with existing institutions to evaluate their performance.

For example, in regulation, the optimal mechanism is equivalent to a non-linear transfer function of the quantity produced, which is either convex or concave, i.e., exhibits either discounts with quantity or an increasing marginal price. Under some particular conditions, Laffont and Tirole (1986) show that the optimal mechanism which is, there, equivalent to a non linear transfer function of observed cost can be replaced by a family of linear cost reimbursement rules within which firms self-select themselves (Picard

(1987), extend the analysis to quadratic reimbursement rules). It is often the case that only a few options are offered instead of a continuum and the loss induced can be evaluated (see Wilson (1993) for some example of such an analysis for the optimal price of a monopolist; see Gasmi et al. (1994) for a comparison of policies through simulations).

In auction theory, the first price auction as well as the second price (Vickrey (1961)) auction with appropriate reserve prices are optimal, i.e., implement the optimal revelation mechanisms for the seller. When risk aversion is introduced, the first price auction becomes better than the second price auction, but neither one is optimal (Holt (1980), Maskin and Riley (1984)).

Implementation in the provision of public goods is usually done with voting mechanisms, i.e. mechanisms without transfers. With single peaked preference, majority voting has excellent incentive properties (dominant strategy) and has good efficiency properties when the median voter is not far from the average voter. Moulin (1980) has shown that the only nonmanipulable social choice functions are those with positional dictators. Recall, that in this framework monetary transfers are not available for compensatory payments.

Recently, the literature has reconsidered the problem in the much easier and less interesting case of complete information between agents (Varian (1994), Jackson and Moulin (1992)) or by extending the concept of subscription equilibrium to the Klemperer and Meyer (1989) or Bernheim and Whinston (1986) supply function equilibria (see Laussel and Le Breton (1995)). The difficulty in this last line of research is the enormous set of equilibria with no really convincing selection criterion available. Some equilibria are Pareto optimal with quasi-linear utility functions. The intuition is that, by committing to a non linear subscription function, a consumer commits to cofinance increases of public goods generated by others. For appropriate beliefs about these co-financings, Pareto optimality can be achieved.

In the economics of environment, Laffont (1995a) shows how in some cases the optimal mechanism for a polluting monopolist can be implemented by the combination of a non linear production subsidy, a non linear pollution tax and a non linear transfer, all functions of the observed cost.

4.   THE NEED FOR AN INCOMPLETE CONTRACT APPROACH

A major implication of the complete contract approach is the superiority of a centralised organisation of the economy, in which all the information flows up to the Centre through incentive compatible mechanisms before commands flow back to the agents. This result contradicts the common sense observation of the relevance of a more decentralised organisation for the economic activities, either at the level of the whole economy, or at the level of organisations such as firms or governments.

Many implicit assumptions lie behind the revelation principle of the complete contract approach in a world of decentralised information. I will stress a few.

The first one is the unbounded rationality of agents and the zero costs of communication, which put no limits on the complexity of contracts. The second one is the availability of benevolent fully rational judges who can enforce all contracts. The third one is the postulated non-cooperative behaviour of the agents, which can be interpreted in various ways such as the ability of the principal to control communication channels between the agents.

Ideally one would like to develop public economics from the maximisation (at the constitutional level) of expected social welfare after relaxing the above assumptions. Each specification of bounded rationality or cost of communication, each constraint on contracts derived when deviating from the benevolence of judges' assumption or from non collusive behaviour will yield a particular public economics.

Economists have been reluctant to relax assumption two because of the lack of a surprising (but in my view momentary) lack of cynicism and to relax assumption three because they did not know how to proceed so far. Consequently various shortcuts have been used to develop some insights about this new world by positing directly implications of relaxing some of these assumptions.

For example, constraints on commitment such as short run commitment only, or renegotiations-proof commitment can be viewed as consequences of the needed simplicity of contracts and the lack of benevolent judges. Multiprincipal governing structures are similarly, either caused by the simplicity of contracts and the costs of communication, or desired because of collusive activities. The political economy of public economics can be viewed similarly as a consequence of the need for simple contracts at the constitutional level.

The future of public economics will be, as long as we are unable to relax the above assumptions in a fundamentalist way, to systematically derive the public economics responses to these derived implications which may look ad hoc to many of us. Probably, a useful guide but no panacea is to take as given the implications which are embodied in some realistic institutions (such as a multiprincipal structure) rather than specifying too directly which variables are supposedly non contractible as the incomplete contract approach relying on non verifiability assumptions has been doing. I do not to deny here the usefulness of this last approach in some cases (for example when some quality dimensions are not supposed verifiable at reasonable cost), but simply stress the lack of discipline and rigor that this line of research has generated.

In the next section, we will show how the literature can be organised along these principles and point out some unexplored areas.

5.   CONSTRAINTS ON COMMITMENT

So far the approach has assumed that principals can commit to mechanisms. This may be acceptable in static models or short periods but is clearly positively inadequate for the long term. Many different reasons explain this inability to commit of public decision makers. They are very much constrained by law and by the democratic rules, which allow a majority to change the rules.

Without asking here the fundamental reasons why commitment must be limited (see Laffont-Tirole 1993 Ch. 16), we can explore the implications for public policy of these limitations.

The literature has considered various types of constraints.

In the regulation context, Laffont and Tirole (1988) study the case where a regulator can commit to only one period in an adverse selection model with perfect correlation of types over time. The model exhibits the ratchet effect. In the first period, the agents hide partially their information, to protect their future rents. They know that, if they reveal completely their information, the principal will fully extract their informational rents in the future because he has not committed not to do it. Laffont and Tirole (1990) treat the case suggested by Dewatripont (1989) where the principal can commit, but not commit not to renegotiate. This realistic constraint on commitment, which is particularly appropriate for private contracts, leads also to pooling in the first periods, but is easier to analyse. Baron and Besanko (1987) simplify the analysis and avoid pooling by assuming that regulators can commit to be fair, i.e., not to use excessively the information they obtain. Finally, Gilbert and Newbery (1988) observe that in a repeated relationship with high discount factors regulators can develop reputations, which enable them to eliminate incentive constraints. The usual multiplicity of equilibria from folk theorems then holds.

Similar issues arise in sequential auctions when buyers are interested in buying several units of the commodities auctioned. In a remarkable paper, Ortega-Reichert (1968) was able to avoid pooling by assuming that buyers learn their willingnesses to pay period after period which are positively correlated over time. Suppressing this assumption, Hausch (1986), in a two-type model obtains mixed strategy equilibria. Waehrer (1992), examining a model of auctions followed by bargaining, makes the link with the ratchet effect of the regulation literature.

If we view the choice of an income tax schedule as the choice of a public good, Roberts (1983) can be interpreted as the pioneered paper discussing commitment in public policy. He showed that redistribution is very much limited by the ratchet effect, as taxpayers hide their true talents to avoid future heavy taxations.

Recently, Laffont and Tirole (1996) have studied the normative properties of markets for pollution rights with and without limits of regulators' ability to commit.

6.   FAVOURITISM

The rent seeking literature has focussed on favouritism issues for a long time. It is only recently that the economics of information and incentives has been introduced in these discussions. The main contribution of information economics is to provide a fundamental explanation of informational rents based on exogenous variables such as the distribution of information. Favouritism can then be viewed as an action which favours the rents of some agents.

It makes particular sense in hierarchical organisations where a principal must use an intermediary, supervisor-regulatory agency-etc, to control agents. Then, the intermediary may develop an informational advantage over the principal and use it to collude with some agents at the expense of the principal's objectives.

In a regulatory context, Laffont and Tirole (1991a) have studied how regulatory agencies may collude with the firm they regulate or with consumers' lobbies, and what should be the regulatory response to these activities. In particular, a weakening of the power of incentives which decreases the rents of asymmetric information is often valuable for the principal.

Laffont and Tirole (1991b) extends the approach to auctions where the organiser of an auction who has soft information on the quality of the offers may be tempted to favour particular bidders. The optimal response is either to provide appropriate incentives to the auctioneer or to prevent him from using his private information in the selection of projects, for example by imposing the choice of the less costly project.

7. COLLUSION

The analysis of collusion in multi-agent structures started in the analysis of the free rider problem for public goods.

Green and Laffont (1979a) showed that the Groves mechanism were not robust to coalitional behaviour, under the assumption that agents share costlessly their private information. This analysis was extended in Laffont and Maskin (1979) (1980) to more general mechanisms and to the Bayesian Nash implementation. Crémer (1996) introduced the limitation that colluders must design incentive compatible mechanisms between themselves with similar negative conclusions for Groves mechanisms.

The auction literature has been also particularly interested in the collusion problem both empirically and theoretically. Graham and Marshall (1987) study collusion both in sealed bid second price and English auctions. In particular, they show that an outside agent can implement efficient collusion by any subset of bidders by using a second-price pre-auction knockout. However, the scheme is ex ante balanced between bidders but not ex post balanced, hence the need for an active third party. McAfee and McMillan (1992) show that efficient collusion with ex post balanced side-payments is possible and easily implementable by an ex ante auction if the ring includes all the bidders. Mailath and Zemski (1991) relax the assumption that bidders are ex ante identical and show that ex post budget balancing efficient collusion in a second price-auction is possible, even among a proper subset of agents. Caillaud and Jehiel (1994) show that in auctions with externalities efficient collusion may not be possible. The optimal response to these collusion activities has been only very partially explored by optimising on the reserve price.

Laffont and Martimort (1997) develop a truly second best theory of collusion proof mechanisms under asymmetric information between colluders in a regulatory context. This general approach can be extended to all public policy problems. This approach enables us to understand why collusion constraints play a role similar to other types of constraints on the available mechanisms, such as renegotiation-proof constraints and put the analysis in the incomplete contracting domain (in particular pooling may occur as an endogenous phenomenon).

8.   MULTIPRINCIPALS

It is often the case that a particular agent is controlled by several principals. In the public policy domain, it reflects an incomplete contracting feature which leads for example to the dual regulation by the Ministry of Industry and the Ministry of Environment (see for example Baron (1985)). Similarly, Laffont and Tirole (1991c) has analysed privatisation as a dual regulation of a firm by the regulator and its stockholders. In their model it leads to a weakening of incentives as, in a sense, multiprincipals free ride on the provision of incentives.

The general theory of multiprincipals in moral hazard or adverse selection models is being developed (see Bernheim and Whinston (1986), Martimort (1992), Stole (1990)) and much remains to be done in public policy to benefit from its insights.

9.   POLITICAL ECONOMY

In addition to the complete information assumption a major weakness of the traditional public policy is its reliance on the benevolent social decision maker.

Even when we recognise the private interest of politicians, this approach can be valid if complete contracting is available at the constitutional level and if we assume that the designers of the constitution wish to maximise expected social welfare. However, if we accept the last assumption, it is clear that constitutions are much too simple to provide a complete contract controlling politicians.

The incompleteness of this constitutional control gives a lot of discretion to politicians. The design of simple policy rules at the constitutional level becomes a trade-off between the desirable flexibility of policies with the undesirable discretion of politicians who have private agendas.

Laffont (1996, 1998) reconsiders public policy for regulation in this way. Boyer and Laffont (1999) follow this line of research for environmental policy. Grossman and Helpman (1994) stress similar phenomena in their analysis of tariff protection.

THIS VOLUME

The contribution of this book can be roughly classified between a set of papers which apply the complete contract approach to new fields and by various explorations of the incomplete contract paradigms (see Table 1).

Table 1

	Contributions		
Applications of the Complete Contract Approach	WATERSON and VAGLIASINDI	JONES and ZANOLA	RIZZO
Collusion and Delegation	LAPECORELLA	PIGNATARO	
Multiprincipals	MAZZA	MARRELLI and STROFFOLINI	
Political Economy	TRIMARCHI		

REFERENCES

Aspremont, C. d' and L.A. Gérard-Varet, 1979, "Incentives and Incomplete Information", *Journal of Public Economics, 11,* 25-45.

Baron, D. , 1985, "Regulation of Prices and Pollution under Incomplete Information", *Journal of Public Economics,* 28, 211-231.

Baron, D . and R. Myerson, 1982, "Regulating a Monopolist with Unknown Cost", *Econometrica,* 50, 911-930.

Baron, D. and D. Besanko, 1987, "Commitment and Fairness in a Dynamic Regulatory Relationship", *Review of Economic Studies,* 54, 413-436.

Bernhelm, D. and M. Whinston, 1986, "Common Agency", *Econometrica,* 54, 923-942.

Boyer, M. and J.J. Laffont, 1999, "Towards a Political Theory of the Emergence of Environmental Incentive Regulation", *Rand Journal of Economics,* 30 1, 137-157.

Branco, F., 1995, "Multi-Object Auctions: On the Use of Combinatorial Bids", DP 1216, CEPR.

Caillaud, B. and P. Jehiel, 1994, "Collusion in Auctions with Externalities", mimeo, CERAS.

Crémer, J., 1996, "Manipulations by Coalitions under Asymmetric Information: The Case of Groves Mechanisms", *Games and Economic Behaviour,* 13, 39-73.

Crémer, J. and R. McLean, 1988, "Full Extraction of the Surplus in Bayesian and Dominant Strategy Auctions", *Econometrica,* 56, 1247-1257.

Dasgupta, R, P. Hammond and E. Maskin, 1980, "A Note on Imperfect Information and Optimal Pollution Control" *Review of Economic Studies,* 47-857-8.

Demsetz, H., 1968, "Why Regulate Utilities", *Journal of Law and Economics,* 11, 55-65.

Dewatripont, M., 1989, "Renegotiation and Information Revelation Over Time in Optimal Labor Contracts", *Quarterly Journal of Economics,* 104, 589-620.

Gasmi, F., M. Ivaldi and J.J. Laffont, 1994, "Rent Extraction and Incentives for Efficiency in Recent Regulatory Proposals", *Journal of Regulatory Economics*, 6, 151-176.

Gilbert, R. and D. Newbery, 1988, "Regulation Games", WP 88-79, University of California, Berkeley.

Graham, D. and R. Marshall, 1987, "Collusive Bidder Behaviour at Single Object Second-Price and English Auctions", *Journal of Political Economy*, 95, 1217-39.

Green, J. and J.J. Laffont, 1977, "Characterization of Satisfactory Mechanisms for the Revelation of Preferences for Public Goods", *Econometrica*, 45, 427-438.

Green, J. and J.J. Laffont, 1979a, Incentives in Public Decision *Making*, Amsterdam , North Holland.

Green, J. and J.J. Laffont, 1979b, "On Coalition Incentive Compatibility", *Review of Economic Studies*, 46, 243-254.

Grossman, G. and H. Helpman, 1994, "Protection for Sale", *American Economic Review*, 84, 833-850.

Groves, T., 1973, "Incentives in Teams", *Econometrica*, 41, 617631.

Hausch, D., 1986, "Multi-Object Auctions: Sequential vs. Simultaneous Sales", *Management Science*, 32 12, 1599-1610.

Holt, C., 1980, "Competitive Bidding for Contracts under Alternative Auction Procedures", *Journal of Political Economy*, 88, 433-45.

Jackson, M. and M. Moulin, 1992, "Implementing a Public Project and Distributing its *Cost Journal of Economic Theory*, 57, 125-140.

Klemperer, P. and M. Meyer, 1989, "Supply Function Equilibria in Oligopoly under Uncertainty", *Econometrica*, 57, 12431278.

Laffont, J.J., 1995a, "Regulation of Pollution with Asymmetric Information", Chapter 2, in Dosi, C. and T. Tomasi, (eds.), *Nonpoint Source Pollution Regulation: Issues and Analysis*, Boston, Kluewer Academic Publishers.

Laffont, J.J., 1996, "Industrial Policy and Politics", *International Journal of Industrial Organization*, 14, 1-27.

Laffont, J.J., 1998, "Frish, Hotelling and the Marginal Cost Pricing Controversy", *Econometrics and Economic Theory in the 20th Century, The Ragnar Frisch Centennial Symposium*, ed. Steinar Strom, Cambridge University Press, 319-342.

Laffont, J.J. and D. Martimort, 1997, "Collusion under Asymmetric Information", *Econometrica*, 65 4, 875-911.

Laffont, J.J. and E. Maskin, 1979, "A Differentiable Approach to Expected Utility Maximizing Mechanisms", in Laffont, J.J. (ed.), *Aggregation and Revelation of Preferences*, Amsterdam, North-Holland.

Laffont, J.J. and E. Maskin, 1980, " A Differentiable Approach to Dominant Strategy Mechanisms", *Econometrica*, 48, 15071520.

Laffont, J.J. and J.C. Rochet, 1998, "Regulation of a Risk Averse Firm", *Games and Economic Behaviour*, 25, 149-173.

Laffont, J.J. and J. Tirole, 1986, "Using Cost Observation to Regulate Firms", *Journal of Political Economy*, 64, 614-641.

Laffont, J.J. and J. Tirole, 1987, "Auctioning Incentive Contracts", *Journal of Political Economy*, 95, 921-937.

Laffont, J.J. and J. Tirole, 1988, "The Dynamics of Incentive Contracts", *Econometrica*, 56, 1153-1175.

Laffont, J.J. and J. Tirole, 1990, "Adverse Selection and Renegotiation in Procurement ", *Review of Economic Studies*, 75, 597-626.

Laffont, J.J. and J. Tirole, 1991a, "The Politics of Government Decision Making: A Theory of Regulatory Capture", *Quarterly Journal of Economics*, 106, 1089-1127.

Laffont, J.J. and J. Tirole, 1991b, "Auction Design and Favouritism", *International Journal of Industrial Organization,* 9, 9-42.

Laffont, J.J. and J. Tirole, 1991c, "Privatization and Incentives", *Journal of Law, Economics and Organization,* 6, 1-32.

Laffont, J.J. and J. Tirole, 1993, *A Theory of Incentives in Procurement and Regulation,* Cambridge, MIT Press.

Laffont, J.J. and J. Tirole, 1996, "Pollution Permits and Compliance Strategies", *Journal of Public Economics,* 62, 85-125.

Loeb, M. and W. Magat, 1979, "A Decentralized Method of Utility Regulation", *Journal of Law and Economics,* 22, 399-404. 16

Laussel, D. and M. Le Breton, 1995, "Efficient Private Production of Public Goods under Common Agency", mimeo GREQAM.

Mailath, G. and A. Postlewaite, 1990, "Asymmetric Information Bargaining Problems with many Agents", *The Review of Economic Studies,* 57, 351-368.

Mailath, G. and P. Zemsky, 1991, "Collusion in Second Price Auctions with Heterogenous Bidders", *Games and Economic Behaviour,* 3, 467-486.

Martimort, D., 1992, "Multiprincipaux avec Anti-Sélection", *Annales d'Economie et Statistique,* 28, 1-37.

Maskin, E. and J. Riley, 1984, "Optimal Auctions with Risk Averse Buyers", *Econometrica,* 52, 1473-1518.

McAfee, P. and J. McMillan, 1987, *Incentives in Government Contracting,* Toronto, University of Toronto Press.

McAfee, P. and J. McMillan, 1992, "Bidding Rings", *American Economic Review,* 82, 579-599.

Moulin, H., 1980, "On Strategy Proofness and Single Peakedness", *Public Choice,* 35, 437-455.

Myerson, R., 1981, "Optimal Auction Design", *Mathematics of Operations Research,* 6, 58-63.

Ortega-Reichert, A., 1968, *Models for Competitive Bidding under Uncertainty,* Ph.D. Dissertation, Stanford University; Technical Report # 8, Operations Research Department.

Picard, P., 1987, "On the Design of Incentive Schemes under Moral Hazard and Adverse Selection", *Journal of Public Economics,* 33, 305-331.

Roberts, K., 1983, "Long Terms Contracts", mimeo, University of Warwick.

Rob, R., 1989, "Pollution Claims Settlements with Private Information", *Journal of Economic Theory,* 47, 307-333.

Stole, L., 1990, "Mechanism Design under Common Agency", mimeo, MIT.

Varian, H., 1994, "A Solution to the Problem of Externalities where Agents are Well Informed", *American Economic Review,* 84, 1278-1293.

Vickrey, W., 1961, "Counterspeculation, Auctions, and Sealed Tenders", *Journal of Finance,* 16, 8-37.

Waehrer, K., 1992, "The Dynamic Effect of Second Stage Bargaining on Competitive Bidding", mimeo.

Wilson, R., 1993, *Nonlinear Pricing,* Oxford, Oxford University Press.

PART 1

THEORY

Chapter 1

INDUSTRIAL POLICY, OPTIMAL MAJORITIES AND HOW THESE CAN PREVENT CAPTURE

Massimo Marrelli and Francesca Stroffolini[*]
University of Napoli "Federico II", Italy

1.   INTRODUCTION

In a recent paper J.J. Laffont (1996) tackled the problem of constructing a positive theory of regulation by "recognizing the uncontrollable nature of the political system in a fine tuning way" and derived "simple constitutional rules which" took "simultaneously into account the inefficiencies of the political system and informational asymmetries".

A similar approach can be found in macro-economics in Persson-Tabellini (1996) and Aghion-Bolton (1994), but is new in Industrial Organisation where the inefficiencies of the political system have effects just as large as those studied in macro-economic policy.

The theory of regulatory capture is, today, a strong argument in favour of less public intervention in the economy; from this point of view, the inherent inefficiency of the political system can be viewed as a form of political capture insofar as the majority maximises its objective function instead of social welfare. Constitutional rules are then needed to take account of this phenomenon. Many of these, examined in Laffont (1996), concern either the proprietary structure (e.g. public vs. private firms) or, more in general, the amount of discretionary power attributed to the regulator (the majority).

Other constitutional rules, however, can be devised; in particular, the requirement of qualified majorities for granting discretionary power of regulation could reduce the expected distortion of capture.

In this paper we intend to examine this problem.

Real world observations suggest that, when the stake is very high, discretionary power of intervention is granted to the government only if qualified majorities are reached; some good examples are, we believe, art. 73 and 79 of the German Fundamental Law (Constitution) which require a majority of 2/3 of voters to privatise some essential public services such as the Postal service, Telecommunications, and Railways, the Portuguese Constitution which requires the absolute majority of the all the *potential* voters for privatisation, and the Charter of the U.N. which requires a majority of 2/3 to pass the budget. Many examples are also to be found in commercial laws of different states: in the Italian law on jointly owned block of flats (condominium), for example, *investment improving expenditures* require the unanimity of the owners.

Regulatory instruments include cost reimbursement and pricing rules; both of them are examined in the paper.

If we consider the first set of instruments, once both informational and political inefficiencies are taken into account in the context of regulation of natural monopoly, it becomes evident how the rent-efficiency trade off is arbitrated at different levels according to the size of the majority and the ownership of the firm; in other words, in the case of public enterprise, where the rent is appropriated by whoever wins the elections, the majority induces effort levels which are higher than optimal and which induce higher rents: the distortion from optimality is higher the slimmer is the majority.

In the case of a private firms, which belongs to one of the groups, the model predicts over-effort if the owner group wins the election and under-effort if the other group wins. "A change of government from 'left' to 'right' (if we assume that right owns the monopoly) is likely to strengthen incentives in the firm, more specifically will lead to a change from a cost plus type of regulation towards fixed price or price cap regulation" (Laffont, 1996).

On the other hand, if we take into account pricing rules, we can examine the distortions of second degree price discrimination due to the inefficiency of the political system; in particular, Laffont shows that, when transfers are valued positively, price discrimination is higher (lower) than optimal when the low (high) valuation consumers have the majority. A testable implication is that the marginal price paid by the low valuation consumers is increasing in the size of their own majority (Laffont, 1996, Proposition 3).

Therefore, in both cases (cost-reimbursement and pricing rules) the distortions introduced by the inefficiency of the political system depend somehow on the size of the majority; a legitimate question to ask is then whether it is not possible to introduce at the constitutional level some decision rule which reduces the welfare loss. One such rule could be to have the decision based on a "qualified" majority: if such a majority is reached implement contract *A* otherwise implement contract *B*. This amounts to endogenising the size of the majority necessary to reach a decision and to couple it with the incentive power of the contract to be implemented.

The problem of finding the optimal majority is not new in the public choice literature: in 1962, Buchanan and Tullock tackled this problem by minimising the expected costs of decision. They assumed that these entailed two components: external costs" which captured the utility loss due to the fact that the decision could be reached without unanimity (and were, therefore, decreasing in the size of the majority) and the decision costs which represented those necessary to convince the voters (assumed to be increasing in the size of the majority).

In this paper, the problem of optimal majority has very different foundations: it attempts at minimising the distortions due to the inefficiency of the political system by introducing constitutional rules which reduce this inefficiency; the question of how implementable these rules are, remains, however, open. In particular, if it turns out to be that the optimal size of majority depends crucially on project dependent variables, the degree of flexibility of the optimal decision rule would be too high to be implemented (this amounts to not recognising the uncontrollable nature of the political system in a fine tuning way), while if this were not the case, then it would be possible to implement a sort of "constitutional built in flexibility" which supplies a set of couples $\{\mu, X\}$, where μ is the required majority and X is a vector of exogenous socio-economic variables.

The paper is organised as follows: in section 2 we present a sketch of Laffont's positive theory of regulation which constitutes the basis of our analysis; in sections 3 and 4 we respectively determine optimal majorities in the case of cost-reimbursement rules and second degree price discrimination for a public and a private firm; in section 5 we show how qualified majorities can prevent collusion between the agency and the firm, and, finally section 6 presents some conclusions and further areas of research.

2.   A POSITIVE THEORY OF REGULATION

In his paper, Laffont examines the question of industrial policy with respect to natural monopolies and shows how the political inefficiencies of a majority system affect the cost reimbursement rules and the incentives of the regulatory institutions. In particular, he examines the case of a single project which can be realised by a single firm and distinguishes between the case of a publicly owned and that of a private firm; in the first case ownership belongs to the group who wins the election, while, in the second, propriety is known a priori and does not change with the result of the election. The firm's cost function is

$$C = \beta - e$$

where β is an efficiency parameter (not known to the regulator and which can take only two possible values: $\overline{\beta}$ and $\underline{\beta}$) and e is management effort whose disutility, in monetary terms, is $\psi(e)$ with positive first and second derivatives.

The population of consumers is a continuum composed of two types, type 1 and type 2, who attribute respectively value S_1 and S_2 to the project, and α (resp. $1 - \alpha$) is the proportion of type 1 (type 2) in the population.

Consider the optimisation of expected social welfare at the stage when economic agents know their types (both consumers and the firm); expected social welfare is:

$$\alpha S_1 + (1 - \alpha)S_2 - (1 + \lambda)[v\underline{t} + (1 - v)\overline{t}] - \lambda(v\underline{U} + (1 - v)\overline{U})$$

with

$$\underline{U} \geq \overline{U} + \Phi(\overline{e}), \ \overline{U} \geq 0, \ \underline{t} = \underline{\beta} - \underline{e} + \psi(\underline{e}) + \underline{U}, \ \overline{t} = \overline{\beta} - \overline{e} + \psi(\overline{e}) + \overline{U}$$

where λ is the shadow cost of public funds, $t = \alpha t_1 + (1 - \alpha)t_2$ is the amount of transfers with t_i levied on type i consumers, $U = t - C - \psi(e)$ is the firm's utility, v is the probability of the firm to be of the efficient type and $\Phi(\overline{e}) = \psi(\overline{e}) - \psi(\overline{e} - \Delta\beta)$ is the rent to be granted to the efficient type.

Given that we have a continuum of consumers, incentive compatibility (for consumers) leads to uniform pricing of the project so that $t_1 = t_2$ and the maximisation program will yield:

$$\psi'(\underline{e}) = 1 \Leftrightarrow \underline{e} = e*$$

$$\psi'(\overline{e}) = 1 - \frac{\lambda}{1+\lambda} \frac{v}{1-v} \Phi'(\overline{e})$$

$$\overline{U} = 0 \tag{1}$$

$$\underline{U} = \overline{U} + \Phi(\overline{e})$$

$$\overline{t} = \overline{\beta} - \overline{e} + \psi(\overline{e})$$

$$\underline{t} = \underline{\beta} - e* + \psi(e*) + \Phi(\overline{e})$$

Do the project iff

$$\text{Min} \left\{ \begin{array}{c} \alpha S_1 + (1-\alpha)S_2 - (1+\lambda)[(\underline{\beta} - \underline{e} + \varphi(\underline{e}))] - \lambda v \Phi(\overline{e}) \\ \alpha S_1 + (1-\alpha)S_2 - (1+\lambda)[(\overline{\beta} - \overline{e} + \psi(\overline{e}))] \end{array} \right\} \geq 0$$

An informational rent is given up to the efficient firm; as it is socially costly because of the excess burden of taxation, a rent-efficiency trade-off leads to a lower effort level $(\overline{e} < e*)$ of the inefficient type.

Consider now what happens when there is first an election in which two candidates commit to govern in favour of type 1 and type 2 respectively; each consumer votes for the candidate representing his type so that, if $\alpha > 1/2$, the candidate of type 1 wins the elections and maximises type 1 consumers' welfare subject to incentive constraints (no discrimination between tax-payers and incentive constraints for the firm).

- If the natural monopoly is public, and the winners appropriate the firms rent, each candidate (say type 1) will maximise his objective function, i.e.:

$$\text{Max} \left\{ \alpha S_1 - (1+\lambda)\alpha[v\underline{t} + (1-v)\overline{t}] + v\underline{U} + (1-v)\overline{U} \right\}$$

under the same set of constraints as above.

Incentive compatibility for consumers prevents price discrimination and therefore saturation of type 2's individual rationality constraint; as type 1 majority wants to minimise transfers, the constraints will be binding and:

$$\overline{t} = \overline{\beta} - \overline{e} + \psi(\overline{e})$$

$$\underline{t} = \underline{\beta} - \underline{e} + \psi(\underline{e}) + \Phi(\overline{e}) \tag{2}$$

Substituting into the objective function and maximising with respect to $\bar{e}$ and $\underline{e}$ we get:

$$\psi'(\underline{e}_G) = 1$$

$$\psi'(\bar{e}_G) = 1 - \frac{v}{1-v} \frac{\lambda}{1+\lambda} \left[1 - \frac{1-\alpha}{\lambda\alpha} \right] \Phi'(\bar{e}_G) \tag{3}$$

where $\alpha \in [1/2, 1]$ and e_G is the equilibrium level of effort when the firm is publicly owned.

The rent of the firm, unlike in the case of the social welfare maximisation program, is now captured only by a fraction of the population while its cost it's spread equally over the whole population; therefore the majority induces a level of effort higher than optimal. If type 2 has the majority we would obtain a similar result with $(1 - \alpha)$ replacing α and $\alpha < 1/2$ in eq. (3). It is easy to check that $\bar{e}_G > \bar{e}$ for $\alpha < 1$ and that $\dfrac{d\bar{e}_G}{d\alpha} < 0$, hence:

"Under public ownership, incentives are affected by the size of the majorities, the distortions from optimality being higher when the majorities are slim" (Laffont, 1996).

- If the firm is private and owned by type 1 consumers, who have the majority, we obtain the same result as in the case of the publicly owned monopoly.

  If, on the contrary, the firm belongs to type 2 consumers and type 1 has the majority, the rent is now more costly to the majority and is therefore defined by a lower choice of effort, such that:

$$\psi'(\bar{e}_P^{-1}) = 1 - \frac{v}{1-v} \Phi'(\bar{e}_P^{-1}) \tag{4}$$

If the natural monopoly is not owned by the political majority, "the allocation selected by majority voting yields an incentive scheme less powerful than that called for by social optimisation" (Laffont, 1996).

3.   OPTIMAL MAJORITY AND REGULATION.

One important implication of Laffont's result is that, since expected distortion from optimality depends on the size of majority, it might be possible to maximise expected welfare by designing a constitutional rule which allows to implement the regulatory contract only if a certain size of majority is reached; the question to ask oneself is then what to do if that majority is not obtained. The constitutional rule therefore has to be constituted by a couple of policies $\{A, B\}$ and a cut-off point μ, such that policy A can be implemented if majority μ or higher is obtained, otherwise policy B is implemented.

One obvious candidate for policy B could be not to do the project. On the other hand, if we assume that the social value of the project is so high as to always justify its production, we could consider, as a benchmark case, a *cost plus* contract in which the power of the incentive scheme and rent are both zero.

Let $F(\alpha)$ be the cumulative distribution function of α, so that $[1 - F(\mu)](F(\mu))$ is the probability of the proportion of type 1 (resp. type 2) in the population being greater than μ.[1]

3.1   Public Firm

Assume the natural monopoly is public and policy B is a *cost plus* contract, then expected social welfare under this rule is:

$$W^G = \int_\mu^1 W(\alpha) f(\alpha) \, d\alpha + \int_0^{1-\mu} W(1-\alpha) f(\alpha) \, d\alpha + [F(\mu) - F(1-\mu)] W^{CP} \tag{5}$$

where $W(\alpha)$ is welfare when type 1 wins and requires the level of over-effort determined by eq. 3, $W(1 - \alpha)$ is welfare when type 2 wins and the level of effort is determined by eq. 3 with α replaced by $1 - \alpha$, and W^{CP} is *cost plus* welfare with $e = 0$.

Maximisation of (5) yields:

$$-W(\mu)[f(\mu) + f(1-\mu)] + W^{CP}[f(\mu) + f(1-\mu)] = 0 \tag{6}$$

Second order conditions $\left[-\dfrac{\partial W^G}{\partial \bar{e}_G}\dfrac{\partial \bar{e}_G}{\partial \mu}\left(f(\mu)+f(1-\mu)\right)<0\right]$ are

satisfied since both $\dfrac{\partial W^G}{\partial \bar{e}_G}$ and $\dfrac{\partial \bar{e}_G}{\partial \mu}<0$.

The meaning of (6) is obvious: optimal majority (μ^*) is such that the marginal cost of reducing the probability of implementing the incentive contract is equal to the marginal benefit of implementing the *cost plus* contract; indeed, $W(\mu^*) = W^{CP}$ or:

$$v\left[\psi(e^*)-e^*+\frac{\lambda}{1+\lambda}\Phi\!\left(\bar{e}_G(\mu^*)\right)\right]+(1-v)\left[\psi\left(\bar{e}_G(\mu^*)\right)-\bar{e}_G(\mu^*)\right]=0 \quad (7)$$

A qualified majority ($\mu^* > 1/2$) obtains iff $W(\mu)\big|_{\mu=1/2} < W^{CP}$. To see what this implies, consider that $W(\mu)\big|_{\mu=1/2} \lessgtr W^{CP}$ iff eq. (7) evaluated at $\mu = 1/2$ is greater or smaller than zero.

The economic intuition behind this result is that, if discretionary power of regulation is granted to the winners whichever the size of the majority, they will implement a high powered incentive scheme which requires the firm to exert over-effort and grant "excessive" rent which can be appropriated by them. Since the rent is socially costly, the over-effort causes a welfare loss which is higher the slimmer the majority. On the other hand the cost plus contract causes a welfare loss due to the fact that the cost of production is higher than the optimal one. A qualified majority exists if there is a range of $\mu > 1/2$, such that the welfare loss of implementing a cost plus contract is lower than the welfare loss of implementing the incentive contract.

Proposition 1. *A constitutional rule, which implements the incentive contract defined in (1) and (2) if the optimal majority of (3) is obtained or, if not, implements a cost plus contract, ensures a level of expected welfare greater or equal to the one obtained with a simple majority rule.*

Proof. Intuitive, if one thinks that the constitutional rule defined above, obtained by the maximisation of expected welfare, includes, as a corner solution, the simple majority case.

Notice that optimal majority does not depend on any project dependent variable (like, for example, $\alpha S_1 + (1 - \alpha)S_2$) and is only dependent on the characteristics of the firm (her disutility of effort) and the shadow cost of public funds. Notice, furthermore, that it does not depend on $F(\alpha)$, the homogeneity of the society, or in other words, the probability of obtaining the required majority.

Remark 1. *A simple comparative statics exercise shows that, if a qualified majority is required then:*

$$\frac{\partial \mu^*}{\partial \lambda} > 0$$

Qualified majorities are higher the higher the shadow cost of public funds: i.e. a more distortionary tax system requires that discretionary power of regulation be granted less frequently. The formal proof of this statement can be found in the appendix.

Not surprisingly, more distortionary tax systems require higher qualified majorities, the obvious reason being that the higher the excess burden of taxation, the higher the welfare cost of the rent, and therefore the greater the interval of $\alpha(1/2 < \alpha < \mu)$ where it is more convenient to implement a *cost plus* contract.

Consider now the case where policy B is "not to do the project"; assume that $S(0) = 0$, eq. (6) now becomes $W(\mu) = 0$, and necessary condition to obtain a qualified majority is $W(\mu)\big|_{\mu < \mu^*} < 0$.

This amounts to saying that the condition in eq. (1) for carrying on the project does not hold; the solution to the ex-ante optimal majority problem is equivalent to that of the maximisation program of expected welfare with a simple majority rule.

3.2   Private Firm

If the firm is private and belongs to type 1, expected social welfare (W^P) becomes:

$$\left\{ \int_\mu^1 W(\alpha) f(\alpha) d\alpha + F(1 - \mu)W^L \right\} + \left[F(\mu) - F(1 - \mu) \right] W^{CP} \qquad (8)$$

Where, W^L is welfare when the firm is owned by the type who does not have the majority, and, therefore, with effort level defined by (4).

Maximisation of (8) with respect to μ yields:

$$-W(\mu)f(\mu) - W^L f(1-\mu) + W^{CP}\big[f(\mu) + f(1-\mu)\big] = 0 \qquad (9)$$

Sufficient conditions for an interior solutions are *CDFC* (Convexity of the Distribution Function) and $W(\mu) > W^L$.[2]

From eqs. (9) and (6), it is easy to see that:

$$\mu^*_{priv} \gtrless \mu^*_{pub}$$

$$iff \qquad\qquad\qquad\qquad\qquad\qquad\qquad (10)$$

$$W(\mu) \gtrless W^L$$

which is the same condition for welfare superiority of public versus private firm in Laffont's paper.

We can summarise the above results in the following proposition

Proposition 2. *If the welfare level induced by the over-effort required by the owners of the firm winning the election is higher than the welfare level induced by the under-effort obtained if the winning group does not own the firm, optimal majority required by privatisation is always greater than the one required by a public firm. The converse is true.*

4.   OPTIMAL MAJORITY AND NON LINEAR PRICING.

Let's assume that the natural monopoly produces q units of a private good with the cost function $C = (\beta - e)q$.

Type 1 and 2 consumers derive utility $S(q_1)$ and $\theta S(q_2)$ from consuming respectively q_1 and q_2 units of the good, $\theta > 1$.

Let $(q_1, T_1), (q_2, T_2)$ be a non linear pricing rule, the socially optimal non linear pricing rule which maximises expected social welfare under incentive and individual rationality constraints is (Laffont, 1996):

$$\theta S'(q_2) = \beta - e$$

$$S'(q_1) = \frac{\beta - e}{1 - (\theta - 1)\dfrac{\lambda}{1 + \lambda}\dfrac{1 - \alpha}{\alpha}}$$

$$T_1 = S(q_1) \tag{11}$$

$$T_2 = S(q_1) + \theta[S(q_1) - S(q_2)]$$

$$\psi'(e) = \alpha q_1 + (1 - \alpha)q_2$$

If type 1 has the majority $(\alpha > 1/2)$ we obtain the same conditions as before with the only exception of the optimal quantity relative to group 1:

$$S'(q_1^{M1}) = \frac{\alpha(\beta - e)}{1 - \theta(1 - \alpha)}$$

While, if type 2 has the majority $(\alpha < 1/2)$, and $(1 + \lambda)(1 - \alpha) > 1$ (Laffont's normal case), this quantity will be:

$$S'(q_1^{M2}) = \frac{(\beta - e)}{1 + \dfrac{(\theta - 1)}{\alpha}\left(\alpha - \dfrac{\lambda}{1 + \lambda}\right)}$$

From the inspection of these condition, Laffont shows that the political system causes distortion from the optimal discriminating policies and, that, if the incentive constraints are binding in the same way in both cases of majorities "pricing discrimination is higher (lower) than optimal when the low (high) valuation consumers have the majority." (Laffont, 1996, Proposition 3).

An alternative constitutional policy could be to prevent second degree pricing discrimination and implement the optimal pooling pricing rule which maximises welfare; this rule yields:

$$T = S(q^{PP})$$

$$S'(q^{PP}) = \frac{\beta - e}{1 + \dfrac{(1 - \alpha)(\theta - 1)}{1 + \lambda}}$$

In our problem of optimal majority, the obvious candidate for contract B will then be the optimal pooling pricing rule, so that the constitutional rule will be: implement second degree pricing discrimination if optimal majority is obtained, if not, implement optimal pooling pricing rule.

Expected social welfare is:

$$w^{PD} = \int_{\mu}^{1} W^{M1}(\alpha)f(\alpha)d\alpha + \int_{0}^{1-\mu} W^{M2}(1-\alpha)f(\alpha)d\alpha + \int_{-\mu}^{\mu} W^{PP}(\alpha)f(\alpha)d\alpha$$

where W^{M1} and W^{M2} are welfare obtained with second degree price discrimination and type 1 and type 2 majorities respectively, and W^{PP} is welfare when pooling pricing is implemented.

Maximisation of the above expression yields:

$$-W^{M1}f(\mu) - W^{M2}f(1-\mu) + \left[f(\mu) + f(1-\mu)\right]W^{PP}(\mu) = 0 \qquad (12)$$

It can be checked that S.O.C. hold.

Proposition 3. *An optimal majority rule improves welfare with respect to a simple majority rule if λ is small; qualified majority will however be "close" to simple majority.*

Proof. Consider that for a qualified majority to exist, there must be some range of α where no discrimination is better than political discrimination. Consider, furthermore, that $\partial\mu^{*}/\partial\theta < 0$, then the proofs of propositions 4 and 5 of Laffont's paper,[3] prove our proposition.

5.   OPTIMAL MAJORITIES AND COLLUSION.

In the previous sections we have examined how the inefficiency of the political system gives rise to some sort of "political regulatory capture", in the sense that the regulatory outcome is the one that maximises the objective function of the group who wins the elections and not Social Welfare.

We have also shown how the introduction of a "qualified majority" requirement can reduce the welfare effects of "capture".

In this section we intend to analyse how the introduction of qualified majorities can reduce the welfare effects of collusion between a monitoring agency and the firm.

Assume that an independent agency has been created by the Constitution to monitor the firm; then notice that, if the firm belongs to the majority, this will appropriate all the rent and therefore it will be in its own interest not to use the information it might obtain on the firm's technology, i.e. it is not in its interest to implement the full information regulatory mechanism. In this sense the majority could alter the firm's rent by favouritism (political capture). Information could be of some use only to the majority who does not own the firm; but in this case there exists a stake of collusion between the firm and the regulatory agency.

Assume that the independent agency observes a signal $\sigma \in (0, \beta)$ with $\xi = prob(\sigma = \beta)$. If β is observed, it is hard information. The agency must receive a payment $s \geq 0$, giving utility s to the agency which, furthermore, has limited liability.

Assume the firm is private and belongs to type 1.[4]

Social welfare will depend on the type of majority and on whether the agency reveals truthfully the technological information; expected social welfare, if there is no collusion between the agency and the firm, is:

$$\xi W^{FI} + (1 - \xi)W^{AI}\left(\bar{e}_P^1\right) \text{ where } \bar{e}_P^1 = \bar{e}_G$$

with type 1 majority, and

$$\xi W^{FI} + (1 - \xi)W^{AI}\left(\bar{e}_P^2\right)$$

with type 2 majority, where W^{FI} (W^{AI}) stands for Welfare under Full Information (Asymmetric Information).

However, if the agency discovers $\beta = \underline{\beta}$ (with probability ξv), and we have a type 1 majority, there is no stake of collusion, while if type 2 wins the elections, then the firm pays a share δ (assumed $= 1$) of its rent to the agency to induce a report $r = 0$.

So with probability $1 - \xi + \xi v$ the government is uninformed and offers an incentive contract which induces a level of effort for the inefficient type

$$e = \hat{e} : \psi'(\hat{e}) = 1 - \frac{v}{1 - v} \frac{1}{1 - \xi} \Phi'(\hat{e}),$$ i.e. it offers a less powerful incentive

than the one in the absence of the agency.

Social welfare is then:

$$W_P^2 = W^{FI} - (1 - \xi)(1 - v)(1 + \lambda)\left[\left(\psi(\hat{e}) - \hat{e}\right) - \left(\psi(e^*) - e^*\right)\right] - \lambda v\Phi(\hat{e}) - \lambda_c \xi v\Phi(\hat{e})w$$

here $\lambda_c \xi v \Phi(\hat{e})$ are the transaction costs of the bribes from the firm to the agency.

While, when majority belongs to type 1, social welfare is:

$$W_P^1 = W^{FI} - (1-\xi)(1-v)(1+\lambda)\big[(\psi(\bar{e}_G)-\bar{e}_G)-(\psi(e^*)-e^*)\big] - \lambda(1-\xi)v\Phi(\bar{e}_G)$$

with $\bar{e}_G : \psi'(\bar{e}_G) = 1 - \dfrac{v}{1-v}\dfrac{\lambda}{1+\lambda}\left[1-\dfrac{1-\alpha}{\lambda\alpha}\right]\Phi'(\bar{e}_G)$.

An obvious instrument to take account of collusion is to provide collusion proof incentive payments according to the rule :

$$s = \frac{\Phi(\bar{e}_P^2)}{1+\lambda_c} \tag{13}$$

if the agency reveals β, where λ_c is the transaction cost of collusion.

Then, with majority 2, expected social welfare is:

$$W_P^3 = W^{FI} - (1-\xi)(1-v)(1+\lambda)[(\psi(\bar{e}_P^2)-\bar{e}_P^2)-(\psi(e^*)-e^*)] - \lambda(1-\xi)v\Phi(\bar{e}_P^2) - \lambda\xi v\frac{\Phi(\bar{e}_P^2)}{1+\lambda_c}$$

and

$$W_P^4 = W^{FI} - (1-\xi)(1-v)(1+\lambda)\big[(\psi(\bar{e}_G)-\bar{e}_G)-(\psi(e^*)-e^*)\big] - \lambda(1-\xi)v\Phi(\bar{e}_G) - \lambda\xi v\frac{\Phi(\bar{e}_P^2)}{1+\lambda_c}$$

with majority 1.

Therefore, setting up constitutionally incentives for the agency is valuable if:

$$W_P^3 + W_P^4 > W_P^1 + W_P^2$$

An alternative, and, in some cases, more efficient instrument would be to introduce a qualified majority rule. Such a constitutional rule can be used in two different ways: a) by coupling it with the organisational structure of an independent agency which monitors the firm and is granted collusion proof incentive payments, and b) by substituting it to the above mentioned organisation.

In the first case:

Proposition 4. *A constitutional rule of the type: "discretionary power of regulation is granted to the government if a majority of, at least, $\mu*$ is reached, otherwise a 'cost plus' contract is implemented", reduces (non strictly) the stake of collusion.*

The proof is intuitive , since qualified majority $\mu*$ which maximises expected welfare, implies that for an interval $1/2 \leq \alpha \leq \mu*$, a cost plus contract is implemented and no rent (stake of collusion) is granted to the firm.

Furthermore, since the expected payment to the agency, in this case,

$$\left\{ \left[F(1 - \mu*) + (1 - F(\mu*)) \right] s \right\}$$

is not higher than the incentive compatible one (s) for the simple majority case, the corresponding expected welfare is not lower.

If the constitutional qualified majority rule is substituted to the two tier hierarchy we have the following proposition:

Proposition 5. *Collusion proof discretionary regulation fares better on welfare grounds than the constitutional rule described in the previous proposition if the level of expected welfare obtained over the suboptimal majorities range net of the total welfare cost of collusion proof incentive payments is greater than the one obtained under non-discretionary regulation.*

A formal proof is to be found in the Appendix.

The economic intuition behind this result lies in the fact that, if you allow regulation to be implemented under a simple majority, you give away incentive payments to the agency whoever wins the elections, but because of the existence of a supervisor, with probability ξ the government is fully informed. On the contrary, if regulation takes place only if a qualified majority is reached expected rent is small but, for sub-optimal majorities, a cost plus contract is implemented.

6. CONCLUDING REMARKS

This preliminary paper shows that one possible way of reducing the distortions due to the combined effect of the inefficiency of the political system and of asymmetric information is to introduce constitutional rules which match industrial policies with qualified majorities. In particular, if one looks at the inefficiency of the political system as a form of "political capture" in the sense that the winning party maximises his own objective function instead of social welfare, the introduction of qualified majorities can be seen as a constitutional device to reduce the stake of capture.

Many of the results obtained depend crucially on the very simplified form of the model; we feel that a key role is played here by the way in which the majority appropriates the rent of the firm: if the rent takes the form of cost-padding (due to employment in excess of the efficient level, for example) the distortion caused by the inefficiency of the political system could probably be different.

We hope to analyse the problem of optimal majorities under different ways of rent extraction on the part of the politicians in future work.

Much remains to be explored. A more ambitious task is to let people vote directly on the form of regulation instead than voting according to their belonging to one of the groups; in this paper, in the distinction by now traditional between voters who behave *a la Mill* and voters who behave *a la Shumpeter*,[5] we took the view that individuals were of the first type, but it would be very interesting to study the effects of qualified majorities in a representative democracy where M.P. vote rationally on single industrial policy issues.

APPENDIX

1) Proof of Remark 1

From (7):

$$
sign\frac{\partial\mu^*}{\partial\lambda} = -sign\left\{\begin{array}{l} v\big(e^*-\psi(e^*)\big)+(1-v)\big(\overline{e}_G(\mu^*)-\psi\big(\overline{e}_G(\mu^*)\big)\big)-v\phi\big(\overline{e}_G(\mu^*)\big)+ \\ -\big[(1+\lambda)(1-v)\big(\psi'\big(\overline{e}_G(\mu^*)\big)-1\big)+\lambda v\phi'\big(\overline{e}_G(\mu^*)\big)\big]\dfrac{\partial\overline{e}_G}{\partial\lambda} \end{array}\right\}
$$

and

$$v(e* -\psi(e*))+(1-v)(\overline{e}_G(\mu*)-\psi(\overline{e}_G(\mu*))-v\phi(\overline{e}_G(\mu*))<0$$

Furthermore, taking account of (1) and considering that $\overline{e}_G(\mu*) > \overline{e}$, it is easy to see that:

$$(1+\lambda)\ (1-v)(\psi'(\overline{e}_G(\mu*))-1)+\lambda\,v\phi'(\overline{e}_G(\mu*))<0$$

Finally $\dfrac{\partial \overline{e}_G}{\partial \lambda} < 0$ from (3).

2) Proof of Proposition 5

For the above proposition to be true we must have:

$$EW^{IP}_{|\mu=1/2} \geq EW^{C}_{|\mu=\mu*} \qquad (14)$$

where

$$EW^{IP}_{|\mu=1/2} \equiv \int_{1/2}^{1} W_P^4(\alpha)d\alpha + F\left(\frac{1}{2}\right)W_P^3$$

is expected welfare with discretionary regulation and collusion proof incentive payments when the decision rule is based on simple majority, and

$$EW^{C}_{|\mu=\mu*} \equiv \int_{\mu*}^{1} W_P^5(\alpha)d\alpha + F(1-\mu*)W_P^6 + [F(\mu*) - F(1-\mu*)]W^{CP}$$

is expected welfare when regulation takes place if majority $\mu*$ is reached and no collusion proof incentive payments are paid, otherwise a cost plus contract is implemented.
Where:

$$W_P^5 = W^{FI} -(1-v)(1+\lambda)[(\psi(\overline{e}_G)-\overline{e}_G)-(\psi(e*)-e*)]-\lambda v\Phi(\overline{e}_G)$$

$$W_P^6 = W^{FI} -(1-v)(1+\lambda)[(\psi(\overline{e}_P^2)-\overline{e}_P^2)-(\psi(e*)-e*)]-\lambda v\Phi(\overline{e}_P^2)$$

Sufficient condition for (14) to be true is:

$$\int\limits_{1/2}^{\mu^*} W_P^4(\alpha)d\alpha + \left[F(\mu^*) - F\left(\frac{1}{2}\right) \right] W_P^3 - \lambda s > \left[F(\mu^*) - F(1 - \mu^*) \right] W^{CP}$$

NOTES

*   Thanks are due to J.J. Laffont , F. Panunzi and the participants to the IGIER seminar in Milan for very helpful comments. The Authors gratefully acknowledge financial support from C.N.R. and M.U.R.S.T. in Rome.

[1]   Notice that a society characterised by F(.) can be said to be more homogeneous than the one characterised by G(.), if F(.) crosses G(.) once from above.

[2]   See Grossman and Hart (1983).

[3]   "For θ close to 1, no discrimination is better than political discrimination if λ is small and majorities are slim; discrimination is better if λ is large enough."

[4]   For a more detailed exposition of the model and for the case of public firm, see Laffont (1996).

[5]   Millian voters vote according to their belonging to one group, while Shumpeterian voters are «rational» in the sense that they vote according to the political platforms they can choose from; for more precise definitions and implications see Galeotti G and A. Breton (1986); Campbell A. et al. (1960) offer a clear definition of the theory of the behaviour of «voters by belonging», while Downs A.(1957) and Ordershook P. (1986) offer sound versions of the theory of the rational choice theory of voters' behaviour.

REFERENCES

Aghion, P. and P. Bolton , 1994, "Government Domestic Debt and the risk of Default: a Political-Economic Model of the Strategic Role of Debt", in Dornbush, R. and M. Draghi (eds.), *Public Debt Management - Theory and History*, Cambridge, C.U.P., Ch.11.

Buchanan, J. and R. Tullock, 1962, *The Calculus of Consent*, Cambridge.

Campbell, A., Converse, P.S.,. Miller, W.S and D.E. Stokes, 1960, *The American Voter*, New York, Wiley.

Downs, A., 1957, *An Economic Theory of Democracy*, New York, Harper and Row.

Galeotti, G. and A. Breton, 1989, "Political Loyalties and the Economy: the U.S. Case", *Review of Economics and Statistics*, 71, 511-517.

Laffont, J.J., 1996, "Industrial Policy and Politics", *International Journal of Industrial Organization*, 14, 1-27.

Ordeshook, P., 1986, *Game Theory and Political Theory*, Cambridge MA, Cambridge University Press.

Persson, T. and Tabellini G., 1996, "Federal Fiscal Constitutions: Risk Sharing and Moral Hazard", *Econometrica*, 64, 623-46.

Chapter 2

ON THE ROLE OF LOBBIES IN POLICY MAKING

Isidoro Mazza
University of Catania, Italy

1.   INTRODUCTION

In the theory of endogenous policy making, government decisions may be influenced by self-interested agents or lobbies, mainly through the transfer of resources or information. Starting from the pioneering studies of Olson (1965), Stigler (1971), Posner (1974), Peltzman (1976), Tullock (1980) and Becker (1983, 1985), which investigated the influence of interest groups in regulatory policy making and rent dissipation for favour seeking, there has been an enormous diffusion of lobbying models in several areas of research, such as: electoral competition [Austen-Smith (1987), Baron (1989ab, 1994), Coughlin et al. (1990), Grossman and Helpman (1996), Morton and Cameron (1992)], international trade [Magee et al. (1989), Grossman and Helpman (1994, 1995), Hillman (1989), Leidy (1994), Mayer (1984)], public procurement [Laffont and Tirole (1993), McLachlan (1985)], fiscal federalism [Hoyt and Toma (1989), Grossman (1989, 1994), Persson and Tabellini (1994)], tax reform [van Velthoven and van Winden (1991), Winer and Hettich (1993)], economic transition [Gelb et al. (1997), Hillman (1994)], economic growth [Olson (1982), Sturzenegger and Tommasi (1994), van Velthoven (1989)].

The vast literature focusing on the activity of lobbies has without doubt substantially improved our understanding of their behaviour and influencing determinants.[1] Nonetheless, there are several issues which deserve further investigation. For example, the influence of lobbying on policy making with respect to *unorganised* voters or ideology remains partly unclear [see Potters and Sloof (1996)]. Similarly, the relevance of community norms on individual choices and the role that social groups and networks may have, for example in the case of elections, are not fully explored [van Winden (1997)]. In addition, relatively little work exists on the formation of interest groups and cartels or about the consequences that the entry of a new group would have on the competition among lobbies [important exceptions are Dougan and Snyder (1996), and Mo (1988), respectively].

An important, but often neglected issue, concerns the characteristics of lobbying in a multi-stage organisation of policy-making. It is easy to conceive that lobbying affects decision making in organisations where decisions are often the result of "a complex set of agency relationships, each of which typically involves multiple principals and multiple agents" [Noll (1989, p.1262)]. In particular, politicians are not only the agents of their electorate, but also the principals of bureaucratic agencies which, in many instances, have the responsibility of implementing a specific policy because of their superior expertise. Authority may also be delegated to committees which initiate the legislative process, especially in congressional systems. In such cases, because of incomplete principal-agent contracts and partial monitoring, the bureaucrat can exploit delegation as well as the *information advantage* and pursue personal goals, such as income and prestige, in direct contrast with the wishes of the legislators. This can lead to an inefficient expansion of the budget or even to a collusion with contractors or regulated firms [Tirole (1992)]. Similar agency relationships exist in federal systems, where the authority of the local governments depends on the degree of decentralisation, or in large companies, where the hierarchy of principal-agent relationships includes, for example: shareholders, board of directors, senior executives, supervisors [Dixit (1996)]. There, the shareholders may be unable to monitor management due to a lack of information and free-riding, and the appointment of a board of directors may not substantially improve the corporate control of ownership [Milgrom and Roberts (1992)].

In principal, when the policy making process results from the interaction of different agents with some degree of authority, several opportunities for lobbying exist. Therefore, the overall influence of an interest group on the decision making process depends on the relative influence of that group at each tier of decision-making and on the hierarchical relationship linking those decisional levels. It is therefore surprising to find that very few works exist which include multi-tier lobbying in the analysis of endogenous policies in hierarchies. A large part of the literature on lobbying concentrates mainly on the demand side, without taking into account a specific institutional setting. Few studies on the organisation of the public sector include the activity of interest groups [see, e.g., Banks and Weingast (1992), Laffont and Tirole (1991, 1993), Spiller (1990)] but where they do, they generally tend to overlook the possibility that lobbies may influence more stages in the organisation [recent surveys of the theory of bureaucracy are provided by Breton (1995) and Wintrobe (1996)].

Since hierarchical decision-making systems are widespread, it appears it would be necessary to adopt a comprehensive analytical framework, with lobbies acting at the relevant decisional stages, in order to improve our understanding of the activity and influence of interest groups. In this paper, after a brief discussion about the characteristics of the political influence of interest groups and the specific role played by information, the attention will be focused on lobbying in organisation with decentralised decision-making. The presentation of recent models of multi-tiered lobbying, aims at highlighting the novelties conveyed by this approach with respect to the traditional models of interest groups and regulatory *capture*. Firstly, it is shown that interest groups play an important role in shaping the horizontal and vertical relationships existing within the organisations. For example, the legislator may have *modest* reasons for spending resources on monitoring subordinate agents, not only when they are already formally under his control [Weingast and Moran (1983)], but also when an autonomous agent is lobbied by the same group influencing the legislator himself. Secondly, the multi-tier approach to lobbying indicates that legislatorial oversight (delegation) may be endogenously induced by the influencing activities of lobbies; for example when they have a strong (weak) influence on the principal but not on the agent. Thirdly, competition for rents among interest groups extends across stages: a group with uneasy access to one stage of the organisation may prefer to shift lobbying investments to another, more favourable, stage. Therefore, lobbying becomes a rather complex problem concerning the allocation of expenditures at the different levels of decision-making.

The paper is organised as follows: Section 2 presents a brief review of the sources of political influence of interest groups and the features of lobbying activities. Section 3 focuses on the organisation of the public sector and lobbying with decentralised decision-making. Section 4 introduces some recent literature investigating multi-stage lobbying and discusses some policy implications of this new general approach. Section 5 concludes the paper with some brief comments and suggestions for further research.

2. THE INFLUENCE OF INTEREST GROUPS ON THE POLICY MAKING PROCESS

One of the main justifications for the political influence of interest groups is the imperfect *(lack of or inaccurate)* information held by a large portion of voters regarding the policy formation process. Elected politicians act as agents to their constituency whose needs should be met if with a view to re-election.

But not all the voters share the same information about their legislatorial activity. Since Downs (1957), voters are considered "rationally ignorant" of politics. A single voter has a negligible influence on the elections; hence, the expected collective benefits of casting the right vote are inferior to the individual costs of acquiring information about the candidates. According to Olson (1965), people do not generally have selective incentives to invest resources in the acquisition of information about the activity of the policymakers. Free-riding and transaction costs hinder the ability of the public and large groups to organise and influence policymaking. Therefore, narrow groups with specific interests, facing low organisation costs and high per-capita stakes, may be more successful than numerically superior groups. Moreover, the smallness of interest groups has two additional advantages. Firstly, they may be substantially favoured with little burden imposed on the rest of the community [Stigler (1971)], up to the point where, the political costs for a majority maximiser politician equate with the benefits at the margin [Peltzman (1976)].[2] Secondly, small groups bear only a small share of the dead-weight losses imposed on the economy, when the redistribution takes place inefficiently, as in the case of regulation or tariffs [Wellisz and Wilson (1986)].

2.1   The influence of interest groups on the incumbent legislator

In a world with many interest groups, Becker (1983, 1985) considers public policy as fully determined by competition among interest groups.[3] Lobbying may lead to efficient outcomes since each group wants to minimise the countervailing opposition of groups suffering dead-weight losses.[4] Groups produce pressure which is assumed to be affected (positively) by the resources invested and (negatively) by the size of the group, and transformed into policy through a generic influence function. The main limitation with the early studies on interest groups is that they do not clearly specify what kind of activities determine the influence of interest groups, and how. A solution to this problem is offered by Grossman and Helpman (1994). Adopting a menu-auction framework developed by Bernheim and Whinston (1986), they assume that interest groups influence the legislative process by offering policy-contingent contribution schedules to the legislator, who has the objective of maximising a weighted sum of contributions and social welfare. In equilibrium, it results in the legislator maximising a weighted social welfare function where the weights are endogenously influenced by the lobbying activities of the groups.

However, the influence of interest groups is, in general, strictly related to the alleged rational disinformation the unorganised voters would have and whose effects may appear rather overstated. For example, Wittman (1989) argues that voters do not have to invest much effort in order to choose their preferred candidate, because organised groups and public lists of campaign contributors constitute valid sources of information and sustain the efficiency of a democratic political system. In addition, voters seem to make use of some information, as the recent performances of the economy [Alesina et al. (1993)]. Therefore, incumbent legislators can find it difficult to redistribute in favour of a minority. In addition, according to Austen-Smith (1991) the assumption that contributions can buy legislatorial votes would imply that the voters do not understand the functioning of politics, failing to recognise that campaign expenditures can be exchanged for redistribution which they may end up paying, as in the case of tariffs. In a rational expectation model it is not acceptable that voters are constantly fooled while contributions are exchanged for policies reducing the level of collective welfare. Fremling and Lott (1995) limit the relevance of this criticism by arguing that politicians, interest groups and voters are all subject to the same problem: to identify which variables are related. Different individuals generally make different identification mistakes which do not cancel out *on aggregate* as happens with the misestimation error considered by rational expectations. In particular, the effect of contributions on the voting choices of politicians is not clear even for public choice scholars.[5] Because of this identification problem, voters could rationally underestimate the strength of the relationship between contributions and the way in which the legislator takes decisions.

There is no doubt, however, that asymmetric information represents an important determinant of the disproportionate influence of interest groups. Lohmann (1994b) combines the concept of imperfect information and the Olsonian argument of free-riding in order to ascertain the political influence of narrow groups. A policy bias towards small groups is due to their superiority, with respect to the general public, in overcoming the free-riding problem of information acquisition and monitoring the legislator. Assuming that the incumbent's moves are not directly observed by the voters and that they are divided into two groups of different size and preference, the small group with specific interests is presumably more informed about the incumbent's actions than the large group.[6] Since any voter in either group wishes to re-elect a competent politician, but is unable to discern whether some advantageous policy is due to luck or ability, the incumbent will find it profitable to bias the policy in favour of the better informed minority. Accordingly, the incumbent mimics a competent politician in front of the well-informed interest group, at the cost of showing less competence to the rest of the public. But the latter group places a lower weight than the more informed group on the possibility that the outcome is due to competence. Thus, the losses of political support by a majority are lower than the gains derived by favouring a better informed minority.

Lobbying can also assume the form of strategic transmission of costly information. Potters and van Winden (1992) consider a signalling game where a lobby has private information about the outcome of specific policies selected by the government. Sending a message costs a fixed amount, but the government cannot verify the accuracy of the message. In the case when there is a possible conflict of interests between the government and the lobby, information cannot be transmitted if a lobby with an incentive to dissemble has a larger stake than a different lobby without conflict of interests. Consequently, in order to have information transmission, the government should not think that information comes from the wrong side. This means that government and lobby must share sufficiently similar interests. If the costs of sending the message are not prohibitive for the lobby with an incentive to dissemble, this will play a mixed strategy, inducing the government to play a mixed strategy, since it still doubts the true state of the world. The subsequent result is that lobbying is more likely to occur when the costs of sending the message is low and the potential benefits are high. Moreover, the responsiveness to lobbying depends (positively) on the costs of sending the message and (negatively) on the stakes of the dissembling lobby. Austen-Smith and Wright (1992) extend the analysis by introducing competitive lobbying by two groups with different interests which can acquire and strategically transmit valuable information to the policy maker. Assuming that the legislator can verify the accuracy of the message, it is shown that lobbying improves the choice of the legislator and can be persuasive, in the sense that a group can induce a disagreeing legislator to adhere to the group's interests.

2.2   The role of interest groups in electoral contests.

There are several models analysing the influence of interest groups in the circumstances of electoral competition. In general, election contests are affected by two types of uncertainty. Candidates are uncertain about the behaviour of voters and voters are relatively uncertain about the policies of candidates.

The first type of uncertainty is usually analysed by making a distinction between whether voting is assumed to be deterministic or probabilistic. With deterministic voting, candidates believe that an electoral outcome can be accurately predicted once the candidates have made their decisions: individuals vote with probability one for the candidate whose platform guarantees higher utility. On the contrary, in the case of probabilistic voting, candidates are uncertain about the voting decision rule of individuals, even when they know their (economic) preferences as well as the competitor's platform. Probabilistic voting models transform the likelihood of voting for a candidate into a continuous function of the utility differences between candidate platforms and voter ideal policy, allowing also votes against the closest candidate.[7] In line with empirical observations, this approach admits the existence of non-policy related factors, such as ideology, candidate characteristics or other idiosyncratic factors, which influence voting as well as economic calculations. Due to the randomness of the non-policy bias, voter choice is treated as a random variable by the candidates. Assuming that voters have a uniformly distributed idiosyncratic bias, Coughlin et al. (1990) are able to endogenise the influence which interest groups can have on policy formation. They show that expected plurality maximising candidates in equilibrium choose policies maximising an additive welfare function, where the weights associated to the utility of each group increase with the group size and are inversely related to the dispersion of the bias [see also Borooah and van der Ploeg (1983)]. In conclusion, interest groups would be more influential than other unorganised groups, because they are more homogeneous, and then convey less uncertainty around their member preferences than the latter. The specific features of probabilistic voting models seem to justify a preference with respect to deterministic voting models, especially when related to elections where voters are uninformed about the alternatives [see Burden (1997)].

Often the probabilistic assumptions are applied to the electorate. Voters can be uncertain about the platform, competence and commitment of a candidate. If voters make idiosyncratic errors in perceiving the different political platforms, candidates can increase the probability of support through campaigning, thus reducing (increasing) the uncertainty of risk-averse voters about their own (the opponent) platform [Austen-Smith (1987), Hinich and Munger (1989), Mayer and Li (1994)]. Alternatively, candidates can try to persuade people to vote in their favour regardless of the platform presented [see Mueller and Stratmann (1994), Myerson and Weber (1993), Nelson (1976)]. In any case, we often observe a large amount of resources invested in campaigning. It is then perfectly reasonable to consider campaign contributions as a relevant instrument for the interest groups to influence the candidates' policies.

Contributions can be provided by interest groups for various reasons: to support the election of the candidate with the most preferred platform (position induced contributions), or as a *quid-pro-quo* to obtain favours (service induced contributions).[8] In the first case, the policy induced contributions are offered to affect the probability of election of the receiving party. We typically obtain that groups contribute in equilibrium only to the candidate offering the most favourable policy. Although policies are taken as given by the interest groups, candidates locate themselves exploiting the trade-off between the loss of votes and the increase in contributions caused by changing policy. Unfortunately, these moves may lead to convergence, in which case no group contributes. In order to avoid such a problem, several different assumptions (such as ideological restraint) have been adopted in the literature [for a survey, see Austen-Smith (1996)].

Alternatively, contributions can be offered in exchange of service to be delivered by the candidate when elected. Baron (1989a) presents a model where candidates use their position to extract contributions from groups in exchange for services provided after being elected. Voting is described in a reduced form where the probability of winning is a function of the relative amount of contributions received. The service-contribution contracts emerge as a Nash equilibrium of the electoral game, with the expectations of the groups equal to the probability of victory. It results in a candidate with an exogenous advantage (such as recognition or incumbency) obtains larger contributions and provides less services than the opponent. This is due the fact that interest groups maximise the return of their investments. Accordingly, they tend to support the candidate with the expected higher probability of winning, whereas the opponent tries to compensate the disadvantage by offering more services per dollar of contribution. However, the services offered are a decreasing function of the recognition advantage, since the latter makes the candidate less dependent on the support of interest groups. Therefore, at some point, the contributions to the favourite candidate become negatively correlated to the probability of winning the election, because the latter increases at a slower rate than the service offered decreases. This result is also empirically supported by Snyder (1990), who finds that candidates with a high probability of winning tended to accept fewer contributions in the elections for the U.S. House of representatives from1980.[9]

Baron (1994) and Grossman and Helpman (1996) extend the above analysis by introducing informed and uniformed voters. The probability of success depends on the announced policy platform and campaigning and voting of the uniformed individuals is probabilistic. The candidates can use the policy-contingent contributions of lobbies to attract the support of uninformed voters. Baron (1994) shows that the choice of being aligned with the interest groups increases the probability of election. In addition, it turns out that an increase in the proportion of uninformed voters has no influence on the probability of winning, but it moves an equilibrium policy away from the median and has a positive effect on the contributions offered. In line with empirical evidence [Snyder (1990)], contributions are higher the closer the election. Interestingly, public financing of elections improves the winning probability of the candidates with the lowest chances and pushes the particularistic policies towards the median. According to Grossman and Helpman (1996), lobbies contribute more to the candidate with better election prospects because the latter would suffer less from serving the interests of the lobbies. As in Baron (1994), the candidates' bias for lobbies is positively affected by the proportion of uninformed voters and their susceptibility to campaign spending. An important problem with this class of models is that the contract between lobbies and the elected candidate are not enforceable. It is then common to assume that the probability of repeating the election game induces the parties to abide by their promises [cf., e.g., Baron (1989ab)]. Inherently to this issue, there is some empirical evidence that contributors tend to establish a long term relationship of mutual trust in several ways. For example, they finance a politician along the years, contribute to junior legislators more often but less generously than to senior legislators and support more representatives with better career prospects [see Snyder (1992) and Stratmann (1997)].[10]

Interest groups may also use multiple instruments of influence, such as contributions and information, simultaneously. Contributions can be offered by the interest groups in order to buy access, by signalling the preferences of the donors, or to enhance the credibility of costless announcements or messages from donors with conflicting interests. In the first hypothesis, Austen-Smith (1993b) finds that contributions may be unable to separate the groups with preferences similar to that of the policy maker from those with very distant preferences. In addition, Ball (1995) shows that lobbying can be welfare-improving when the distortions associated to lobbying are inferior to the improvement in efficiency caused by excessive information. In the second case, Lohmann's (1995a) results show that, due to free-riding, the contributions offered will be smaller than those offered as a *quid-pro-quo*: since the probability that the information provided by each group will be decisive is very small, it is also expected that benefits, as well as contributions, will be small.

Finally, interest groups may also directly endorse a candidate, as an alternative or in addition to contributions. Grossman and Helpman (1996) consider public endorsement as a form of communication between well-informed group leaders and other members of the group, who are uncertain about the effect that the different political platforms would have on their welfare.[11] Potters et al. (1997) show under which conditions lobbies can decide to support a candidate with campaign contributions instead of directly endorsing the latter through costly signalling, and vice versa. It turns out that, when there is sufficient conflict of interest between the contributing lobby and the voters, direct information transmission is not possible. By offering contributions, the donor can thus exploit the stronger congruence between the candidate and the voters.

2.3 Empirical foundations

As described, the main instruments that lobbies have to influence policy-making are information transmission and monetary contributions. Although it is clearly difficult to get knowledge on the amount and quality of information provided, data for campaign contributions are available. There is a large debate questioning the theoretical and empirical foundations of the claim that campaign contributions affect the legislator vote. Empirical results concerning the hypothesis that money can buy votes are rather ambiguous [cf. Potters and Sloof (1996)]. Leaving aside bribes - which can be limited by social and legal constraints [cf. Nas et al. (1986), Shleifer and Vishny (1993), Thompson (1993)]- there is more evidence that contributions can buy votes when voting is on issues with narrow interests, than on policies with wider benefits [see Morton and Cameron (1992)].[12] This result is quite intuitive, because redistribution may be hard to notice in the case of concentrated benefits and widely spread costs. In addition, it should be noticed that money transfers influence and are influenced by the legislator position. The lack of empirical evidence for the influence hypothesis may be due to the fact that some econometric estimates do not take correctly into account the endogeneity of contributions and decisions.

Furthermore, the common assumption that contributions can improve the chance of a candidate's success is rather controversial. Actually, in many democratic systems we observe that electoral competitions involve substantial expenditures for campaigning, which would be useless if voters were fully informed about competing candidates. On the other hand, voters may not be influenced by advertising because they have an idiosyncratic bias for one of the candidates or are informed about the different political platforms. Elections are not fully equivalent to fund raising contests, since it is not always true that the candidate spending more money is the winner. More importantly, the argument that contributions increase the probability of electoral success has been criticised because it would imply irrational expectations of the voters [cf. section 2.1.].

3.   LOBBYING IN A DECENTRALISED SYSTEM OF POLICY-MAKING

So far the analysis has concentrated on lobbying directed at political representatives. However, the power of the legislator to enact the preferred policy may be limited by other subjects having a voice in the definition of a political outcome and being subject to lobbying.

In the previous literature, the supply side is highly simplified and generally constituted by a single policy-maker. In reality, legislation is the result of the bargaining among several actors with different interests. The composition of the variety of interests in the legislature raises problems of enforcement which can be solved by appropriate institutional organisation.[13]

Information asymmetries are an important feature of the complex system of reciprocal influences existing in the public sector. This constitutes a complicate governance structure characterised by overlapping agency relationships. Different legislators, for example the Congress and the President, are agents of the voters and principals of bureaucratic agencies. The degree of agent compliance with the objectives of the principal(s) may depend on different elements, such as: the diversity of interests, the availability of incentive contracts and/or monitoring instruments, as well as the pervasiveness of information asymmetries [Noll (1989)].

In this paper, the horizontal transactions among legislators will not be discussed. Instead, I will refer to the hierarchical relationships between elected representatives and bureaucrats, paying special attention to the role played by the interest groups.

3.1   The effects of the delegation of authority

Domestic policies are a result of the combination of choices made by several agents. Often politicians are not willing or able to follow all the intermediate steps necessary to implement a specific policy. Delegation may be justified in several ways. For example, the legislator may not have the expertise and time needed to supervise the realisation of specific projects [Fiorina (1982, 1985)]. The presence of a large number of specific problems requiring specific knowledge and the costs of acquiring, processing and transmitting information, induce the constitution of hierarchical organisations -also in the private sector- characterised by decentralised information managing [Radner (1992, 1993)].[14] Moreover the legislator may be willing to delegate in order to shift the responsibility of possible failures to his bureaucrats [Fiorina (1982, 1985)], to allow a ready solution to unpredicted events [Epstein and O'Halloran (1994)] as well as to overcome the legislator's inability to commit [Gatsios and Seabright (1989)]. Finally delegation may represent an instrument to elude the inefficiencies connected with logrolling.[15]

However, it can also be expected that the delegation of authority causes a loss of legislatorial control over the outcomes of government policy. With complete information, the monopoly power of initiating legislation by presenting a proposal and the right of excluding proposals made by other actors (gatekeeping) provide the bureaucrat with a substantial power over a policy outcome [see Baron and Ferejohn (1989), Hill (1985), McKelvey (1976), Romer and Rosenthal (1978, 1979), Steunenberg (1996)].[16] With asymmetric information, agencies have an additional instrument to control the public decision process. Taking advantage of their superior knowledge, agencies may try to deceive the legislator and pursue personal objectives in contrast to those of the legislator. In order to reduce the risk of bureaucratic drift, or even abdication, caused by delegation and lack of information, the legislator could resort to police-patrol oversight, but that hardly seems feasible for the high costs in terms of time and resources. Instead, the legislator can design an appropriate system of *ex-ante* incentives/constraints and *ex-post* penalties [see Bendor et al. (1985, 1987)]. Moreover, the introduction definition of criteria and procedures that restrict *de facto* the autonomy and range of activity improves the effectiveness of ongoing controls [Epstein and O'Halloran (1994)].[17]

Accordingly, the hypothesis of bureaucratic discretion would mainly depend on the cost of defining laws and incentive schemes to limit it. When direct monitoring is not feasible, Weingast and Moran (1983) suggest that there are other instruments which can be successfully used to limit bureaucratic discretion under asymmetric information, without turning to complicated schemes.[18] Firstly, the competition among bureaucrats can force them to provide services that satisfy the constituency of the their political principal [cf. also Breton and Wintrobe (1982)]. Secondly, the legislator can design a judicial system which allows the consumers of bureaucratic services (especially interest groups) to act as watchdogs protecting their rights against the abuses of the administrative system [see McCubbins and Schwartz (1984)].[19] Thirdly, bureaucratic managers are often appointed by politicians who consequently have some influence on their career [Fiorina (1981), Peacock (1994), Tirole (1994)]. According to Weingast and Moran (1983), these instruments would be sufficient for an effective legislatorial control without needing frequent monitoring. Consequently, the lack of hearings and investigations, usually presented as evidence of bureaucratic discretion, could on the contrary, prove legislatorial dominance. In reply to these arguments, it is worth noting that they are not sufficient to dismiss the hypothesis of bureaucratic discretion. Competition may not be desirable when it represents a burden for policy implementation. Therefore, the legislator may prefer to restrain competition among agencies to reduce the costs of organisation and of duplication of roles.[20] In addition, the ability of the legislator to control bureaucrats by exploiting the patrolling oversight of his constituents should not be exaggerated. In fact to separate true alarms from false warnings can be problematic.[21] Finally, the power of appointing trusted bureaucrats does not guarantee against future unloyal behaviour, especially when an official has become so powerful (or indispensable) that they will be very costly to sack. Career concerns and appointing power alone may not be sufficient to control bureaucrats under asymmetric information. In particular, the principal(s) should be able to detect the performance of the agent. This information may not be available because signalling is too costly or not fully indicative of the agent's competence, for example.

As mentioned at the beginning of this section, the literature on lobbying has devoted relatively little attention to the relationships linking the main actors of the public sector. One hypothesis considers the constitution of an "iron triangle", a sub-government where lobbies collude with the bureaucrats being able, through the provision of contributions, to obtain from the legislator a support to their interests as well as a large budget for the bureaus [Wilson (1989)]. This interpretation of the political decision making process seems rather simplistic, as the actors outside the triangle (e.g. the voters) are assumed unable to influence policy making. More importantly, within the triangle, the conjecture of homogeneous interests -which does not appear to be empirically defendable- has the effect of blurring the problems deriving from information asymmetries among the actors.

3.2   The activity of interest groups

In the last decade, several works have tried to reduce the gap between the theory of interest groups and the theory of bureaucracy. This new strand of analysis explicitly introduces lobbying in the interaction between politicians and regulatory agencies. In particular, we can identify two distinct types of models which have a principle-agent structure in common, where the information advantage provides the bureaucrat with the power of autonomous decisions while costly monitoring hinders legislatorial control.

One type of analysis describes a positive theory of regulatory capture and focuses on the reaction of the legislator in order to block collusion between lobbies and the agency through the definition of appropriate incentive schemes [cf. Laffont and Tirole (1993, ch.11)].

Spiller (1990) considers a bureaucrat as the common agent of two principals an interest group and a legislator.[22] The agent can extract rents from the competition between the principals to obtain their favours. At the same time, the existence of those rents implies a competition among individuals applying to become the agent. The legislator, having the authority of appointing the regulator, can eventually appropriate the rents. In this case, the legislator may allow the interest group to lobby the bureaucrat because that will increase the rents offered to the regulator that can be subsequently seized by the legislator. This model is particularly interesting for the presentation of the bureaucrat as an agent of more principals and for the effects that lobbying indirectly exerts on the relationship between bureaucrat and legislator. The main shortcoming is represented by the fact that it overlooks the possibility for the principals (i.e. legislator and lobby) to cooperate and offer one contract to the agency [see Tirole (1992)]. Excluding co-operation, or collusion, between politicians and interest groups may appear rather surprising since, as discussed in the previous section, there is a great deal of evidence which they strictly interact and which interest groups have several instruments to influence the decisions of the legislator.

Laffont and Tirole (1991) consider a situation where a firm has an informational rent represented by the private information about its technology. The regulatory structure is formed by a regulatory agency which can obtain information on the firm's technology and a principal, the legislator, counting on the message given by the agency. In the case of asymmetric information, since the rent of the efficient firm increases with the incentives offered to the inefficient type, the legislator is induced to use less powerful incentive schemes than in the full information case. Therefore, the rent for the efficient firm by mimicking the inefficient type is reduced. Due to their superior information and expertise, the agency can hide information from the legislator and collude with the private firm (in exchange for bribes, revolving-door, etc). The control of the principal is then exerted through the definition of collusion-proof schemes for the agent and the firm. Interestingly, it is shown that an interest group can be hurt by its own power. In fact, under the threat of producer protection, the firm enjoys a rent lower than that obtained without collusion and incurs the risk of shutdown.

It should be noticed, however, that interest group collusion with bureaucrats may mitigate the incentives for the legislator to limit the agency discretion. There are at least two explanations for this "tolerant" behaviour. Firstly, lobbies and agency "can sign agreements that are contingent on more information than the ones they sign with the principal" [Tirole (1992, p.172)]. Secondly, by allowing regulatory capture, the legislator can favour politically influential groups without assuming direct responsibility for it.

Another group of papers follows a different approach, where interest groups favour the supervision of the legislator, by acting as "watch-dogs" of the latter and providing valuable information on an agency performance [cf. Laffont and Tirole (1993) ch.15]. This information can be helpful for the re-election of the incumbent, since his constituency also includes consumers of the agency's services. The value of the information transmitted by the groups may induce the legislator to create agencies which can be more easily monitored [Banks and Weingast (1992)]. However, informed parties may behave strategically and sound "fire alarms" even when they are not needed. Lupia and McCubbins (1994) show that the legislator can learn from fire alarms if there are sufficient penalties from lying and a similarity between the preferences of the monitoring parties and the legislator. Therefore, the information on the agency performance may be collected and strategically provided by interest groups with the objective of lobbying the legislator.

Epstein and O'Halloran (1995) study this class of problems in a paper where lobbying is modelled as strategic provision of information concerning the outcome of an agency proposal. The result is that lobbying is often informative (i.e. it reduces the agency informational advantage) and influential, as it affects the legislator decisions and induces the agency to moderate the proposal to obtain the interest group support. This also happens in case where lobby and agency have a combined interest to collude against the legislator. Notice that the interest group influences the policy without needing to sound the alarm.[23] The work of Epstein and O'Halloran (1995) reveals that lobbies improve legislatorial oversight and indicates that interest groups can indirectly influence the agent's behaviour by lobbying the principal. If bureaucratic proposals are in contrast with the preference of an interest group, this can lobby the legislator to veto them. In many cases just the threat of pulling the alarm is sufficient to obtain favourable proposals.

4.   HIERARCHIES AND MULTI-TIERED LOBBYING

Both the approaches presented in the previous section postulate that interest groups can lobby only one policy maker: either the regulating agency or the legislator. As explained below, this assumption represents an important shortcoming of the analysis, unless decisions taken at different tiers of decision making are independent, or the legislator fully controls a regulating agency. However, in hierarchical structures, a policy often results from the decisions of several actors and interest groups have more opportunities to influence the policy making process. In this case, there is no clear reason to assume *a priori* that lobbying can be directed only at one policy maker.

4.1   A general approach

The adoption of a political economic approach considering, in an integrated fashion, the multiple stages of influence, can provide important new insights for the study of the influence of lobbies in policy-making and political control of bureaucracy. Listed below are some of them. Firstly, the cost of the legislator of the bureaucratic drift is generally considered in the political economic models without taking into account the effect that legislatorial monitoring may have on the allocation of lobbying resources. For example, a legislator may be induced to exert control in order to shift lobbying expenditures at his stage. A legislator with a strong hold on an agency activity may attract more lobbying expenditure, such as campaign contributions, than a politician with poor ability to control bureaucracy. Secondly, if lobbies can influence both legislators and bureaucrats, the legislatorial incentive to avoid collusion between the regulating agency and the regulated firm(s) can be altered, with respect to the case where lobbying is directed to one governmental stage only. As we have seen in the previous section, when a group can lobby only the regulating agency but not the legislator, it is reasonable to expect that the latter will try to obstruct collusion between the regulated actor and the agency, unless he is able to extract the agency rent, for example through the designation of power. However, if a lobby also has access at the legislatorial stage and acquires a political bias, the principal may be reluctant to invest resources to monitor the subordinate agency when the latter colludes with friendly groups. The opposite could happen when regulatory collusion originates with groups unable to influence the legislator. Thirdly, it is evident that, in the presence of a hierarchical organisation, the political strength of an interest group would be measured by its ability to influence the final outcome of the hierarchy of decisions. Accordingly, competition among lobbies would extend across stages. Lobbying at one decisional level may easily be affected by the access that the group and its opponents have at another level. For example, if a group increases the lobbying efforts to influence one decision maker, countervailing opposition can be exerted by other groups at a different decision stage. In that sense, it would be interesting to verify whether the finding that the entry of an opponent increases the expenditure of a single rent-seeker [cf. Fabella (1995)] also holds when there is the possibility of shifting lobbying to other decision levels. Fourth, if lobbying is also based on strategic transmission of information on an agency performance, this provision is likely to depend on the ability of that group and its opponents to influence the agency outcome. Therefore, the allocation of lobbying expenditures at each decisional stage becomes a rather complex problem which may depend on several elements, such as: the information of lobbies and decision makers, the timing of choices in the policy-making process and the access of lobbies to each stage and the legislatorial control over bureaucratic agencies.

4.2   Models of multi-tiered lobbying

One of the earlier studies introducing multi-tiered lobbying is Hoyt and Toma (1989). In that paper, it is shown that the existence of two stages of lobbying has an effect on the efficiency of the redistribution system. Hoyt and Toma (1989) consider, in a perfect information framework, two levels of government, local and state. The local government determines the expenditure for public services, whereas the state government has the authority to alter that decision. For simplicity, the effect of local provision on the state-mandate level is exogenously determined. Each local jurisdiction has two groups of residents bearing a different cost from the provision of local services. Each group can produce political influence, according to Becker's (1983) model, at each governmental tier. It is shown that countervailing lobbying at the state level reduces the inefficiency caused by local lobbying, such as the over-provision of public services.

Hillman and Katz (1987) and Katz and Tokatlidu (1996) investigate multi-stage rent-seeking contests. The main objective of these works is to assess the effect of the examined multiple contests on rent dissipation. In Hillman and Katz (1987) there exists a hierarchical bureaucracy, where the official at the lowest stage obtains a rent in the form of bribes. In order to keep their position, they can influence the outcome by investing real resources and/or transferring a portion of the rent in the form of bribes to the hierarchy above them, which is composed by n-1 incumbents. All positions are contestable and contenders may invest resources or bribe the hierarchy of superiors with a share of the transfer that they receive in order to influence the appointment. Therefore, we have one contest for the initial rent and n-1 contests for the positions in the hierarchy. At each stage the official receives a bribe from the subordinate which is partially passed on to the superiors, and so on until we reach the top. The portion of transfer paid as a bribe is exogenously given and equal for all contests. Notice that bribery is implicitly preferable to the use of real resources because it does not entail a social cost. It turns out that rent dissipation depends on the number of contests. If this is very large, the rent dissipation tends to be complete, with the upper limit for the expenditures given by the rent. If we limit the number of contenders and contests (not necessarily equal), it results in the rent dissipation being lower than in the competitive case. In addition, the more prominent the use of real resources in the contest the fewer the number of tiers that can be added before rent dissipation is maximised. Therefore, this work offers interesting insights about the benefit of limiting the expansions of governmental bureaucracies. Unlike the previous work, Katz and Tokatlidu (1996) do not consider a hierarchical organisation of governmental decision makers. They refer to a two-stage contest where, at the first stage, two interest group compete for the assignment of a given rent, whereas, at the second stage, the members of the winning group contend the distribution of the prize. The main characteristic of this model is that the marginal benefit for each individual of investing resources for winning the initial rent (public good) depends on the probability of winning the second contest (private good). Katz and Tokatlidu (1996) indicate that the relative size of the contestant groups become relevant for the rent dissipation. Large groups benefit less than small group from entering in the second round contest, because the prize of the fist round is diluted among many members and because rent dissipation is larger. In addition, changes in the size of one group affects the first-round rent seeking expenditures of the other group. The result is an asymmetry between groups which reduces dissipation. However, when only the size of one group changes, the effect depends on the direction of the change and the relative size of the group. An increase in the size of the large group may reduce rent-seeking, whereas an enlargement of the small group definitely increases dissipation.

Mazza and van Winden (1998) present a model of endogenous policy in a hierarchical government. At the upper stage a legislator chooses the tax revenue to finance the provision of two public goods. At the lower level, a bureaucrat decides the distribution of the budget into the two projects. Therefore, we have two distinct governmental levels of decision and at each level, the agent can be influenced by two interest groups, through the offer of policy contingent transfers as in Grossman and Helpman (1994) (see sect. 2.1). The political influence of interest groups can be different and it is endogenously affected by the decision of lobbying. The autonomy of the bureaucrat approximates their superior expertise, but she may pursue personal objectives only at some cost. The degree of legislatorial control is exogenously given by a weight that the bureaucrat gives to the objective of the legislator.[24] Unlike the above mentioned studies, rents and lobbying expenditures are endogenously determined in this work, which also investigates the effect of lobbying on the relationship between the two public decision makers. The main results of this work concern the effects that multi-stage lobbying may have on the relationship between the public decision makers. In that sense, it offers some indications on the consequence of delegation, or imperfect control, when lobbies are active at the upper and lower levels of decision.[25] Mazza and van Winden (1998) maintain that an unpressured equilibrium (with complete legislatorial control) can coincide with an equilibrium reached under competitive lobbying. Therefore, delegation and bureaucratic capture may not lead to worse outcomes, from the legislator's point of view. In addition, in a fully competitive framework, where both interest groups are able to lobby the bureaucrat for the allocation of a given budget, the degree of legislatorial control does not have an effect on the bureaucratic decision. The reason for this is, that the interest groups define their schedules of policy contingent transfers in such a way that their respective utilities are maximised and therefore, the legislator cannot induce a better policy. Not surprisingly, however, legislatorial control reduces lobbying expenditures at the lower stage. This result suggests that political supervision may be endogenously induced by the same lobbies. Accordingly, the analysis is extended to endogenise legislatorial control, showing that interest group could find profitable paying contributions to the legislator in order to induce costly monitoring. For what concerns the effect of competitive lobbying on the decision of the governmental agencies, it is interesting to notice that an increase of the influence of a group at the bureaucratic stage, may lead to a *worse* policy outcome for that group, when this does not have a sufficient relative influence at the legislatorial stage. The reason behind this is that, the reaction of the legislator, who can use the size of the budget as a second-best instrument of control and then limit the bureaucratic redistribution by reducing the available budget.

Sloof (1996) analyses the influence of interest groups on the delegation of political authority to a bureaucrat with preferences different from those of the legislator, when both public actors can be lobbied through strategic and costly transmission of information. It is assumed that only the bureaucrat has sufficient expertise to understand the technical information which can be sent by the interest group. Delegation, therefore implies a trade-off, for the legislator, between the advantages of a more informed policy and the risks of bureaucratic drift. It results in the interest group lobbying the legislator for delegation if the cost of lobbying the politician is larger than the cost of lobbying the bureaucrat. Moreover, delegation needs the preferences of legislator, bureaucrat and interest group to be sufficiently aligned. In signalling models, the similarity of preferences between sender and receiver is important in order to have information revealed in equilibrium. It is then interesting to notice that the legislator may prefer a biased bureaucrat over an unbiased one.[26] The reason for this is, that more information is transferred when the interests of the bureaucrat and lobby are more aligned; and where the informational gains may outweigh the losses due to bureaucratic drift.

Austen-Smith (1993) considers the case where a bureaucratic agency acts at the beginning of the decisional process, by making a proposal to the legislator that can either accept or reject it, in which case the status quo is preserved (closed rule). There is uncertainty on how policies map into outcome. The interest group may decide on acquiring private information and lobbying each decision maker before he or she acts. Lobbying is performed through strategic transmission of costly information and is modelled as a cheap-talk: the lobby can prove without cost to be informed, when it has acquired information, but not the type of information acquired. Therefore, the interest group lobbies only if informed but, since it has preferences over the policy consequences, the incentive to dissemble is discounted by the receiver. The main objective of the paper is to investigate at which stage the group will decide to lobby and the effects of lobbying on the outcome. It is found that if information is acquired, that this happens at the agenda setting stage; and if lobbying is influential (meaning that the receiver's decision is not constant in the message) that is more likely to happen at the agenda-setting stage. On the other hand, since under closed rule the legislator can only accept or refuse the proposal, but cannot amend it, at that stage lobbying is often informative (i.e. it affects the beliefs) without being influential; although influential lobbying can exist at both stages of the process.

5. CONCLUDING COMMENTS

In this paper the relevance of interest groups in the policy making process has been investigated. After a brief presentation of the sources of the disproportionate influence that narrow groups may have on elections and the legislative process, and the available instruments of lobbying, I have considered the activity of interest groups in a decentralised organisation of decision making. In that section two opposite situations have been considered: when interest groups try to capture a regulatory agency and when they instead act as providers of information about the performance of that agency. Finally, this paper has addressed the topic of multi-tiered lobbying in hierarchical public organisation. The models presented suggest that this approach, although it has often been neglected, can shed an important light on our understanding of the activity of interest groups. The results discussed show that the existence of multiple levels of lobbying has an impact on, for example, the welfare costs of lobbying, the amount of lobbying expenditure, the outcome of legislatorial control, the benefits (or costs) of delegation and the effect of lobbying on the policy outcome. In addition, the approach of multi-tiered lobbying represents a useful instrument for studying endogenous policy making in federal systems and private enterprises [see Mazza and van Winden (1997)]. In particular, the political economic analysis of firms hardly considers the role of lobbying, in spite of the existence of several agency relationships, such as those between the board and the managers or between different managers, which can be influenced by specific groups, such as the shareholders.

NOTES

[1] There are several surveys on the theory of interest groups. Among the most recent ones, Austen-Smith (1996), Potters and van Winden (1996) and van Winden (1997) review the main theoretical models of lobbying; Nitzan (1994) focuses on rent-seeking models, placing particular attention on the effect of some variables, such as the nature of the contested prize or the number of participants, on the amount of rent-dissipation. Potters and Sloof (1996) examine the empirical literature trying to assess the influence of interest groups on policy making.

[2] The political support of interest groups may require a barrier against the entry of other groups. Otherwise a monopolistic rent can attract more beneficiaries and lead to its dissipation as well as the disappearance of support [see Hillman (1982)].

[3] The influence of unorganised groups is not taken into account. On the contrary, Denzau and Munger (1986) suggest that the policy supply price faced by the interest groups may be affected by the legislator attachment to voters [cf. also Snyder (1991)]. Therefore, the

preferences of unorganized voters can be represented. Accordingly, interest groups would choose to offer contributions to those legislators whose constituency is either indifferent (or ignorant), or well informed but with preferences similar to the interest group. This hypothesis is empirically supported by Stratmann (1992).

[4] We can identify two broad categories of influence models. The so-called "Chicago School" of political economy [in particular, Becker (1983, 1985) and Wittman (1989)] assert that competitive lobbying would lead to efficient redistribution. On the contrary, the "Virginia School" [in particular, Tullock (1983, 1989)] argues that resources are wasted in rent-seeking activities and politicians choose inefficient transfer mechanisms in order to disguise redistribution in favour of other groups. Baba (1997) suggests that efficient rent-seeking is more likely than the inefficient one when the cost of informing voters is either very low or very high. However, if the cost is low only for efficient redistribution and high for inefficient redistribution, then we obtain inefficiency. Coate and Morris (1995), in a model where voters are imperfectly informed about the policy outcome and the politicians' propensity to accept bribes, show that corrupted politicians may prefer to serve interest groups in a disguised but inefficient way, in order to increase their reputation. Dixit and Londregan (1995) suggest that the use of inefficient protection of declining industries instead of direct transfers, constitutes a commitment device to guarantee politicians that the voters will still support them in the future. Accordingly, the workers face a disincentive to relocate because the net economic gains do not exceed the political benefits.

[5] Incidentally, it could be the case that legislator and interest groups have the same preferences, to the point where there is no need to influence expenditures. *Then, it may seem strange the empirical finding that interest groups lobby also friendly legislators.* Austen-Smith and Wright (1994) explain this behaviour with another finding: interest groups also lobby legislators who are going to vote against them. Therefore friendly legislators can be lobbied to counteract the efforts of the opposing group.

[6] Lohmann (1993, 1994a, 1995b) shows that if the policy maker takes into account the free-riding problem, then the political action of a small group of people can also be decisive, as it provides information on the preferences of a larger number of individuals. The efficacy of a political action is based on the legislator awareness of the (weak) incentives to undertake it and on the influence that it can exert on the preferences of other individuals.

[7] This characteristic also allows for the existence of equilibria in cases where no equilibria exist with deterministic voting [Coughlin (1992)]. In addition the resulting equilibria can be efficient and have appealing normative properties. In particular, in a binary Luce model of voting (where the likelihood of making a choice on any pair of platforms depends only on the values assigned, in a probabilistic fashion, to the platforms by a scaling utility function) the outcome of the electoral competition implicitly maximises a Nash social welfare function [Coughlin and Nitzan (1981)], or a Benthamite social welfare function in the case of exponential utility functions [Coughlin (1986)].

[8] Incidentally, several papers find that campaign expenditures would have a negative effect on the probability of winning for the incumbents and a positive effect for the challengers [cf. Morton and Cameron (1992)]. This rather disturbing result would indicate an irrational behaviour of incumbents, who are generally able to obtain the largest portion of contributions. Further analysis, after correcting for the simultaneity problem (i.e. the candidate who is more likely to win receives a larger share of contributions), also shows the expected positive effects of campaign expenditures for the incumbent.

[9] It is worth remembering that the decisions of a candidate and, consequently, his ability to attract contributions depend also on the preferences of his political party [cf. Baron and Mo (1993)]. Parties may also have the important function of bargaining with interest groups on behalf of the legislator [Lindsay and Maloney (1988)].

[10] However, McCarty (1996) indicates that the elected representatives do not seem to punish strongly the former supporters of opponents.

[11] Eichenberger and Serna (1996) argue that voters make random estimation errors, whose size is decreased by the acquisition of "clean" information and increased by the exposition to "dirty" (i.e. irrelevant or wrong) information. Therefore, organised groups could have the strategic role of providing clean information to voters with similar preferences preserving them from dirty information.

[12] For example, examining votes on agricultural policy in the U.S., Stratmann (1991, 1995) finds that they are quite strongly affected by contributions.

[13] One example is the committee system in the US Congress which, according to Weingast and Marshall (1988), would solve many of the enforceability problems related to logrolling.

[14] Decentralisation and specialisation can reduce the time to process information but imply some costs in terms of delay in the communication within an organisation. On the basis of this trade-off, Bolton and Dewatripont (1994) design efficient communication networks to the point that, for a given degree of specialisation, the number of communication links cannot be reduced without having a negative effect on the performance of the organization.

[15] The separation of powers between the executive and the legislature, may represent an instrument of the voters to improve the accountability of elected officials [see Alesina and Rosenthal (1996) and Persson et al. (1996)].

[16] When the bureaucrat can make a take-it-or-leave-it proposal, their ability to control the decision-making process depends on the reversion level, which is the outcome occurring when the proposal is refused [Romer and Rosenthal (1978, 1979)]. In the specific case where only the agenda-setter, unlike the voters, knows the reversion level, the former may have less influence on the equilibrium outcome than in the case of complete information [cf. Banks (1990)]. This apparently counter-intuitive result is due to the agenda setter's inability to signal the true reversion level. Therefore, the information advantage of a bureaucrat mitigates the strategic advantage due to monopoly agenda-setting power. Gilligan and Krehbiel (1989) argue that one reason for conceding this monopoly power could be the information advantage of bureaucrats with respect to the political principal. An open rule which allows for amendments can be an inferior to a closed rule, where the agency proposal can be either approved or rejected in favour of the status quo (in which case a new proposal can be submitted), because the latter procedure *would information* benefits exceeding the costs for the authority loss.

[17] Notice that the legislator may strategically impose strict procedures ("hard-wire" or "stack the deck") in order to obstacle future legislatorial control. The uncertainty about future elections can induce the incumbent to *enact* an agency with limited discretionary authority and scarce ability of implementing current policies [see Langbein and Crewson (1996)]. In this way, the incumbent would exclude the possibility of an agency serving the winning opposition in the future. On the contrary, with low probability of coalitional drift, as in the case where the preferences of opposition and agency move apart, the incumbent would prefer to "soft-wire" the agency, using the latter to limit the activity of the opponent, in case of defeat.

[18] Weingast and Moran (1983) find evidence of changes in the policy of the Federal Trade Commission determined by variations in the preferences of the congressional committee. Weingast (1984) obtains similar results for the Security and Exchange Commission. These results indicate that the preferences of the agency do not matter at the margin. Muris (1986) criticises that analysis because it overlooks the relevance of ideology and career goals in the agency performance. Empirical analysis shows that PACs give disproportionately to committee members with jurisdiction over their activities [see, e.g., Munger (1989)]. This suggests that committee member may indeed have larger control on regulation than other representatives. Grier et Munger (1991) find that the committee assignment has a positive effect on contributions; but they also notice that legislators sort themselves out in the committees where they have more preference affinity. Then, the evidence that the committee membership has a positive and significant effect on contributions may be biased by that affinity. Finally, Krehbiel (1990) shows that the preferences of committee members do not differ substantially from those of the legislature, and Grier et al. (1990) show that the comparative advantage of committee membership is very weak in the Senate.

[19] In models of constituency monitoring, consumers of agency services are considered able to check the activity of bureaucratic regulators [cf. Laffont and Tirole (1993, ch.15)]. Konrad and Torvsik (1994) assume that consumers/voters perceive the regulation problem between politicians and bureaucrats; then the probability for the incumbent of being re-elected depends on the information extracted from the agency. In this way, through elections, voters indirectly influence the legislator selection of incentive schemes and the bureau choice of effort.

[20] Desveaux (1995, 157-8) remarks that: "Competitiveness and resource scarcity among public agencies may be especially problematic in comprehensive and innovative policy-making. [...] If they are to succeed in putting forth innovative policies, agencies must attempt to render the process as efficient as possible. This often entails controlling many of the critical assets necessary to designing and implementing a policy. Where resources are limited, the efficiency criterion may be so important in policy-making that potential abuses stemming from bureaucratic power are seen as less salient".

[21] Lupia and McCubbins (1994) present a model where, in order to learn from fire-alarm, it is necessary that there exists either a penalty for pulling a false alarm or some amount of similarity between the preferences of the legislator and those of the constituents watching the bureaucrat.

[22] More often a bureaucratic agency is considered the common agent of two political principals, such as the President and the Congress [see Krause 1996].

[23] An exception is when an extreme group prefers the status quo to any agency proposal. Then it does not convey any useful information to the legislator, even if it sounds the alarm, unless there are more interest groups predisposed to take actions against the agency choices. In that case even extremist groups may reinforce the signal sent by more moderate groups.

[24] Although the case where the superior has perfect control over the subordinate is not excluded, it is in general assumed that the delegation mechanism is imperfect: the superior is unable to determine incentives inducing a behaviour perfectly matching his preferences.

[25] Mazza (1995) extends the analysis introducing uncertainty on the way in which policies map into outcomes and considering more channels of influence (e.g. money and information).

[26] Where the bias is represented by a parameter expressing how the bureaucrat weighs the welfare of the interest group with respect to the objective of the legislator.

REFERENCES

Alesina, A. and H. Rosenthal, 1996, "A theory of divided government", *Econometrica*, 64, 1311-41.

Alesina, A., Londegran, J. and H. Rosenthal, 1993, "A model of the political economy of the United States", *American Political Science Review*, 87, 12-33.

Austen-Smith, D., 1987, "Interests groups, campaign contributions, and probabilistic voting", *Public Choice*, 54, 123-139.

-          , 1991, "Rational consumers and irrational voters: A review essay on Black Hole Tariffs and Endogenous Policy Theory", *Economics and Politics*, 3, 73-91.

-          , 1993, "Information and influence: Lobbying for agendas and votes", *American Journal of Political Science*, 37, 799-833.

-          , (1993) "Campaign contributions and access", *mimeo.*

-          , 1996, "Interest groups: Money, information and influence", in: Mueller, D.C. (Ed.), *Perspectives on Public Choice*, Cambridge, CUP.

-          and J.R., Wright, 1992, "Competitive lobbying for a legislator's vote", *Social Choice and Welfare*, 9, 229-257.

-          and -   , 1994, "Counteractive Lobbying", *American Journal of Political Science*, 38, 25-44.

Baba, S.A., 1997, "Democracies and inefficiency", *Economics and Politics*, 9, 99-114.

Ball, R., 1995, "Interest groups, influence and welfare", *Economics and Politics*, 7, 2, 119-146.

Banks, J.S., 1990, "Monopoly agenda control and asymmetric information", *Quarterly Journal of Economics*, 105, 445-464.

-      and B.R. Weingast, 1992, "The political control of bureaucracies under asymmetric information", *American Journal of Political Science*, 36, 509-524.

Baron, D.P., 1989, "Service-induced campaign contributions and the electoral equilibrium", *Quarterly Journal of Economics*, 104, 45-72.

-      , 1989, "Service-Induced Campaign Contributions, Incumbent Shirking, and Reelection Opportunities", in Peter C. Ordeshook (Ed.), *Models of Strategic Choice in Politics*, Ann Arbor, U. of Michigan Press, 93-120.

-      , 1994, "Electoral competition with informed and uninformed voters", *American Political Science Review*, 88, 33-47.

-      and J. Ferejohn, 1989, "The power to propose", in: P.C. Ordeshook (Ed.), *Models of Strategic Choice in Politics*, Ann Arbor, University of Michigan Press, 343-366.

-      and J. Mo, 1993, "Campaign Contributions and Party-Candidate Competition and Services and Policies" in: Barnett, W.A., Hinich, M.J. and N.J. Schofield (Eds.), *Institutions, Competition, and Representation*, Cambridge, CUP, 313-354.

Becker, G.S., 1983, "A theory of competition among pressure groups for political influence", *Quarterly Journal of Economics*, 98, 371-400.

-     , 1985, "Public policies, pressure groups and deadweight cost", *Journal of Public Economics*, 28, 329-347.

Bendor, J., Taylor, S. and R. Van Gaalen, 1985, "Bureaucratic expertise versus legislative authority: A model of deception and monitoring in budgeting", *American Political Science Review*, 79, 1041-1060.

-     , -   and -   , 1987, "Stacking the deck: Bureaucratic missions and policy design", *American Political Science Review*, 81, 873-896.

Bernheim, D.B. and M.D. Whinston, 1986, "Menu auctions, resource allocation, and economic influence", *Quarterly Journal of Economics*, 101, 1-31.

Bolton, P. and M. Dewatripont, 1994, "The Firm as a Communication Network", *Quarterly Journal of Economics*, 109, 4, 809-839.

Borooah, V.K. and F. van der Ploeg, 1983, *Political Aspects of the Economy*, Cambridge, Cambridge University Press.

Breton, A., 1995, "Organizational hierarchies and bureaucracies: An integrative essay", *European Journal of Political Economy*, 11, 411-440.

-     and R. Wintrobe, 1982, *The logic of bureaucratic conduct*, Cambridge, Cambridge University Press.

Burden, B.C., 1997, "Deterministic and probabilistic voting models", *American Journal of Political Science*, 41, 1150-69.

Coate, S. and S. Morris, 1995, "On the form of transfers to special interests", *Journal of Political Economy*, 103, 1210-1235.

Coughlin, P.J., 1986, "Elections and Income Redistribution", *Public Choice*, 50, 27-91.

-     , (1992) *Probabilistic Voting Theory*, Cambridge, Cambridge University Press.

-     and S. Nitzan, 1981, "Electoral Outcomes with Probabilistic Voting and Nash Social Welfare Maxima", *Journal of Public Economics*, 15, 113-121.

-     , Mueller, D.C. and P. Murrell, 1990, "A model of electoral competition with interest groups", *Economic Letters*, 32, 307-311.

Denzau, A.T. and M.C. Munger, 1986, "Legislators and interest groups: How unorganized interests get represented", *American Political Science Review*, 80, 1, 89-106.

Desveaux, J.A., 1995, *Designing bureaucracies*, Stanford, Stanford University Press.

Dixit, A., (1996) *The Making of Economic Policy. A Transaction-Cost Politics Perspective*, Cambridge, MIT Press.

-     and J. Londregan, 1995, "Redistributive politics and economic efficiency", *American Political Science Review*, 89, 856-866.

Dougan, W.R. and J.M. Snyder, 1996, "Interest-group politics under majority rule", *Journal of Public Economics*, 61, 49-71.

Downs, A., 1957, *An economic theory of democracy*, New York, Harper and Row.

Eichenberger, R. and A. Serna, 1996, "Random errors, dirty information, and politics", *Public Choice*, 86, 137-156.

Epstein, D. and S. O'Halloran, 1994, "Administrative procedures, information, and agency discretion, *American Journal of Political Science*, 38, 697-722.

-     and -   , 1995, "A Theory of Strategic Oversight: Congress, Lobbyists, and the Bureaucracy", *Journal of Law, Economics, and Organization*, 11, 227-255.

Fabella, R.V., 1995, "The social cost of rent seeking under countervailing opposition to distortionary transfers", *Journal of Public Economics*, 57, 235-247.

Fiorina, M.P., 1982, "Legislative choice of regulatory forms: Legal process or administrative process?", *Public Choice*, 39, 33-66.

-          , 1985, "Group concentration and the delegation of legislative authority", in Roger G. Noll (Ed.), *Regulatory policy and the social sciences*, Berkeley, University of California Press, 175-197.

Fremling, G.M. and J.R. Jr. Lott, 1996, "The bias towards zero in aggregate perceptions: An explanation based on rationally calculating individuals", *Economic Inquiry*, 34, 276-295.

Gatsios, K. and P. Seabright, 1989, "Regulation in the European Community", *Oxford Review of Economic Policy*, 5, 37-60.

Gelb, A., Hillman, A.L. and H.W Ursprung, 1997, "Rents as distractions: Why the exit from transition is prolonged", in: Nicolas Baltas, George Demopoulos and Joseph Hassid (Eds.), *Economic Interdependence and Cooperation in Europe*, Berlin, Springer Verlag.

Gilligan, T. and K. Krehbiel, 1989, "Collective choice without procedural commitment" in: P. Ordeshook (Ed.), *Models of Strategic Choice in Politics*, Ann Arbor, U. of Michigan Press, 295-314.

Grier, K.B. and M.C. Munger, 1991, "Committee assignments, constituent preferences, and campaign contributions", *Economic Inquiry*, 29, 24-43.

Grier, K.B., Munger, M.C. and G.M. Torrent, 1990, "Allocation patterns of PAC monies: The U.S. senate", *Public Choice*, 67, 111-128.

Grossman, G.G. and E. Helpman, 1994, "Protection for sale", *American Economic Review*, 84, 833-850.

-          and -   , 1995, "Trade wars and trade talks", *Journal of Political Economy*, 103, 675-708.

-          and -   , 1996, "Electoral competition and special interest politics", *Review of Economic Studies*, 63, 265-286.

-          and -   , 1996, "Competing for endorsements", *CEPR Discussion Paper* n.1546.

Grossman, P.J., 1989, "Federalism and the size of government", *Southern Economic Journal*, 55, 580-93.

-          , 1994, "A political theory of intergovernmental grants", *Public Choice*, 78, 295-303.

Hill, J.S., 1985, "Why so much stability? The impact of agency determined stability", *Public Choice*, 46, 275-287.

Hillman, A.L., 1982, "Declining industries and political-support protectionist motives", *American Economic Review*, 72, 1180-1187.

-          , 1989, *The political economy of protection*, London, Harwood Academic Publishers.

-          , 1994, "The political economy of migration policy" in: H. Siebert (Ed.), *Migration: A Challenge for Europe*, 263-282.

-          and E. Katz, 1987, "Hierarchical structure and the social costs of bribes and transfers", *Journal of Public Economics*, 34, 129-42.

Hinich, M.J. and M.C. Munger, 1989, "Political Investment, Voter Perceptions, and Candidate Strategy: An Equilibrium Spatial Analysis", in: P. Ordeshook (Ed.), *Models of Strategic Choice in Politics*, Ann Arbor, U. of Michigan Press, 49-67.

Hoyt, W.H. and E.F. Toma, 1989, "State mandates and interest group lobbying", *Journal of Public Economics*, 38, 199-213.

Katz, E. and J. Tokatlidu, 1996, "Group competition for rents", *European Journal of Political Economy*, 12, 599-607.

Konrad, K.A. and G. Torvsik, 1995, "Regulation and reelection", *paper presented at the Annual Meeting of the Public Choice Society*, Long Beach March 24-26,.

Krause, G.A., 1996, "The institutional dynamics of policy administration: Bureaucratic influence over securities regulation", *American Journal of Political Science*, 40, 1083-1121.

Krehbiel, K., 1990, "Are congressional committees composed of preference outliers?", *American Political Science Review*, 84, 149-163.

Laffont, J.J. and J. Tirole, 1991, "The politics of government decision-making: A theory of regulatory capture", *Quarterly Journal of Economics*, 106, 1089-1127.

- and - , 1993, *A theory of incentives in procurement and regulation*, Cambridge, MIT Press.

Langbein, L.I. and P.E. Crewson, 1996, "The Causes and Consequences of Administrative Discretion: Some Empirical Evidence", *Paper presented at the Public Choice Society Meeting, Houston*.

Leidy, M.P., 1994, "Trade policy and indirect rent seeking: A synthesis of recent work", *Economics and Politics*, 6, 97-118.

Lindsay, C.M. and M.T. Maloney, 1988, "Party politics and the price of payola", *Economic Inquiry*, 203-221.

Lohmann, S., "1993, A signalling model of informative and manipulative political action", *American Political Science Review*, 87, 319-333.

- , 1994, "Information aggregation through costly political action", *American Economic Review*, 84, 518-530.

- , 1994, "Electoral incentives, political intransparency and the policy bias toward special interests", *mimeo*.

- , 1995, "Information, access, and contributions: A signalling model of lobbying", *Public Choice*, 85, 267-284.

- , 1995, "A signalling model of competitive political pressures", *Economics and Politics*, 7, 181-206.

Lupia, A. and M. McCubbins, 1994, "Learning from oversight", *Journal of Law, Economics, and Organization*, 10, 1, 96-125.

Magee, S.P., Brock, W.A. and L. Young, 1989, *Black Hole Tariffs and Endogenous Policy Theory*. New York, Cambridge University Press.

Mazza, I. and F. van Winden, 1998, "An endogenous policy model of hierarchical government", *Tinbergen Institute Discussion Paper* n.98-007/1.

Mayer, W., 1984, "Endogenous tariff formation", *American Economic Review*, 74, 970-985.

- and J. Li, 1994, "Interest groups, electoral competition, and probabilistic voting for trade policies", *Economics and Politics*, 6, 59-77.

McCarty, N., 1996, "Commitment and the campaign contribution contract", *American Journal of Political Science*, 40, 872-904.

McCubbins, M. and T. Schwartz, 1984, "Congressional oversight overlooked: Police patrols vs. fire alarms", *American Journal of Political Science*, 28, 165-179.

McKelvey, R.D., 1976, "Intransitivities in multidimensional voting models and some implications for agenda control", *Journal of Economic Theory*, 12, 472-482.

McLachlan, D.L., 1985, "Discriminatory Public Procurement, Economic Integration and the Role of Bureaucracy", *Journal of Common Market Studies*, 23, 357-372.

Milgrom, P. and J. Roberts, 1992, *Economics, organization and management*, Englewood Cliffs, NJ, Prentice Hall.

Mo, J.-P., 1988, "Entry and structures of interest groups in assignment games", *Journal of Economic Theory*, 46, 66-96.

Morton, R. and C. Cameron, 1992, "Elections and the theory of campaign contributions: A survey and critical analysis", *Economics and Politics*, 4, 79-108.

Mueller, D.C. and T. Stratmann, 1994, "Informative and persuasive campaigning", *Public Choice*, 81, 55-77.

Munger, M.C., 1989, "A simple test of the hypothesis that committee jurisdiction shape corporate PAC contributions", *Public Choice*, 62, 181-186.

Muris, T.J., 1986, "Regulatory policymaking at the Federal Trade Commission: The extent of congressional control", *Journal of Political Economy*, 94, 2, 884-889.

Myerson, R. and R.J Weber, 1993, "A theory of voting equilibria", *American Political Science Review*, 87, 1, 102-114.

Nas, T.F., Price, A.C. and C.T. Weber, 1986, "A policy-oriented theory of corruption", *American Political Science Review*, 80, 1, 107-119.

Nelson, P., 1976, "Political information", *Journal of Law & Economics*, 19, 79-108.

Nitzman, S., 1994, "Modelling Rent-Seeking Contests", *European Journal of Political Economy*, 10, 41-60.

Noll, R.G., 1989, "Economic perspectives on the politics of regulation", in: Schmalensee, R. and R. Willig (Eds.), *Handbook of industrial organization*, II, Amsterdam, North Holland, 1253-1287.

Olson, M., 1965, *The logic of collective action*, , Cambridge, Harvard University Press.
-      , 1982, *The Rise and Decline of Nations*, Yale U. Press, New Haven.

Peacock, A., 1994, "The utility maximizing government economic adviser: A comment", *Public Choice*, 80, 191-197.

Peltzman, S., 1976, "Toward a more general theory of regulation", *Journal of Law and Economics*, 19, 211-240.

Persson, T. and G. Tabellini, 1994, "Does centralization increase the size of government?", *European Economic Review*, 38, 765-773.
-      , Roland, G. and G. Tabellini, 1996, "Separation of powers and accountability: Towards a formal approach to comparative politics", *CEPR Discussion Paper*, n.1475.

Posner, R.A., 1971, "Taxation by regulation", *Bell Journal of Economics and Management Science*, 2, 22-50.
-      , 1974, "Theories of Economic Regulation", *Bell Journal of Economics and Management Science*, 5, 335-358

Potters, J. and R. Sloof, 1996, "Interest groups. A survey of empirical models that try to assess their influence", *European Journal of Political Economy*, 12, 403-442.
-      and F. van Winden, 1992, "Lobbying and asymmetric information", *Public Choice*, 74, 269-292.
-      and -   , 1996, "Models of interest groups: Four different approaches", in Schofield, N. (Ed.), *Collective Decision-Making: Social Choice and Political Economy*, Boston, Kluwer, 337-362.

Potters, J., Sloof, R. and F. van Winden, 1997, "Campaign expenditures, contributions and direct endorsements: The strategic use of information and money to influence voter behavior", *European Journal of Political Economy*, 13, 1-31.

Radner, R., , 1992, "Hierarchy: The economics of managing", *Journal of Economic Literature*, 301382-1416.
-      , 1993, "The organization of decentralized information processing", *Econometrica*, 61, 1109-1146.

Romer, T. and H. Rosenthal, 1978, "Political resource allocation, controlled agenda and the status quo", *Public Choice*, 33, 27-44.
-      and -   , 1979, "Bureaucrats versus voters: on the political economy of resource allocation by direct democracy", *Quarterly Journal of Economics*, 93, 563-587.

Shleifer, A. and R.W. Vishny, 1993, "Corruption", *Quarterly Journal of Economics*, 108, 599-617.

Sloof, R., 1997, "Interest group influence and the internal organization of government", *mimeo.*

Snyder, J.M., 1990, "Campaign Contributions as Investments: The U.S. House of Representatives 1980-1986", *Journal of Political Economy*, 98, 1195-1227.

- , 1992, "Long-term investing in politicians; or, give early, give often", *Journal of Law and Economics*, 35, 15-43.

Spiller, P.T., 1990, "Politicians, Interest Groups, and Regulators: A Multiple -Principals Agency Theory of Regulation, or 'Let Them Be Bribed'", *Journal of Law and Economics*, 33.

Steunenberg, B., 1996, "Agent Discretion, Regulatory Policymaking, and Different Institutional Arrangements", *Public Choice*, 86, 309-339.

Stigler, G.J., 1971, "The theory of economic regulation", *Bell Journal of Economics and Management Science*, 2, 137-146.

Stratmann, T., 1991,"What do campaign contributions buy", *Southern Economic Journal*, 57, 606-620.

- , 1992, "Are contributors rational? Untangling strategies of political action committees", *Journal of Political Economy*, 100, 647-664.

- , 1995, "Campaign contributions and congressional voting: Does the timing of contributions matter?", *Review of Economics and Statistics*, 77, 127-136.

- , 1997, "Contributions patterns and voting behavior over legislators' careers: How legislators align themselves with interest groups" *mimeo.*

Sturzenegger, F. and M. Tommasi, 1994, "The Distribution of Political Power, the Costs of Rent-Seeking, and Economic Growth", *Economic Inquiry*, 32, 236-248.

Thompson, D.F., 1993, "Mediated corruption: the case of the Keating Five", *American Political Science Review*, 87, 369-381.

Tirole, J., 1992, "Collusion and the theory of organizations", in Laffont, J.J. (Ed.): *Advances in Economic Theory. Sixth World Congress*, II, Cambridge, Cambridge University Press, 151-206.

- , 1994, "The internal organization of government", *Oxford Economic Papers*, 46, 1-29.

Tullock, G., 1980, "Efficient Rent-Seeking", in: Buchanan, J.M., Tollison, R.D. and G. Tullock (eds.), *Toward a Theory of the Rent-Seeking Society*, Texas A. & M. University Press, 97-112.

- , 1983, *Economics of Income Redistribution*, Boston, Kluwer.

- , 1989, *The Economics of Special Privilege and Rent-Seeking*, Boston, Kluwer.

Ursprung, H.W., 1990, "Public Goods, Rent Dissipation and Candidate Competition", *Economics and Politics*, 2, 115-132.

van Velthoven, B., 1989, *The Endogenization of Government Behaviour in Macroeconomic Models*, Springer-Verlag, Heidelberg.

- and van Winden F., 1991, "A positive model of tax reform", *Public Choice*, 72, 61-86.

Weingast, B.R., 1984, "The congressional-bureaucratic system: A principal agent perspective", *Public Choice*, 44, 147-191.

- and M.J. Moran, 1983, "Bureaucratic discretion or congressional control? Regulatory policymaking by the Federal Trade Commission", *Journal of Political Economy*, 91, 765-800.

- and W.J. Marshall, 1988, "The industrial organization of Congress; or, why legislatures, like firms, are not organized as markets", *Journal of Political Economy*, 96, 132-163.

Wellisz, S. and J.D. Wilson, 1986, "Lobbying and tariff formation: A deadweight loss consideration", *Journal of International Economics*, 20, 367-375.

Wilson, J., 1989, *Bureaucracy: What government agencies do and why they do it*, New York, Basic Books.

van Winden F., 1997, "On the Economic Theory of Interest Groups. Towards a Group Frame of Reference in Political Economics", *CREED* Discussion paper.

Winer, S.L. and W. Hettich, 1993, "Optimal Representative Taxation, Information and Tax Reform", *mimeo*.

Wintrobe, R., 1996, "Modern bureaucratic theory", in: Mueller, D.C. (Ed.), *Perspectives on Public Choice*, Cambridge, CUP.

Wittman, D., 1989, "Why democracies produce efficient results", *Journal of Political Economy*, 97, 1395-1426.

Chapter 3

DELEGATED CONTROL OF INCENTIVES IN REGULATED INDUSTRIES

Fabrizia Lapecorella[*]
University of Bari, Italy

1. INTRODUCTION

We study the incentive problem faced by a regulator who controls only one of two privately informed firms belonging to a monopolistic industry and relies on this firm for provision of correct incentives to the other.

The regulation of multiproduct monopolies structured as hierarchies with one firm controlling the activity of the other(s) is a relevant and yet overlooked regulatory issue[1]. On policy grounds, a government wishing to regulate this type of industries may have no choice other than direct control of the firm at the top of the hierarchy and indirect control of the other(s). Alternatively, individual control of firms belonging to a monopolistic industry may be technically feasible but not desirable on political grounds: the growing concern for the size and the scope of government intervention in production that currently characterizes many capitalist economies can lead regulators to "prefer" limited control and indirect provision of incentives[2]. Finally, regulation through delegating control of incentives to a privately informed firm has interesting theoretical implications for the regulator's mechanism design problem. Since the final equilibrium in the industry depends on the outcome of the contracting game played by the firms, the optimal regulatory policy must satisfy additional implementability constraints relative to the case where each firm is directly controlled.

For the specification of the regulatory setting we follow Dana (1993). In particular, his analysis of regulation with decentralized production is the benchmark to which we compare our regulation with delegation. Ruling out the possibility that one firm can produce all the industry products, we focus on different ways of coordinating the activities of two firms each endowed with a piece of private information[3].

A regulatory problem similar to ours is studied in Baron and Besanko (1992) who derive the optimal regulatory policy for a firm organized as a two-tier hierarchy with each unit privately informed about its cost. Under the assumption that the contract signed by the units as well as the communication between them are observable, their mechanism design problem is shown to have a solution always identical to that obtained with direct provision of individual incentives[4].

An inherently different mechanism design problem arises under our assumption that the contractual relation between the two firms is unobservable. For this case, we first define the set of incentive constraints required to prevent the firms from strategic use of both their private information and contracting opportunities, then we derive the optimal incentive scheme that fully implements the desired regulatory outcome[5].

We show that regulation trough delegation is costly in terms of expected welfare only when industry costs are positively correlated. In all other cases, optimal incentive schemes with direct and delegated provision of incentives turn out to be identical. This non obvious equivalence result is due to the relation between the firms' ex-post profits established in equilibrium under centralized control of incentives. In fact, with uncorrelated or negatively correlated costs, there are no incentives for strategic contracting between firms because the profits that each of them is allowed to make are a non-increasing function of the other's cost report.

The paper is organized as follows. In sections 2 and 3 we describe the regulatory setting and summarize the features of the optimal regulatory policy with centralized control of incentives. The regulator's mechanism design problem under delegated control of incentives is discussed in Section 4 where we define the implementability constraints that prevent strategic contracting between the firms. The optimal regulatory policy is derived in Section 5 and discussed in Section 6. Section 7 concludes.

2.   THE MODEL

The regulator contracts for two goods, q_i, produced by two different firms at a constant marginal cost c_i, $i \in \{1,2\}$. The realized costs of firm i may be either low or high, i.e. $c_i \in \{c_i^L, c_i^H\}$, with $c_i^L < c_i^H$. We denote by

$j \in \{L, H\}$ the set of firm *1*'s types and by $k \in \{L, H\}$ the set of firm *2*'s types. To simplify notation we let $\Delta c_i = c_i^H - c_i^L, \forall i$.

Each firm can only produce one output and is privately informed on its marginal cost. Firm *1*, whose marginal cost is c_1^j believes that firm *2* has low costs with probability x_1^j, i.e. $x_1^j = pr\left(c_2 = c_2^L \middle| c_1 = c_1^j\right)$; x_2^k denotes the corresponding conditional probability for firm *2* of type k.

The regulator's beliefs about firms' costs are represented by the joint probability distribution function $\phi(c_1, c_2)$ with $\phi^{jk} = pr(c_1 = c_1^j \text{ and } c_2 = c_2^k)$, $\sum_j \sum_k \phi^{jk} = 1$. Costs may be correlated and

$$\frac{\phi^{LL}}{\phi^{HL}} > \frac{\phi^{LH}}{\phi^{HH}} \text{ if } cov(c_1, c_2) > 0,$$ with the sign of the inequality reversed for negative correlation. All other information is assumed to be common knowledge.

Firm *i*'s total revenue, $T_i = t_i + p_i(q_i)q_i$, is the sum of revenue from sales, $p_i(q_i)q_i$, and a net transfer payment received from the government, t_i [6]. Given the demand for its product, each firm chooses the level of production that maximizes profits, $\pi_i = T_i - c_i q_i$. Assuming that production in the industry depends on government demand only, we require that the regulated firms' profits be non-negative for any possible cost realization.

Total benefit accruing to consumers from consumption of good q_i, is the area underneath the inverse demand curve, $S_i(q_i) = \int p_i(q_i)dq_i$, assumed to be increasing and concave in output. Hence, the inverse demand function, $p_i = p_i(q_i) = S_i'(q_i)$, is decreasing.

The regulator is benevolent and its objective is to maximize social welfare defined as a weighted average of consumers' surplus and profits [7]:

$$SW = \sum_{i=1,2} \{S_i(q_i) - T_i + \alpha(T_i - c_i q_i)\}, \quad 0 < \alpha < 1 \tag{1}$$

As customary, it is assumed that firms have no opportunity to bargain with the regulator over the form of R.

3.   REGULATION WITH CENTRALIZED
CONTROL OF INCENTIVES

With no asymmetry of information, the regulator achieves its objective by imposing marginal cost pricing to each firm in the industry[8]. However, with imperfect information about costs, the regulator can only use quantities q_i (or, equivalently, prices p_i) and transfers, T_i to design a contract where each firm's output and total revenue are specified as a function of both firms' announced costs[9]. Denoting the cost contingent quantities and transfers by $q_i^{jk} = q_i(c_1^j, c_2^k)$ and $T_i^{jk} = T_i(c_1^j, c_2^k)$ for $i \in \{1,2\}$ and $j,k = H,L$, the regulatory contract is the set of values $R = \{q_i^{jk}, T_i^{jk}\}$.

The optimal pricing policy for the case where the regulator has direct control on each firm in the industry is the benchmark for our analysis of delegated control of incentives[10].

Under centralized control of incentives the timing of the game played by the regulator and the firms is the following:

Nature draws the value of each firm's cost c_i for $i \in \{1,2\}$. Each firm learns only its own cost.

The regulator proposes R.

Each firm accepts or refuses R. If one firm refuses, both get their reservation level of profits.

If both accept, R is implemented.

With this timing and given the assumption that regulated firms cannot make negative profits, R must be chosen so as to maximize expected social welfare under *ex-post* participation constraints and *interim* incentive constraints for each firm:

$$\underset{R}{MAX} \ \sum_j \sum_k \phi^{jk} \left\{ \sum_{i=1,2} \left[S_i\left(q_i^{jk}\right) - (1-\alpha)T_i^{jk} \right] - \alpha\left(c_1^j q_1^{jk} + c_2^k q_2^{jk}\right) \right\} \qquad [CENT]$$

$$s.t.: x_1^j\left(T_1^{jL} - c_1^j q_1^{jL}\right) + \left(1 - x_1^j\right)\left(T_1^{jH} - c_1^j q_1^{jH}\right) \geq x_1^j\left(T_1^{mL} - c_1^j q_1^{mL}\right) + \left(1 - x_1^j\right)\left(T_1^{mH} - c_1^j q_1^{mH}\right)$$

$$j,m = L,H; j \neq m \qquad [IC1]$$

$$x_2^k\left(T_2^{Lk} - c_2^k q_{21}^{Lk}\right) + \left(1 - x_2^k\right)\left(T_2^{Hk} - c_2^k q_2^{Hk}\right) \geq x_2^k\left(T_2^{Ln} - c_2^k q_2^{Ln}\right) + \left(1 - x_2^k\right)\left(T_2^{Hn} - c_2^k q_2^{Hn}\right)$$

$$k, n = L, H; k \neq n \qquad [IC2]$$

$$T_1^{jk} - c_1^j q_1^{jk} \geq 0 \qquad\qquad j, k = L, H \qquad [P1]$$

$$T_2^{jk} - c_2^k q_2^{jk} \geq 0 \qquad\qquad j, k = L, H \qquad [P2]$$

At the optimum of this problem the binding constraints are the *ex-post* participation constraints for the inefficient firms and the Bayesian incentive constraints for the efficient firms.

The first effect of the non-negative *ex-post* profits constraints is that in equilibrium each firm chooses to report its true costs as a dominant strategy[11]. The second effect of these constraints is that the Cremer and Mc Lean (1988) result on *first best* implementation in correlated environments does not apply and the optimal regulatory policy always commands prices above marginal costs for the inefficient firms. In particular, with uncorrelated costs the regulator can do no better than in the case where it faces a single privately informed monopolist: each firm's optimal level of production is set independently of the other firm's cost, and the departure from marginal cost pricing allowed to inefficient firms has the purpose of limiting the informational rent of the efficient ones[12]. With correlated costs equilibrium allocations are qualitatively similar. However, the regulator achieves a higher expected social welfare by allowing a more significant output distortion relative to the *first best* level in the state of the nature that is relatively less likely to occur and, simultaneously, reducing the rents paid in the state that is relatively more likely.

The features of the *second best* regulatory outcome can be summarized as follows:

Proposition 1: *Under centralized control of incentives firm 1 and firm 2 are treated symmetrically:*
each efficient firm produces the first best level of output:

$$p_1\left(q_1^{Lk}\right) = c_1^L \qquad\qquad \forall k,$$

$$p_2\left(q_2^{jL}\right) = c_2^L \qquad\qquad \forall j \; ;$$

each inefficient firm produces a level of output lower than the first best level. When costs are correlated the magnitude of the distortion allowed to each firm depends on the cost of the other:

$$p_1\left(q_1^{Hk}\right) = c_1^H + \frac{\phi^{Lk}}{\phi^{Hk}}(1-\alpha)\Delta c_1 \qquad\qquad k = L, H \; ,$$

$$p_2\left(q_2^{jH}\right) = c_2^H + \frac{\phi^{jL}}{\phi^{jH}}(1-\alpha)\Delta c_2 \qquad\qquad j = L, H \; ;$$

i.e. $\overset{\bullet}{q_1^{Hk}}, q_2^{jH}$ *are increasing (decreasing) functions of the other firm's cost if correlation is positive (negative);*

informational rents for the efficient firms are proportional to the level of output that they should have produced if they had reported $c_i = c_i^H$ *:*

$$\pi_1^{Lk} = \Delta c_1 q_1^{Hk} \qquad\qquad k = L, H \; ,$$

$$\pi_2^{jL} = \Delta c_2 q_2^{jH} \qquad\qquad j = L, H \; ;$$

inefficient firms make no profits:

$$\pi_1^{Hk} = 0 \qquad\qquad \forall k \; ,$$

$$\pi_2^{jH} = 0 \qquad\qquad \forall j \; .$$

4.   MECHANISM DESIGN WITH DELEGATED CONTROL OF INCENTIVES

We now consider the case where the government can only buy q_1 and q_2 from one of the two firms, say firm *1*. Since each firm can only produce one output, firm *1* buys q_2 from firm *2* at a price $T_2 = T_2(q_2)$, and has a total revenue $T = t_1 + \sum_{i=1,2} p_i(q_i)$, where the first term is a net transfer from the government and the second is the revenue from sale of the two products. This amounts to assume that direct communication with both firms is too costly for the regulator. On the other hand, the two firms can communicate between them at no cost. This time the regulatory policy is a triplet $R' = \{q_1^{jk}, q_2^{jk}, T^{jk}\}$ with q_i^{jk} and T^{jk} contingent on the values of c_1 and c_2 reported by firm *1* to the regulator. Given R', firm *1* offers a contract $C = \{q_2, T_2\}$ to firm *2*.

The firms' profits are $\pi_1 = T - T_2 - c_1 q_1$ and $\pi_2 = T_2 - c_2 q_2$. As before, no firm in the industry can make losses, therefore, both R' and C must satisfy *ex-post* participation constraints.

The net surplus accruing to consumers is given by the difference between $\sum_{i=1,2} S_i(q_i)$ and firm *1*'s total transfer, T, and social welfare is a weighted average of consumers' and producers' surplus:

$$SW = \sum_{i=1,2} [S_i(q_i) - \alpha c_i q_i] - (1 - \alpha)T \qquad 0 < \alpha < 1. \tag{2}$$

We assume that C cannot be observed or verified by the regulator, whereas the cost report made by firm *2* is verifiable. By imposing that firm *1* transmits to the regulator the whole vector of types we focus on the issue of opportunistic behavior on the part of the firm that is directly controlled and do not consider the effects of limited communication that have been analyzed elsewhere in the literature[13]. If firm *1* accepts R', the two firms play a principal-agent game where firm *1* is an *informed principal* in the sense of Myerson (1983)[14]. The regulator mechanism design problem is complicated by the fact that under R' the informed middle principal has the right to design and offer an unobservable contract to firm *2*. This implies that firm *1* can deviate from the regulator's preferred behavior by lying on its marginal cost and/or offering to firm *2* a contract that is not incentive compatible.

Under delegated control of incentives the timing of the overall game is the following:

Nature draws the value of each firm's cost c_i for $i \in \{1,2\}$. Each firm learns only its own cost.

The regulator proposes R' to firm *1*.

Firm *1* accepts or refuses R'. If *1* refuses, both firms get their reservation level of profits.

If R' is accepted, firm *1* offers to firm *2* an unobservable contract C.

Firm *2* accepts or refuses C. If *2* refuses, both firms get their reservation level of profits.

If C is accepted, firm *2* reports c_2 to firm *1*. This report is verifiable.

Firm *1* reports c_1 and c_2 to the regulator. R' and C are implemented.

This timing - in the presence of cost correlation – may induce the informed middle principal to use strategically its contracting opportunities: when firm *1* - before contracting with firm *2* - has already signed an agreement that conditions its *ex-post* profits to the reported value of c_2, this firm may find it profitable to offer a contract such that firm *2* is not given proper incentives to reveal c_2. In this case firm *1* offers a contract $C_P = \{q_2^{jk}, T_{2P}^k\}$ where T_{2P}^k only satisfy firm *2*'s *ex-post* participation constraints. Alternatively, firm *1* can induce truthful reporting of c_2 by offering an incentive compatible contract $C_{IC} = \{q_2^{jk}, T_{2IC}^k\}$ where T_{2IC}^k satisfy firm *2*'s incentive compatibility constraints as well as *ex-post* participation constraints[15]. The form of the transfers paid to firm *2* under these two contracts is the following:

$$T_{2P}^k = c_2^k q_2^{jk} \tag{3}$$

$$T_{2IC}^L = c_2^L q_2^{jL} + \Delta c_2 q_2^{jH} \tag{4}$$

$$T_{2IC}^H = c_2^H q_2^{jH} \tag{5}.$$

If firm *1* pays firm *2* according to reported costs without providing incentives for truthful cost revelation, the latter will consistently pretend that its costs are high and the quantities q_i^{jL} will never be produced in equilibrium. Therefore, full implementation of the desired regulatory outcome requires that the regulator designs a grand-mechanism that in equilibrium induces firm *1* to report the true value of c_1 and offer an incentive compatible contract C_{IC} to firm *2*. Since the generalized version of the Revelation Principle[16] applies to the overall game, the regulator can select such a mechanism from the class of direct mechanisms that induce truthtelling and honest behavior, without loss of generality. We call mechanisms with these properties *incentive and contract compatible*.

The implementability constraints that must be satisfied by any incentive and contract compatible regulatory policy $R' = \left\{ q_1^{jk}, q_2^{jk}, T^{jk} \right\}$, are defined as follows:

(i) contract compatibility:

the expected profits of firm *1* that reports the true c_1 and offers C_{IC} to firm *2* must be at least as great as its profits if - for any reported value of c_1 - it offers to firm *2* the contract C_P:

$$x_1^j \left(T^{jL} - T_{2IC}^L - c_1^j q_1^{jL} \right) + \left(1 - x_1^j \right)\left(T^{jH} - T_{2IC}^H - c_1^j q_1^{jH} \right) \geq T^{mH} - T_{2P}^H - c_1^j q_1^{mH}$$

$$j = L, H; \forall m = L, H . \qquad [CC]$$

(ii) incentive compatibility:

the expected profits of firm *1* that reports the true c_1 and offers C_{IC} to firm *2* must be at least as great as its expected profits if it lies on the value of c_1:

$$x_1^j \left(T^{jL} - T_{2IC}^L - c_1^j q_1^{jL} \right) + \left(1 - x_1^j \right)\left(T^{jH} - T_{2IC}^H - c_1^j q_1^{jH} \right) \geq x_1^j \left(T^{mL} - T_{2IC}^L - c_1^j q_1^{mL} \right) + \left(1 - x_1^j \right)\left(T^{mH} - T_{2IC}^H - c_1^j q_1^{mH} \right)$$

$$j, m = L, H; m \neq j \qquad [IC]$$

Constraints *CC* ensure that firm *1* can never profit from offering to firm *2* a contract that is not incentive compatible. Constraints *IC* are, instead, standard incentive compatibility constraints.

5. REGULATION WITH DELEGATED CONTROL OF INCENTIVES

When only one firm in the industry is directly regulated and this firm is given the right to design and offer an unobservable contract to the other firm, the optimal regulatory policy is the set of cost contingent values

$R' = \{q_1^{jk}, q_2^{jk}, T^{jk}\}$, $j, k = L, H$, that maximizes expected social welfare under implementability constraints CC and IC, *ex-post* participation constraints P, and feasibility constraints F. Accordingly, R' solves the following program:

$$MAX \sum_j \sum_k \phi^{jk} \left[S_1(q_1^{jk}) + S_2(q_2^{jk}) - T^{jk} + \alpha(T^{jk} - c_1^j q_1^{jk} - c_2^k q_2^{jk}) \right] \quad [DEL]$$

s.t.:

CC, IC

$$T^{jk} - T_{2IC}^k - c_1^j q_1^{jk} \geq 0 \qquad\qquad j, k = L, H \qquad\qquad [P]$$

$$q_2^{jL} \geq q_2^{jH} \qquad\qquad \forall j \qquad\qquad [F]$$

where constraints F impose a standard monotonicity restriction on the output produced by firm *2* that is required for feasibility of the incentive compatible contract C_{IC} [17].

The central result of our analysis is that delegated control of incentives does not affect the efficiency of the regulatory outcome so long as the two firms' costs are not positively correlated.

Proposition 2: *With negative cost correlation the optimal regulatory mechanism R that implements the second best outcome under centralized control of incentives is incentive and contract compatible.*

Proof: See the Appendix.

This equivalence result is simply due to the fact that under the incentive scheme that is optimal with direct control of incentives and negative cost correlation, the *ex-post* profits for any type of firm *1* are a decreasing function of the cost report of the other firm. In this case the contract compatibility constraints CC have no role to play because it is in the interest of firm *1* that the regulator be able to observe outputs q_2^{jL} when the realized costs of the firm that is indirectly regulated are low [18].

When firms' costs are positively correlated the regulator anticipates that any type of firm *1* faced with an incentive scheme that promises *ex-post* profits $\pi^{jH} > \pi^{jL}$ will prefer that firm 2 reports high costs always. In this case, implementation of the allocations desired by the regulator in the four possible states of nature is subject to binding contract compatibility constraints and the *second best* outcome obtained with centralized control of incentives is no longer implementable.

In equilibrium, the regulatory outcome has the following features:

Proposition 3: *With positive cost correlation, the optimal incentive and contract compatible regulatory mechanism is such that:*
efficient firms are treated symmetrically. Each firm produces the first best level of output regardless of the value of the other firm's cost:

$$p_1\left(\hat{q}_1^{Lk}\right) = c_1^L \qquad \forall k$$

$$p_2\left(\hat{q}_2^{jL}\right) = c_2^L \qquad \forall j ;$$

inefficient firms produce a level of output lower than the first best level but they are not treated symmetrically: the output produced by firm 1 is constant across the realized costs of firm 2, whereas output of firm 2 is an increasing function of firm 1's cost:

$$p_1\left(\hat{q}_1^{Hk}\right) = c_1^H + \frac{\left(\phi^{LL} + \phi^{LH}\right)}{\left(\phi^{HL} + \phi^{HH}\right)}(1 - \alpha)\Delta c_1 \qquad \forall k$$

$$p_2\left(\hat{q}_2^{jH}\right) = c_2^H + \frac{\phi^{jL}}{\phi^{jH}}(1 - \alpha)\Delta c_2 \qquad j = L, H$$

and $\hat{q}_2^{HH} > \hat{q}_2^{LH}$ implied by $\mathrm{cov}(c_1, c_2) > 0$;
the efficient firm 1 enjoys informational rents. The optimal transfers T^{Lk} are such that this firm's ex-post profits are constant across the realized values of c_2, i.e. $\hat{\pi}_1^{LL} = \hat{\pi}_1^{LH} = \Delta c_1 \hat{q}_1^H$;
the inefficient firm 1 makes zero profits always, i.e. $\hat{\pi}_1^{HL} = \hat{\pi}_1^{HH} = 0$.

Proof: See the Appendix.

In this model the efficiency loss associated to indirect control of incentives is due to the fact that in order to eliminate firm *1*'s incentive to offer the "wrong" contract to firm *2*, the regulator can no longer exploit the positive cost correlation and must offer an incentive scheme that grants to the efficient firm *1* the same informational rent in the two states $\left(c_1^L, c_2^L\right)$ and $\left(c_1^L, c_2^H\right)$. At the optimum, the two participation constraints for the efficient firm are slack, whereas all the incentive constraints for this firm, *IC* and *CC*, are binding. This implies that the least costly way for ensuring that in fact an incentive compatible contract is offered to firm *2* is to choose net transfers for the efficient firm *1* that satisfy:

$$T^{LL} - T_{2IC}^{L} - c_1^L q_1^{LL} = T^{LH} - T_{2IC}^{H} - c_1^L q_1^{LH} = \pi_1^L \tag{6}.$$

Equation (6) is the binding constraint *CC* for $j = m = L$, written using (3) and (5), i.e. $T_{2P}^{H} = T_{2IC}^{H}$. Given (6) and the binding participation constraints for $j = H$, the other two binding incentive constraints are:

$$\pi_1^L = \Delta c_1 \left[x_1^L q_1^{HL} + \left(1 - x_1^L\right) q_1^{HH} \right] \tag{7}$$

$$\pi_1^L = \Delta c_1 q_1^{HH} \tag{8}.$$

(7) and (8) imply that $\hat{q}_1^{HL} = \hat{q}_1^{HH} = \hat{q}_1^{H}$. The optimal net transfer for the efficient firm *1* is independent of the value of c_2 and is given by:

$$\hat{t}_1^L = c_1^L q_1^{LL} + \Delta c_1 \hat{q}_1^{H} = c_1^L q_1^{LH} + \Delta c_1 \hat{q}_1^{H} \tag{9}.$$

From (9) follows that at the optimum of $[DEL]$ $\hat{q}_1^{LL} = \hat{q}_1^{LH} = \hat{q}_1^{L}$; moreover, the efficient firm has an informational rent $\Delta c_1 \hat{q}_1^{H}$ that, as usual, is proportional to the level of output that should be produced if realized costs were high. This time, however, the magnitude of the optimal departure from marginal cost pricing is directly related to the regulator's probabilistic assessment that the regulated firm is efficient given by the marginal probability that $c_1 = c_1^L$.

This result has an interesting implication in terms of the regulator's preference for the firm that is to be controlled directly. If the regulator, believing that the directly controlled firm is likely to be efficient (inefficient) reduces the welfare loss due to his imperfect information by setting as high (low) a price as possible for the output to be produced when the reported cost is high, he will do so more effectively if the price elasticity of demand for the firm's output is high (low).

Finally, since the optimal regulatory policy sets $\hat{q}_2^{jL} > \hat{q}_2^{jH}$, contract compatibility implies that the equilibrium allocations of firm *2*'s output and profits are exactly identical to those described in Proposition 1 with the net transfers paid by (accruing to) the regulator through firm *1*.

6. DELEGATED VS. CENTRALIZED CONTROL OF INCENTIVES

Under regulation with delegated provision of incentives the strategy space of the firm that is directly regulated is enlarged relative to the case where individual incentives are provided to each firm and this creates additional opportunities for strategic deviations from the regulator's preferred behavior. Proposition 2 establishes that there are circumstances in which this bears no consequences for the regulator's mechanism design problem. When firms' costs are negatively correlated, firm *1*'s incentives for strategic contracting with firm *2* are eliminated by the relationship between firm *1*'s profits and firm *2*'s announced costs established by the incentive scheme that is optimal under centralized regulation.

A similar result is derived by Baron and Besanko (1992) who study the same two types of regulation using a different model of multiproduct monopoly[19]. As pointed out in the introduction, the chief difference between this study of indirect regulation and ours relates to the assumed observability of the contract offered by one firm to the other. Under this assumption the incentive schemes appropriate in each regulatory setting can only differ if firm *1*'s choice of the incentive contract offered to firm *2* signals its privately known cost parameter. Analysis of the equilibrium in the subgame played by the two firms shows that, in fact, this is not the case. Thus, there are never efficiency losses in bringing about the desired regulatory outcome by simply ordering firm *1* to pass to firm *2* the same incentive compatible payments that the regulator would have paid if it had contracted with firm *2* directly.

In our model the form of the contract signed by the firms is independent of the true value of c_1 (see the Appendix). However, when this contract is unobservable this is not in itself sufficient to establish equivalence of the two regulatory regimes. In fact, when cost correlation is positive decentralized incentives are such that the efficient firm can always profit by allowing firm *2* to exaggerate its costs. In this case the same incentive constraints that are binding at the optimum of problem $[CENT]$ bind at the optimum of $[DEL]$. In addition, the two contract compatibility constraints for the efficient firm *1* bind at the optimum of $[DEL]$ and, therefore, expected social welfare under regulation through delegation is strictly lower than expected social welfare with direct regulation. This suggests that in the presence of positive cost correlation a benevolent regulator who can freely choose the scope of direct control over the firms belonging to an industry to be regulated, will never choose to delegate provision of incentives to one of the two firms comprising the industry.

7.   CONCLUSIONS

In this paper we have characterized the nature of the incentive problem faced by a regulator who controls directly only one of two privately informed firms. The regulator wishes that this firm reveals its private information and provides the other firm with proper incentives for truthful cost revelation of its costs, but cannot observe the contract agreed upon by the firms.

While it is well known that in the presence of asymmetric information limiting the scope of direct control can never be beneficial, we have shown that there are circumstances in which this indirect form of regulation can be as (in)efficient as direct regulation. In fact, when industry costs are negatively correlated implementation of the desired regulatory outcome does not require use of costly incentives. In this case delegated control of incentives can be an effective choice to achieve other important objectives. It might, for example, allow saving on transaction costs associated to each individual regulatory agreement, or help to ease political concern about the size of government intervention in private production.

The equivalence between centralized and delegated provision of incentives no longer holds if there is positive cost correlation. In this case the regulator's incentive problem is compounded and expected social welfare is lower than in the case where both firms are directly controlled by the regulator.

APPENDIX

The contracting game between the firms.

The game between firm *1* (*principal*) and firm *2* (*agent*) is an informed principal problem with "private values" since the private information of the principal is not an argument of the agent's objective function. In addition, the agent has a finite number of types and the prior information of the principal is such that the probability of each type is positive. For this type of problems, Maskin and Tirole (1990) prove that when the agent's objective function is linear in the payment received from the principal:

a) the principal employs the same mechanism when it has private information about its type as it would if its type were known to the agent;

b) the equilibrium mechanism is the same for whatever information the agent may have about the principal's type.

Our analysis of the contracting game between the firms uses these results.

Given a regulatory mechanism $R' = \left\{ q_1^{jk}, q_2^{jk}, T^{jk} \right\}$, firm *1* sets payments for firm *2* so as to minimize the expected cost of the contract offered to firm *2*. If firm *1* offers the contract $C_P = \left\{ q_2^{jk}, T_{2P}^k \right\}$ that is not incentive compatible, the cost minimizing transfers T_{2P}^k are obtained by solving the following program:

$$MIN \ x_1^j T_{2P}^L + \left(1 - x_1^j\right) T_{2P}^H \qquad \forall j$$

$$s.t.: \ T_{2P}^k - c_2^k q_2^{jk} \geq 0 \qquad\qquad k = L, H \qquad\qquad [P2]$$

In this case the optimal transfers are simply set equal to announced total costs, i.e.:

$$T_{2P}^k = c_2^k q_2^{jk} \qquad\qquad k = L, H \qquad\qquad (A.1).$$

If firm *1* offers the incentive compatible contract $C_{IC} = \left\{ q_2^{jk}, T_{2IC}^k \right\}$, the cost minimizing transfers T_{2IC}^k are obtained by solving the following program:

$$MIN \ x_1^j T_{2IC}^L + \left(1 - x_1^j\right) T_{2IC}^H \qquad\qquad \forall j$$

$$s.t.: \quad T_{2IC}^k - c_2^k q_2^{jk} \geq T_{2IC}^k - c_2^k q_2^{jn} \qquad k,n = L,H, n \neq k \qquad [IC2]$$

$$T_{2IC}^k - c_2^k q_2^k \geq 0 \qquad\qquad k,n = L,H \qquad\qquad [P2]$$

The solution is found via standard Lagrangean techniques and has the following features:

the set of incentive compatible transfers $\left\{T_{2IC}^k\right\}$ is non-empty if and only if the optimal regulatory mechanism sets $q_2^{jL} \geq q_2^{jH}$, $\forall j$;

if the set of incentive compatible transfer is non-empty, the general form of the cost minimizing transfers paid to firm 2 is:

$$T_{2IC}^L = c_2^L q_2^{jL} + \Delta c_2 q_2^{jH} \qquad\qquad \forall j \qquad\qquad\qquad (A.2)$$

$$T_{2IC}^H = c_2^H q_2^{jH} \qquad\qquad \forall j \qquad\qquad\qquad (A.3);$$

the efficient firm 2 enjoys an informational rent proportional to the level of output that it should have produced if it had reported $c_2 = c_2^H$:

$$\pi_2^{jL} = \Delta c_2 q_2^{jH} \qquad\qquad \forall j \qquad\qquad\qquad (A.4);$$

the inefficient firm 2 makes zero profits:

$$\pi_2^{jH} = 0 \qquad\qquad \forall j \qquad\qquad\qquad (A.5).$$

Proof of Proposition 2.

We prove that the solution to $[CENT]$ for the case of $\text{cov}(c_1,c_2) < 0$ solves the more constrained problem $[DEL]$ by checking that the contract compatibility constraints CC are satisfied when:

(i) $T^{jk} = T_1^{jk} + T_2^{jk}$, where T_i^{jk}, $i \in \{1,2\}$, are the transfers paid to the firms under the optimal centralized mechanism R;

(ii) q_i^{jk}, $i \in \{1,2\}$, are the optimal output levels as set in R.

Note first that for a given q_2^{jH}, $T_{2IC}^H = T_{2P}^H$ (see A.1 for $k = H$, and A.3). Therefore, constraints CC can be rewritten as:

$$T^{jL} - T_{2IC}^L - c_1^j q_1^{jL} \geq T^{jH} - T_{2IC}^H - c_1^j q_1^{jH} \qquad m = j; j, m = L, H \qquad (A.6)$$

$$x^j \left(T^{jL} - T_{2IC}^L - c_1^j q_1^{jL} \right) + \left(1 - x^j \right) \left(T^{jH} - T_{2IC}^H - c_1^j q_1^{jH} \right) \geq T^{mL} - T_{2IC}^L - c_1^j q_1^{mL}$$

$$m \neq j; j, m = L, H \qquad (A.7).$$

Furthermore, $T_2^{jk} = T_{2IC}^k \ \forall j$. Therefore, if firm 1 is paid $T^{jk} = T_1^{jk} + T_2^{jk}$, its profits are those given in Proposition 1:

$$\pi_1^{Lk} = \Delta c_1 q_1^{Hk} \qquad\qquad k = L, H \qquad\qquad\qquad (A.8)$$

$$\pi_1^{Hk} = 0 \qquad\qquad\qquad k = L, H \qquad\qquad\qquad (A.9)$$

We use A.8 and A.9 to rewrite A.6 and A.7 respectively as follows:

$$m = j; j = L: \qquad\qquad \Delta c_1 q_1^{HL} \geq \Delta c_1 q_1^{HH} \qquad\qquad (A.10)$$

$$m = j; j = H: \qquad\qquad 0 \geq 0 \qquad\qquad\qquad\qquad (A.11)$$

$$m \neq j; j = L: \qquad\qquad \Delta c_1 q_1^{HL} \geq \Delta c_1 q_1^{HH} \qquad\qquad (A.12)$$

$$m \neq j; j = H: \qquad\qquad \Delta c_1 q_1^{LH} \geq \Delta c_1 q_1^{HH} \qquad\qquad (A.13).$$

A.11 is trivially satisfied; A.13 is always strictly satisfied since R sets $q_1^{Lk} > q_1^{Hk}$, $\forall k$, irrespective of the relation between the firms' costs; A.10 and A.12 are satisfied if and only if $\text{cov}(c_1, c_2) \leq 0$, since in these cases R sets $q_1^{jL} \geq q_1^{jH}$, $\forall j$. In particular, with negative correlation firm I's profits are a decreasing function of c_2 and A.10 and A.12 are strictly satisfied. *Q.E.D.*

Proof of Proposition 3.

The solution of problem $[DEL]$ is found via standard Lagrangean techniques; the full Khun-Tucker analysis is in Lapecorella (1995). We check that the only binding constraints are the incentive compatibility constraint IC for the efficient firm, the contract compatibility constraints CC for the efficient firm and the participation constraints P for the inefficient firm:

$$x^L \left(T^{LL} - T_{2IC}^L - c_1^L q_1^{LL} \right) + \left(1 - x^L \right) \left(T^{LH} - T_{2IC}^H - c_1^L q_1^{LH} \right) =$$
$$x^L \left(T^{HL} - T_{2IC}^L - c_1^L q_1^{HL} \right) + \left(1 - x^L \right) \left(T^{HH} - T_{2IC}^H - c_1^L q_1^{HH} \right) \qquad \text{(A.14)}.$$

$$x^L \left(T^{LL} - T_{2IC}^L - c_1^L q_1^{LL} \right) + \left(1 - x^L \right) \left(T^{LH} - T_{2IC}^H - c_1^L q_1^{LH} \right) = T^{LL} - T_{2P}^H - c_1^L q_1^{LL}$$
$$\text{(A.15)}$$

$$x^L \left(T^{LL} - T_{2IC}^L - c_1^L q_1^{LL} \right) + \left(1 - x^L \right) \left(T^{LH} - T_{2IC}^H - c_1^L q_1^{LH} \right) = T^{HL} - T_{2IC}^H - c_1^L q_1^{HH}$$
$$\text{(A.16)}$$

$$T^{HL} - T_{2IC}^L - c_1^H q_1^{HL} = 0 \qquad\qquad\qquad\qquad\qquad\qquad \text{(A.17)}$$

$$T^{HH} - T_{2IC}^H - c_1^H q_1^{HH} = 0 \qquad\qquad\qquad\qquad\qquad\qquad \text{(A.18)}$$

Inserting into the regulator's objective function the values of the transfers T^{jk} obtained from the equations above and the values of T_{2P}^k and T_{2IC}^k given by A.1 to A.3 and optimizing yields the regulatory mechanism described in Proposition 3. *Q.E.D.*

NOTES

* I would like to thank Jean Jacques Laffont and Massimo Marrelli for helpful comments on earlier versions of this paper.

1   Most papers in the literature on multiproduct monopoly regulation are based on the implicit assumption that the regulator has the ability to exert direct control on the productive activity of each firm (see, for example, Sappington (1983b), or Laffont and Tirole (1990), and subsequent studies based on these).

2   It is a well known result of the incentive literature that there can be no losses in controlling the activities of privately informed agents by means of individual complete contracts (see Tirole (1988) or Holmstrom and Tirole (1989)). Hence, the regulator's preference for regulation through delegation - when direct control is available - cannot be rationalized in terms of expected cost of providing incentives.

3   In general, with this assumption we study a problem where the organizational structure of production does not affect the underlying structure of private information. Regulation with delegated control is, in this respect, different from Dana's integrated production case (where the regulator deals with one firm possessing two-dimensional private information), and from other similar studies (see, for example, Riordan and Sappington (1987)).

4   In fact, when the regulator observes both the mechanism ruling the interaction of the units and their cost reports, he actually deals with a problem of one-dimensional uncertainty (with respect to each unit) that is no different from that he faces when each unit is regulated directly (we say more on this point in section 6). Unlike us, Baron and Besanko use fixed coefficient technologies and focus on the case of independent costs. Their equivalence result, however, does not follow from these assumptions.

5   A thorough account of the mechanism design problem with limited control of incentives and unobservable subcontracting, in a more general setting, is given in De Fraja and Lapecorella (1995).

6   Note that t_i can be a tax or a subsidy depending on whether it is negative or positive respectively. Government net transfers are assumed to be lump sum so that consumers' surplus just varies by an equivalent amount.

7   A theoretical rationalization of this social welfare function, frequently used in the literature to represent regulator's objective, is given in Baron (1988).

8   Constant marginal costs imply that marginal cost pricing is the full information benchmark. So long as the assumption of no social cost of public funds is retained, marginal cost pricing is the relevant benchmark even if a known fixed cost is added to the specification of the cost functions.

9   The derivation of the optimal regulatory policy in terms of the aggregate transfers t_i is based on the implicit assumption that consumers' demand for each good depends only on the price of the good considered.

10 The solution of the regulator's problem for the case of direct control of incentives is in Dana (1993).

11 For a general discussion of full implementation in multiple agents settings with risk neutrality and limited liability see Demski, Sappington and Spiller (1988).

12 See Baron and Myerson (1982).

13 See Baron and Besanko (1992), Melumad, Mookherjee and Reichelstein (1995), Gilbert and Riordan (1995) and Laffont and Martimort (1998, 1999).

[14] The informed principal problem that arises in our model is discussed in the Appendix. There we use the analysis of this type of agency problems developed by Maskin and Tirole (1990, 1992).

[15] These transfers are derived in the Appendix. Note that the functions $l_{2P}^{..}$ and l_{2IC}, $K = L, H$, are not indexed with the superscript j because we know from Maskin and Tirole (1990) that with private values and risk neutrality, the form of the contracts offered to firm *2* does not depend on firm *1*'s type (equivalently, the outcome of the contracting game is the same as if firm *2* were informed on firm *1*'s type).

[16] See Myerson (1982).

[17] This follows from the solution of the contracting game played by the two firms (see the Appendix).

[18] As usual, here it is implicitly assumed that when indifferent between two courses of action the agent selects the one preferred by the principal.

[19] Another equivalence result is obtained by Melumad, Mookherjee and Reichelstein (1995); however, unlike us, they study only an uncorrelated environment.

REFERENCES

Baron, D.P, 1988, "Regulation and Legislative Choice", *RAND Journal of Economics*, 19, 467-477.

Baron, D.P. and R.B. Myerson, 1982, "Regulating a Monopolist with Unknown Costs", *Econometrica*, 53, 911-930.

Baron, D.P. and D. Besanko, 1992, "Information, Control and Organizational Structure", *Journal of Economics & Management Strategy*, 1, 237-275.

Cremer, J. and R. Mc Lean, 1988, "Full Extraction of the Surplus in Bayesian and Dominant Strategy Auctions", *Econometrica*, 56, 1247- 1258.

Dana, J.D.jr., 1993, "The Organization and the Scope of Agents: Regulating Multiproduct Industries", *Journal of Economic Theory*, 59, 288-310.

De Fraja, G. and F. Lapecorella, 1995, "Optimal mechanism Design in Vertical Hierarchies with Unobservable Subcontracting", *mimeo*, University of York.

Demski, J.S. and D.E.M. Sappington, 1984, "Optimal Incentive Contracts with Multiple Agents", *Journal of Economic Theory*, 33, 152-171.

Demski, J.S., D.E.M. Sappington and P. Spiller, 1988, "Incentive Schemes with Multiple Agents and bankruptcy constraints", *Journal of Economic Theory*, 44, 156-167.

Gilbert, R. and M. Riordan, 1995, "Regulating Complementary Products: A Comparative Institutional Analysis", *RAND Journal of Economics*, 26, 243-256.

Holmstrom, B.R. and J. Tirole, 1989, "The Theory of the Firm", in R. Schmalensee and R.D. Willig, eds., *Handbook of Industrial Organization*, v.1, Amsterdam: North Holland, 61-133.

Laffont, J.J. and D. Martimort, 1998, "Collusion and Delegation", *RAND Journal of Economics*, 29, 280-305.

Laffont, J.J. and D. Martimort, 1999, "Mechanism Design under Collusion and Correlation", forthcoming *Econometrica*.

Laffont, J.J. and J. Tirole, 1990, "The Regulation of Multiproduct Firms, Part I: Theory", *Journal of Public Economics*, 43, 1-36.

Lapecorella, F., 1995, "Multiproduct Monopoly Regulation with Delegated Control of Incentives", *Discussion Paper* n.95/47, University of York.

Maskin, E. and J. Tirole, 1990, "The Principal-Agent Relationship with an Informed Principal, I: Private Values", *Econometrica*, 58, 379-410.

Chapter 4

FIRMS, UNIONS AND REGULATORS

Giacomo Pignataro[*]
University of Catania, Italy

1. INTRODUCTION

Over the last fifteen years there has been an extensive revision of the theory of optimal pricing in regulated industries. The traditional concern was with the design of optimal pricing rules, looked at as a problem of maximising a social welfare function subject to some basic constraints, represented by consumers' demand and firm technology. The main criticism to this approach is that it completely overlooks the limits to perfect regulation, mainly arising from the asymmetric distribution of information between the regulator and the regulated firm. The new economics of regulation is, therefore, built upon the assumption of asymmetric information, and it has contributed to the establishment of new theoretical benchmarks for optimal pricing. One of the main achievements of this literature is, however, that it does not consider the firm as a passive subject in a "command-and-control" scheme, but as a strategic player in the regulatory game. Given the point we are up to now, there is, however, the need to extend this literature further, to take account of a wider spectrum of determinants of the strategic behaviour of the firm. In fact, the models belonging to the new economics of regulation are usually based on a very simple scheme of interaction between two parties only: the regulator and the firm, generally regarded as single entities. However, the regulatory relationship usually operates within a complex web of interactions of the firm with other actors in other markets. The main implication of considering these other interactions is that what is generally regarded as exogenous in the models of regulation is then endogenous to regulation. The outcome of regulation is affected not only by the distribution of information between the firm and the regulator, but also by the objectives pursued by other actors in other markets.

The extension of regulatory models to the analysis of firm and regulator interactions (other than the direct one, between the firm and the regulator) can be considered then a sort of logical corollary of one of the basic rationales of the new economics of regulation. Of course, modelling this spectrum of strategic interactions within the regulatory game is not an easy task since one cannot pretend to bring in the models *all the complexity of regulatory practice*. It is useful to adopt a sort of piecemeal approach and consider separately some of the relevant interactions with specified actors.

Actually there are a few recent models which consider an enlarged set of strategic determinants of the firm's behaviour within the regulatory game, looking at situations where a monopolist operates in both regulated and deregulated markets. Two examples are a paper by Anton and Gertler (1988) and another one by Vickers (1995). There is, however, a more general analytical problem connected to the neo-classical paradigm of the firm as a "black box": the equilibrium outcome of all the interactions characterising the internal organisation of a firm are considered as exogenous to regulation, while they are actually affected by, and affect regulation too.

There can be different ways of analysing the interactions within the firm. A possible way is to take account of situations where the different actors operating inside the firm share the same information and are able to make binding agreements. One very important example, as it will be extensively shown in this paper, is given by the existence of imperfectly competitive input markets. Workers, for instance, are usually paid a wage, which is bargained over between the firm and a union representing them.

The analysis of the role of a union in a firm, which is regulated in its output market, is a good case for different reasons. First of all, because the theoretical analysis of union behaviour is now well established and it offers different models which can be employed in our research to provide a consistent modelling of an enlarged regulatory game. Secondly, it is a topic of relevant interest in the regulatory practice and in the empirical analysis of the effects of regulation on factor prices. The paper just starts with a brief survey of this empirical analysis to show that the work done along these lines does not achieve any conclusive result. The lack of a sound theoretical framework does not allow for an understanding of the interrelation between output regulation and wage bargaining. The paper then summarises the results of two works by Pignataro (1995a, 1995b), which present two models of regulation of an output market, controlled by a monopolistic firm which bargains over workers' wage with a union.

In section 3, the first of the two works is discussed. It is a model characterised by the assumption of symmetric information among all the players in the game. The reason for beginning with a very simple, even if unrealistic assumption is, firstly, the usual one, that the complete information case can be regarded as a benchmark for examining situations which depart from this assumption. Secondly, this is a necessary step to extend the optimal pricing literature and to identify the specific control problems (different from those connected with asymmetric information), related to a regulatory setting in which the firm is not treated as a single entity and the regulator does not have a comprehensive authority on all players in the game. The main implication is that the contracting activity between the firm and the union may interfere with the optimality of the policy designed by the regulator, and therefore the analysis must identify the control problems related to this potential interference.

The objective of section 4 is extending the previous analysis to a setting where the regulator does not have complete information on the firm's technology and, therefore, computing the optimal regulatory policy. One of the main results achieved by the literature on regulation and asymmetric information is the fact that the firm, because of its superior information with respect to the regulator, is able to enjoy some rents. Within the context of this work, it becomes important to study how informational rents are shared with union, and how the level of these rents is affected by the bargaining activity between the firm and the union.

Section 5 summarises the main results of the analysis.

2. THE EMPIRICAL ANALYSIS OF THE EFFECTS OF REGULATION ON WAGES

Even if not considered by the theoretical literature on regulation, some empirical works, studying the effects of price regulation on workers wages, have introduced the assumption of imperfectly competitive input markets. We will briefly examine the results of the studies by Hendricks (1975, 1977), Moore (1978), Ehrenberg (1979) and Rose (1987).

The first of Hendricks' works studies the impact of regulation on collective bargaining in regulated electric utilities. He ran two empirical tests: in the first one, he compared wage levels within the regulated sector; in the second one he confronted wages of regulated and unregulated firms. What Hendricks wanted to show was that there is no guaranteed direction of the effect of price regulation on the level of wage and that this direction depends on the type of regulation. The basic mode of regulation considered in the paper is the rate of return, within different frameworks characterised by different factors affecting the probability of reviewing the allowed profit constraint. In the "profit boundary" case, there are profit levels (either high or low) beyond which a review is very likely. In the "firm initiated" case, it is the firm which puts forward the case for a review, but the regulator's decision on the revision still depends on the firm's profit level. Finally, the "commission resistance" hypothesis states that the current level of profits of a regulated firm depends on the toughness of regulators. In each of these three cases, the firm's resistance to wage increases depends on the profit level of the firm and it can be different in all three cases.

The analysis of data about wage levels in different electric utilities should help to ascertain the impact of the different hypotheses regarding the likelihood of rate review on wages. However, the route followed in the empirical section of Hendricks' paper is not to differentiate the utilities according to the different hypotheses regarding the probability of revision, but on the basis of their profit level to "impute the predominant mode of regulation from the resulting wage patterns". The result drawn by Hendricks from the analysis of the data is that, since low profit firms present higher wages than the other firms, this suggests that "the type of regulation which is most pervasive corresponds to the second case put forth".

The other relevant result stems from the comparison of wages between regulated electric utilities and non-regulated firms in other manufacturing industries. The finding is that wages are lower in regulated firms than in other non-regulated firms. A subsequent paper by Hendricks (1977), comparing earnings in seven occupations in fourteen regulated industries with earnings in other manufacturing industries, confirms this result. Hendricks' conclusion is that even if regulation can give unions more power because of entry restrictions, employment stability and managerial incentives to resist union claims can offset this effect.

Moore (1978) studies the effects of regulation on wages in the trucking industry. Like Hendricks, Moore considers a type of regulation based on a profit constraint but his results are completely different. Average wages are higher in regulated trucking firms than in non-regulated trucking firms.

Ehrenberg (1979) examines the case of the New York Telephone Company. It is important to clarify the object of Ehrenberg's study, which was not aimed at estimating the impact of regulation on wages, but at finding out whether NYT workers' wages were "just and reasonable". The interest shown in a "just and reasonable" wage was related to the regulatory practice of passing costs on to output prices. The effect of this practice is, according to Ehrenberg, to alter the bargaining structure in the labour market giving more power to unions. The wage scale, for Ehrenberg, could be considered as just and reasonable "if on average across occupations, the wage rate did not exceed the average wage rates for comparable-quality employees of other firms in the same labour markets from which NYT drew its employees". Then Ehrenberg carried out a comparison between wages paid by NYT and wages earned by other employees in the same labour market, using different sources of data. The conclusion of all comparisons was that "NYT was a high-wage employer". This result does not imply, according to the objectives of his study, that high wages for NYT workers were the effect of regulation, since he did not take account of other factors such as unionisation, which could have influenced wages.

Finally, the paper by Rose (1987) investigates the effects of deregulation in the trucking industry on wages. The idea is that regulation can create rents "over which workers and firms may negotiate". Since deregulation causes a reduction in rents the analysis of the variations of wages after such changes in the regulatory environment can prove to be a good empirical test of union rent sharing hypothesis. The results of Rose's empirical tests are consistent with this hypothesis: "microdata estimates of union premia over non-union wages in the trucking industry indicate declines of roughly 40 percent in the size of union differential" since the beginning of deregulation.

The brief survey of the work done in this field shows how, because of its empirical nature, it does not allow for the drawing of definite conclusions on the interdependence between economic regulation in the output market and wage setting in the labour market. Moreover, the regulatory scheme considered in all the works previously reviewed is represented by a constraint on profits, that is, it is an *ad hoc* regulatory scheme. The absence of conclusive empirical results thus emphasises the need for some theoretical work focusing on the main problems related to the inter-relation between regulation in the output market and wage bargaining in the labour market. We need to answer at least to two basic questions. First of all, is it true that regulation of prices in the output market does lead to high wages and, if so, under what circumstances? The model discussed in section 3 tries to answer this question. Secondly, how wage bargaining and the firm-union relationship can affect the firm's strategic interaction with the regulator and, therefore, the regulatory outcome. This latter question is relevant when the regulatory relationship is studied within a framework characterised by asymmetric information on the regulator's side, as it is assumed to be in the model presented in section 4. Then, with a sound theoretical framework, exploring different hypotheses on information and regulatory structures, it may be possible to provide some explanations for the empirical observations.

3.   PRICE REGULATION UNDER SYMMETRIC INFORMATION AND WAGE BARGAINING

In one of two papers, Pignataro (1995a) shows the optimal regulatory policy in the context of a very simple model, characterised by symmetric distribution of information between a regulator and a firm. As a matter of simplicity, a monopolistic firm is assumed to produce its output using labour only. Workers are not hired in a competitive labour market: they are paid a wage which is bargained over between the firm and a union representing them. The agreement over wage is incorporated into a binding agreement. This allows for the modelling of wage bargaining as a co-operative game, whose outcome can be found using the so called Nash generalised solution: the wage that maximises the weighted[1] product of the incremental utilities of the firm and the union with respect to their fall back levels. The union's utility function is assumed to be:

$$U(w,L) = (w - \overline{w})L(q) \tag{1}$$

where $\overline{w}$ represents the wage (or other income) workers could earn outside the firm and L is the number of workers employed by the firm. L depends on the output produced by the firm, according to a production function q (L).

The firm maximises profits[2], which are computed as

$$\pi(p,w) = pq(p) - L(q(p)) \tag{2}$$

where q(p) represents the demand for the firm's output. The firm's reservation level of profits is assumed to be zero.

The bargaining power of the firm is measured by a parameter $\mu, 0 \le \mu \le 1$. The measure of the union's bargaining power is $(1 - \mu)$.

It is possible to show that a benevolent regulator, maximising a social welfare function, represented as weighted sum of consumers' and producer's surplus[3], that is

$$W(p,w) = \int_{p}^{\infty} q(\widetilde{p})d\widetilde{p} + \alpha\pi(p,w) \tag{3}$$

with $0 \leq \alpha \leq 1$, wishing to move first, setting the output price before the firm and the union bargain over the workers' wage. The equilibrium outcome, in terms of regulated output price and wage is as follows[4]:

$$p^* = \overline{w} \frac{dL}{dq} \qquad (4)$$

$$w^* = \overline{w} \qquad (5)$$

The regulated output price does not depend on the actual wage paid to workers and it is equal to the minimum marginal cost (i.e. the one corresponding to the union's reservation wage). The consequence of such a pricing policy for the outcome of wage bargaining is obvious: the wage will be equal to the union's reservation level. The firm's profits will be equal to zero (which is assumed to be the firm's reservation level of profits).

The equilibrium outcome of this enlarged regulatory game (price setting by the regulator and wage-bargaining between the firm and the union) would be quite different should the sequence of moves be different. If the firm and the union bargained over wage before the regulator set the price in the output market, this would give a first-mover advantage to the union. The equilibrium wage and price would be determined according to the following equations[5]:

$$\frac{dL}{dq} q(p(w^*)) + (w^* - \overline{w}) \left(\frac{dL}{dq} \right)^2 \frac{dq}{dp} = 0 \qquad (6)$$

$$p^*(w) = w^* \frac{dL}{dq} \qquad (7)$$

It is possible to show that the wage agreed on by the firm and the union is above the reservation wage[6]. The regulated output price is equal to the actual marginal costs of the firm. Profits, again, will be equal to zero. The main consequence is that output price regulation creates rents for the union, for two reasons. First, the regulatory pricing policy changes the trade-off between employment and wage, allowing for a larger employment for any given wage, since it eliminates the output restriction arising from monopolistic pricing behaviour. Secondly, it makes the firm indifferent to wage, transforming the union in a monopoly union, since it eliminates the entire firm's rents.

The regulator's control problem is then twofold. On one side, he wants to control the firm in the output market, so that its monopolistic power of setting prices is not used against consumers. On the other side, he is also concerned with the union's behaviour in the labour market, whereas, when the latter is perfectly competitive, this control is exercised by the dynamics of competition. If instead, it is not perfectly competitive, cost endogeneity may lead to factor prices above their marginal social cost. The result, affecting social welfare, is then a restriction of output, even when monopoly power is perfectly controlled[7]. If the regulator wants to achieve a first-best outcome in the output market, he must commit, in advance, to setting a price equal to the minimum marginal cost[8]. Otherwise, whenever the regulator is able to extract all the rents from the monopolist (as happens when we assume that information is symmetrically distributed), a union will extract rents from consumers, behaving as a monopoly union, because the monopolist becomes indifferent to the wage level.

From a positive analysis perspective, this result should confirm the traditional claim that a cost-of-service type of regulation gives no incentive to cost-reduction and that it can create rents for some groups, such as workers. However, the reason why the union can get such a high rent is not only that the regulator sets the price after the union sets the wage (and, therefore, prices are based on actual costs, according to a cost-of-service regulatory scheme), but also because the firm, whatever the wage, will earn no profits and, therefore, will lose any interest in resisting to the union's claims.

4. PRICE REGULATION UNDER ASYMMETRIC INFORMATION AND WAGE BARGAINING

The extension of the previous model to the case of asymmetric information is presented in Pignataro (1995b). The interest for this extension, apart from the obvious reason of adopting a more realistic assumption on the regulator's information, arises from the remarks made in the previous section. With symmetric distribution of information between the firm and the regulator, and if the regulator can commit to a fixed-price type of policy, it is possible to achieve the first-best outcome. The regulator is able to eliminate the monopolist's rents and, at the same time, he leaves no room for the union to get a wage above its reservation level. The asymmetric information case, however, is different in as much as the regulator is not able to extract all the rents from the firm and, therefore, these are at stake in the bargaining between the firm and the union. This has at least two drawbacks for the design of the regulatory policy: on one hand, the rents given to the firm because of its information advantage produce the effect of raising the wage and, therefore, marginal costs which, in turn, reduces social welfare. On the other hand, the existence of a union, which erodes the firm's rents, also affects the strategic behaviour of the firm with respect to the issue of revelation of information to the regulator.

The production function for the firm's output is the following: $q = f(\theta, L)$. θ is a technology parameter which can take on only two values, θ_H and θ_L. We assume that the production function exhibits constant returns to scale and, moreover that $f_L(\theta_H) < f_L(\theta_L)$, which is the marginal product of labour of a firm of type θ_H is lower than that of a firm of type θ_L. Only the firm and the union know the actual realisation of θ, but not the regulator. The regulator has prior beliefs surrounding the distribution of the parameter according to the probability ϕ_H that $\theta = \theta_H$, and the probability ϕ_L that $\theta = \theta_L$. L is the quantity of labour employed by the firm.

The regulator is assumed to be able to make a take-it-or-leave-it offer to the firm, represented by a contract specifying a price schedule and a tax schedule, based on revelation of θ by the firm, that is (p_L, T_L ; p_H, T_H)[9]. Subsequently, the union and the firm bargain over a wage. Finally, the firm will announce its cost parameter and the corresponding price and tax will be implemented.

The union's objective function and profits are defined as in (1) and (2). As far as the regulator's objective function is concerned, expression (3) is changed to take into account the fact that its *ex-ante* specification is in terms of expected welfare, that is:

$$EW(p_i, T_i; w, \theta_i) = \sum_i \phi_i \left[\int_p^\infty q(\tilde{p}) d\tilde{p} + \alpha\pi(p_i, T_i; w, \theta_i) \right] \qquad i = L, H \quad (8)$$

The equilibrium outcome is derived in Pignataro (1995b) by use of backward induction, looking at the equilibrium path, along the different stages of the game, which will result in truthful reporting by the firm[10]. The main results are summarised here, looking at the players' decisions in the three stages of the game.

4.1   The firm's revelation decision

In the final stage of the game, the firm of type i will choose the regulatory policy designed for its type if, given the price-tax pairs (p_i, T_i; i = L,H) and a wage w:

$$p_i q_i + T_i - w L_q^i q_i \geq p_j q_j + T_j - w L_q^i q_j$$

with $L_q^i = \dfrac{dL(q;\theta_i)}{dq}$, i = L,H

The firm's reporting decision depends, not only on the regulatory policy chosen by the regulator, but also on the wage agreed on with the union in the previous stage. The firm will correctly report its type if:

$$w L_q^i (q_i - q_j) \leq (p_i q_i + T_i) - (p_j q_j + T_j) \qquad (9)$$

with q_i and q_j, the quantity demanded as function of the regulated prices p_i and p_j.

Inequality (9) allows for a quite straightforward interpretation of the impact of wage-bargaining on the strategic behaviour of the firm, as far as the revelation of information is concerned. If the second term of inequality is positive and $q_i > q_j$ [11], the firm will find it convenient to tell the truth if the wage is not so high that the additional cost of producing the greater output does not offset the additional revenues. In other words, the regulatory policy is giving the firm a premium for telling the truth that, if captured by the union in the wage-bargaining stage, will not be enough for the firm to behave according to the regulator's plan. If the second term of the inequality is negative and $q_i < q_j$ [12], the firm will tell the truth if the wage is not so low that it finds convenient to produce the higher quantity q_j and get the larger revenues.

The regulator must, therefore, take into account the determinants of the wage-bargaining outcome in the design of his regulatory policy so that, given this policy, the wage is such that the firm finds convenient to reveal its costs correctly.

4.2 The wage bargaining

The outcome of the wage-bargaining is computed in Pignataro (1995b), according to the aim of finding the equilibrium path for truth-telling in the enlarged regulatory game. Therefore, the bargaining is modelled as a Nash bargaining, such that, given a regulatory policy (p_i, T_i; i = L,H), the equilibrium wage will generate truthful reporting by the firm in the following stage of the game[13]. The expression for the equilibrium wage is:

$$w_i^* = \frac{\mu \bar{w} L_q^i q_i + (1-\mu)(p_i q_i + T_i)}{L_q^i q_i} \qquad i = L, H \qquad (10)$$

Two things clearly emerge from the analysis of expression (10). Firstly, as expected, the larger the total revenues arising from the regulatory policy, the larger the wage. Secondly, as long as T is positive, the wage is increasing in price (and decreasing in quantity)[14]. The pricing rule determines the trade-off between wage and employment: for any given wage, a lower price produces a larger employment. Therefore, the lower the price-cost margin set by the regulator, the higher, for the union, the cost, in terms of employment, of getting a given increase above the reservation wage.

4.3 The optimal regulatory policy

The following table summarises the optimal regulatory pricing policy[15], and the equilibrium values of profits and wage, according to different values of μ.

Table 1. Summary of the equilibrium values

	P	π	W
$\mu = 1$	$P_H > MC_H$	$\pi_H = 0$	$w_H^* = \bar{w}$
	$P_L = MC_L$	$\pi_L > 0$	$w_L^* = \bar{w}$
$0 < \mu < 1$	$P_H > MC_H$	$\pi_H = 0$	$w_H^* = \bar{w}$
	$P_L < MC_L$	$\pi_L > 0$	$w_L^* > \bar{w}$
$\mu = 0$	$P_H = p_L = MC_H = MC_L$	$\pi_H = \pi_L = 0$	$w_H^* = \bar{w}$
			$w_L^* > \bar{w}$

1. $\mu = 1$

The union has no bargaining power and therefore the wage is set at the reservation level. The regulatory policy looks exactly like the one designed by Baron and Myerson (1982) in their seminal paper. The regulated output price is equal to marginal costs in the good state of the world and above marginal costs in the other state. The distortion from marginal costs depends on the regulator's beliefs, the weight given to the firm's profits in the social welfare function and the difference between the two marginal costs. The profits of a firm of type θ_H are zero, while the other type of firm will earn positive profits. This result is not surprising since in this case the regulator's problem is exactly the same as the one analysed by Baron and Myerson. Their model can be considered as a special case of this model (when the union has no bargaining power).

2. $\mu = 0$

When the firm has no bargaining power at all, the union behaves as if it was a "monopoly union", that is it sets the wage without bargaining with the firm. This implies that the union captures the rents arising from the regulatory policy. This will change quite dramatically. The price is unique and equal to the minimum marginal cost when $\theta = \theta_H$. The reason for this result is that, since the union is able to extract all the firm's rents, there is no way for the regulator to make convenient for the firm a truthful report. The regulator knows that the union will capture any transfer to the firm and, therefore, he gives up the two separating prices, sustained by appropriate subsidies to the firm. However, since the lowest price he can set is equal to the minimum marginal cost for a firm of type θ_H, this gives the union, whose members work for a firm of type θ_L, the opportunity to capture the rents created by this pricing policy.

3. $0 < \mu < 1$

When μ is positive but different from one, the output price, in both states of nature, is distorted from actual marginal costs. When the firm reports to have high costs, it has to charge a price above actual marginal costs. As in Baron and Myerson (1982), this distortion is partly justified by the need, for the regulator, to limit the low cost firm's rents. However, even when $\alpha = 1$, that is when profits are not costly, the distortion still exists. As expression (10) for the equilibrium wage clearly shows, the wage is positively related with the firm's rents. Inequality (9) also shows that the reporting strategy of the firm is affected by the wage: given a price-tax pair set by the regulator, if the wage is too high, the firm will misreport.

Therefore, the distortion of the output price from marginal costs is used to limit the firm's rents when it has low costs, even when these rents are not socially costly. There is, however, another cost related to rents, which arises from wage. Wages are costly because they directly reduce social welfare and also, because they affect the firm's report to the regulator.

When the firm reports to have low costs, the output price is below actual marginal costs . Again, the explanation of this distortion is related to the costs arising from a high wage, as already pointed out above, and the regulator's interest in limiting the wage. Discussing the equilibrium wage in (10), it was mentioned that the wage is increasing in the output price. Therefore, lowering the price, below marginal costs, has the effect of lowering the wage.

The equilibrium wage is different according to the firm's type. It is always equal to the union's reservation level, for a high cost firm; it is above that level, for the other type of firm. Then, regulation *per se* does not induce high wages, but, comparing this outcome with the one derived in the previous section, it is the existence of the asymmetry of information between the regulator and the firm which makes the difference. Moreover, high wages do not originate from cost-of-service regulatory schemes. The wage is above the union's reservation level, even if the regulator is moving first. The existence of asymmetric information creates the rents for the firm and, consequently, the possibility for the union to capture a share of these rents.

5.   CONCLUSIONS

This paper has mainly summarised the results of two works which are an attempt to enlarge the theory of regulation, moving beyond the paradigm of the firm as a black box. In doing so, it is possible to take account of a wider spectrum of determinants of the firm's behaviour in the regulatory game. We have considered the case of wage bargaining between the firm and a union representing workers. The firm and the union share the same information and they sign binding agreements. Two models have been presented, corresponding to different assumptions about the regulator's information. The basic questions, which have been addressed, are connected to the effects of regulation on wage bargaining and with the way the interaction, and the agreement between the firm and the union interferes with the firm's behaviour in the regulatory relationship.

The model presented in section 3 has allowed the identification of a specific control problem arising from the introduction of wage bargaining in a model of regulation. Even if the regulator is able to restrain the firm's monopoly power completely (as in the case he has perfect information), other rents can be extracted from consumer's surplus by the union. A fixed-price type of regulatory scheme reveals to be a "high-powered" incentive scheme, not only when the regulator wants to give an incentive to the firm for its effort to reduce costs. It is also useful to control the behaviour of other actors in other markets indirectly, through the use of the output price. Therefore, a cost-of-service type of regulation may originate high wages for the workers: this effect can be even greater when the regulator is very tight on firm's profits, since the firm looses any incentive to resist the union's claims.

However, the union can get positive rents, even when the regulator does not use such regulatory pricing schemes. Looking at the optimal regulatory policy with asymmetric information, the regulator needs to provide the firm with incentives for a correct revelation of its superior information. These rents are partly captured by the union, according to its bargaining power, which will result in higher wages. Moreover, the regulator must also consider how the informational rents are shared between the firm and the union, since the wage level arising from this sharing agreement is an important determinant of the revelation strategy of the firm. Therefore, the existence of a union is a problem for two reasons: it captures a share of the informational rents of the firm and increases the wage, reducing social welfare; and it also interferes with the reporting strategy of the firm. The consequence of such control problems for the optimal regulatory policy is that different efficiency distortions arise to limit the wage through a modification of the wage-employment trade-off and of the informational rents attributed to the firm.

The work surveyed in this paper shows how, proceeding along a piecemeal approach and modelling the different interactions of the firm one by one, it is possible to take account of the complexity of real world firms. The results produced with this approach do not exclude other important results already established in the literature, but they are even more general. This approach, however, also pushes the analysis towards the realm of incomplete contracting, since considering the interactions within the firm puts forward the limits of the regulator's authority and the constraints to complete contracts. One has then to value the trade-off between the improvement of the explanatory power of theoretical models, with the risk of building very specific and *ad hoc* theories.

APPENDIX

Proof of (4) and (5)

First of all, let's find the wage-bargaining outcome. It corresponds to the solution of the following maximisation problem:

$$\max_{w} \left[(w - \overline{w})L_q q(p)\right]^{1-\mu} \left[q(p)(p - wL_q)\right]^{\mu}$$

$L_q q$ is equal to L, because of the assumption of constant returns to scale (see footnote 2 in the text).

The first-order condition for this problem is:

$$q(p)\left[(1 - \mu)(p - wL_q) - \mu(w - \overline{w})L_q\right] = 0$$

The equilibrium value of the wage, as a function of the pricing policy can be written as:

$$w^*(p; \mu, \overline{w}) = \frac{(1 - \mu)p + \mu \overline{w} L_q}{L_q} \qquad (A1)$$

The regulator's problem can be written as:

$$\max_{p} \left[S(p) + \alpha \mu q(p)(p - \overline{w} L_q)\right]$$
$$s.t. \mu q(p)(p - \overline{w} L_q) \geq 0$$

Profits are computed substituting w with the expression (A1).
The first-order condition for the regulator's problem is:

$$-q(p) + \mu(\alpha + \lambda)\left[q(p) + q'(p - \overline{w} L_q\right] = 0$$

The only possible solution is with $\lambda > 0$ and, consequently, with the constraint binding. If $\lambda = 0$, the first-order condition would become: $(\mu\alpha - 1)q + \mu\alpha(p - \overline{w} L_q)q' = 0$. Since $\lambda = 0$ implies that the constraint is not binding and, therefore $(p - \overline{w} L_q)$ is always positive, the first-order condition would never be satisfied, whatever values of μ and α. Then, if the constraint is binding the optimal price is $p = \overline{w} L_q$ and computing the wage according to (A1) gives $w = \overline{w}$.

Proof of (6) and (7)

Firstly, we derive the optimal regulatory policy for any given wage bargained over between the firm and the union in the previous stage of the game. By the observation that social welfare, as defined in (3), is non-increasing in the output price, it is maximised for the lowest price compatible with non-negativity of profits, that is $p^*(w) = wL_q$, as in (7). At the wage bargaining stage, the use of the Nash generalised solution reduces the maximisation of the union's utility subject to the pricing policy $p^*(w)$, that is:

$$\max_w U(w) = (w - \overline{w})L_q q(p^*(w))$$

The first order condition for this problem is just equation (6).

The wage bargaining problem for the model in section 4.

Since we are looking for the equilibrium path for truth-telling, we can represent the firm-union bargain over wage according to a Nash generalised solution where, given a regulatory policy $(p_i, T_i; i = L,H)$, the parties' incremental utilities are those arising from truth-telling. Therefore the equilibrium wage is the solution of the following problem, and it will be such that t will generate truthful reporting by the firm in the following stage of the game:

$$\max_w \left[p_i q_i + T_i - w L_q^i q_i \right]^\mu \left[(w - \overline{w}) L_q^i q_i \right]^{-\mu}$$

The regulator's problem for the model in section 4.

The optimal regulatory policy, inducing truth-telling by the firm, is the solution of the following problem:

$$\max_{p_i, T_i} \sum_i \phi_i \left[\int_p^\infty q(\tilde{p})d\tilde{p} - T_i + \alpha(p_i q_i + T_i - w_i^* L_q^i q_i) \right]$$

$$s.t. (p_i q_i + T_i - w_i^* L_q^i q_i) \geq (p_j q_j + T_j - w_i^* L_q^i q_j)$$

$$(p_i q_i + T_i - w_i^* L_q^i q_i) \geq 0$$

$$i, j = L, H; i \neq j$$

The regulator's problem can be rewritten substituting w_i^* with the expression (10) in the text:

$$\max_{p_i, T_i} \sum_i \phi_i \left[\int_p^\infty q(\widetilde{p}) d\widetilde{p} - T_i + \alpha\mu(p_i q_i + T_i - \overline{w} L_q^i q_i) \right]$$

$$s.t. \left[(1-\mu)q_j + \mu q_i \right] \left[p_i q_i + T_i - \overline{w} L_q^i q_i \right] \ge q_i \left[p_j q_j + T_j - \overline{w} L_q^i q_j \right]$$

$$\mu(p_i q_i + T_i - \overline{w} L_q^i q_i) \ge 0$$

$$i, j = L, H; i \ne j$$

The optimal regulatory policy, according to Proposition 1 in Pignataro (1995b), is $(p_L, T_L; p_H, T_H)$ such that:

$$p_H - \overline{w} L_q^H - \frac{\phi_L \phi_H^{-1}(1-\alpha\mu)}{\left[(1-\mu)q_H + \mu q_L\right]^2} \left[\mu q_L^2 \overline{w}(L_q^H - L_q^L) \right] = 0$$

$$T_H + \frac{\phi_L \phi_H^{-1}(1-\alpha\mu)}{\left[(1-\mu)q_H + \mu q_L\right]^2} \left[\mu q_L^2 q_H \overline{w}(L_q^H - L_q^L) \right] = 0$$

$$p_L - \overline{w} L_q^L - \frac{(1-\alpha\mu)}{\left[(1-\mu)q_H + \mu q_L\right]^2} \left[(1-\mu)q_H^2 \overline{w}(L_q^H - L_q^L) \right] = 0$$

$$T_L - \frac{\mu \overline{w} q_L q_H \left[\alpha(1-\mu)q_H + q_L \right](L_q^H - L_q^L)}{\left[(1-\mu)q_H + \mu q_L\right]^2} = 0$$

NOTES

* I wish to thank Jean-Jacques Laffont and Massimo Marrelli for their comments on a previous version of this paper. The usual caveat applies

1 The weight is represented by the relative bargaining power of the firm and the union.

2 Fixed costs are assumed away to leave out of our analysis any problem of efficient funding of subsidies for the firm. As a further simplification of the analysis, we will also assume that marginal costs are constant, so as to have $dL/dq \equiv L_q$ constant.

3 One of the main arguments for using such a welfare function is laid out by Baron (1989), who argues that any measure of social welfare is the outcome of a political process. Therefore, because of political reasons (related, for instance, to the relative size of different groups in a constituency), consumers' surplus is weighted more than profits. However, there can be efficiency reasons for weighting profits less than consumers'

surplus. If the regulator had to subsidise firms, there could be efficiency distortions to be taken into account, arising from the taxes levied to finance these subsidies. See Caillaud et al. (1988). There is no union surplus included in (3). Here, we could use Baron's argument again. We could think of a social welfare function as a weighted sum of consumers, producer and union surplus, where, for political or any other reason, the union's weight is restricted to being zero. This reflects a common observation in regulation, whereas the regulator is usually assigned a limited task, to protect the welfare of consumers, guaranteeing, at the same time, conditions of financial viability for the firm. There are also other models which use a similar approach: Anton and Gertler (1988) deal with a firm operating in two output markets, only one of which is regulated. The regulator is assumed to be interested only in the welfare of consumers in the regulated market.

[4] For a proof, see the Appendix.

[5] For a proof, see the Appendix.

[6] Since $\dfrac{dL}{dq} > 0$ e $\dfrac{dq}{dp} < 0$, equation (6) is satisfied iff $(w - \overline{w}) > 0$.

[7] It is possible to find examples whereas, for a strong union's preference for wage as compared to employment, a regulatory pricing based on actual costs originates an output even lower than the one produced by an unregulated monopolist. The reason is quite intuitive. When the output market is not regulated, the firm tends to keep wages as low as possible, and its success obviously depends on its relative bargaining power. The firm's resistance to increase wages will avoid a further restriction of output, beside that related to the exercise of monopoly power by the firm. The effect of regulation (when the firm's rents are completely extracted by a perfectly informed regulator) is, instead, that of eliminating any interest of the firm in keeping wages low. It may happen then that the increase in output arising from an efficient pricing rule is completely offset by the consequential increase in wage, when compared to an unregulated situation where the firm has a strong bargaining power and keeps wage very low.

[8] The alternative would be that the regulatory authority was extended to the labour market, so as to impose a wage equal to the union's reservation wage. This solution, however, looks very difficult to implement, because of political and institutional difficulties connected with it.

[9] Therefore, if the firm reports to be of type θ_L, it will charge a price p_L and receive (pay) a subsidy (tax) T_L. If it declares to be of type θ_H, it will charge p_H and receive (pay) a subsidy (tax) T_H.

[10] Given a regulatory policy (p_i, T_i) and a wage w agreed on by the firm and the union, the optimal reporting strategy by the firm is derived first. Then, the outcome of wage bargaining is determined using the Nash generalised solution and, finally, the optimal regulatory policy is computed. To find the optimal regulatory policy, it is possible to use the revelation principle (there is no loss in generality in focusing on a regulatory policy inducing truthful revelation of information by the firm). Therefore, values of p_i, T_i and w are found, for which truth-telling is a sub-game perfect equilibrium of the game. The detailed computation of the equilibrium outcome can be found in Pignataro (1995b).

[11] If the second term of the inequality is positive and $q_i < q_j$, the firm is paid more if it correctly reports its costs to produce less. The firm is obviously willing to tell the truth

independently of the wage, but this regulatory policy is completely inconsistent with the maximisation of social welfare as defined in (3) (not to tell that it violates the revelation principle).

[12] If the second term of the inequality is negative and $q_i > q_j$, the regulatory policy would never induce truthful revelation of costs, since the firm would have larger revenues and less costs from cheating.

[13] For the analytical format of the Nash bargaining outcome, see the Appendix.

[14] The sign of $\dfrac{\partial w_i^*}{\partial p_i}$ when T is negative is not clear cut.   However, when T is negative, the regulator is taxing the firm to take its rents and, therefore the wage will be equal to the reservation wage.

[15] For the analytical format of the regulator's problem, see the Appendix.

REFERENCES

Anton, J. And P. Gertler , 1988, "External Markets and Regulation", *Journal of Public Economics*, 37, 243-260.

Baron, D.P., 1989, "Design of Regulatory Mechanisms and Institutions", in Schmalensee, R. and R.D. Willig (eds.), *Handbook of Industrial Organization*, vol. II, Amsterdam, Elsevier Science Publishers, 1347-1447.

Baron, D.P. and R.B. Myerson, 1982, "Regulating a Monopolist with Unknown Costs", *Econometrica*, 50, 911-930.

Caillaud, B., Guesnerie, R., Rey, P. and J. Tirole, 1988, "Government Intervention in Production and Incentives Theory: A Review of Recent Contributions", *Rand Journal of Economics*, 19, 1-26.

Ehrenberg, R.G., 1979, *The Regulatory Process and Labor Earnings*, New York, Academic Press.

Hendricks, W., 1975, "The Effects of Regulation on Collective Bargaining in Electric Utilities", *Bell Journal of Economics*, 6, 451-465.

Hendricks, W., 1977, "Regulation and Labor Earnings", *Bell Journal of Economics*, 8, 483-496.

Laffont, J.J. and J. Tirole, 1993, *A Theory of Incentives in Procurement and Regulation*, Cambridge MA, MIT Press.

Moore, T.G., 1978, "The Beneficiaries of Trucking Regulation", *Journal of Law and Economics*, 21, 327-343.

Pignataro, G., 1995a, "Regulation of a Monopolist with an Imperfectly Competitive Labour Market", University of York Discussion Papers in Economics, 95/28.

Pignataro, G., 1995b, "Optimal Regulation of a Monopolist with Collusive Agents", University of York Discussion Papers in Economics, 95/29.

Rose, N.L., 1987, "Labor Rent Sharing and Regulation: Evidence from the Trucking Industry", *Journal of Political Economy*, 95, 1146-1178.

Vickers, J., 1995, "Competition and Regulation in Vertically Related Markets", *Review of Economic Studies*, 62, 1-17.

PART 2

APPLICATIONS

Chapter 5

IMPLEMENTATION PRACTICES IN REGULATION

An Analysis of the UK Experience

Michael Waterson[1] and Maria Vagliasindi[2*]
[1]University of Warwick, UK; [2]European Bank for Reconstruction and Development

1.   INTRODUCTION

It is undoubtedly true that the theoretically superior approach to creating a price regulation scheme is to characterise the problem in terms of maximand and constraints, then to devise rules on the basis of the solution to implement as a regulatory scheme. Yet in practice a very different approach is commonly used - create an ad hoc scheme whose properties are largely unexplored which is then adapted as circumstances dictate. The two prime examples of recent years are rate of return regulation and price cap regulation.

There is little doubt as to why a straightforward scheme was initially chosen for regulation in the UK. What is a little surprising is the method chosen. In the rush to privatise British Telecom (the first such major network industry to be privatised) the government neglected development of any regulatory framework until very late. It then asked Professor Stephen Littlechild to report. His report (1983) is in many ways a remarkable document. He was given two models to compare, a maximum rate or return scheme (similar to US rate of return regulation) proposed by an Inter-Departmental working Group, and an output-related profits levy scheme proposed by Professor Alan Walters. In the event, he chose neither, instead developing his own "local tariff reduction scheme". He also emphasised the development of competition where possible.

His approach was to "focus precisely on those services of particular concern" (p. 34). These were defined as business rentals, residential rentals and local call charges, these being monopoly services with no prospect of competition in the medium term. Also "for the present it seems simpler to leave trunk calls out of any tariff reduction scheme". (p. 34). BT would be constrained not to increase tariffs on the basket of services (the Local Tariff index, LTI) thus defined by more than the retail price index, RPI-X percent. Quality of service in these areas would not be allowed to deteriorate. These conditions were assumed to hold for the first five years of the licence. Two other conditions, to apply for longer were: BT not to discriminate anti-competitively in setting its tariff, and BT to be required to publish its tariffs. Littlechild considered his scheme outshone the others he considered in terms of protection against monopoly, encouraging efficiency and innovation, low burden of regulation, promotion of competition, and prospects for the industry.[1]

One particular attraction Littlechild saw in this approach was that the burden of regulation was relatively light: "Monitoring of the LTI would impose a negligible burden ... The DGT [Director General of Telecommunications] does not have to make any judgements or calculations with respect to capital, allocation of costs, rates of return, future movements of costs and demand, desirable performance, etc. He will need to monitor the non-discrimination clause, but he would need to do so anyway..." (1983:36).

This pricing scheme was adopted, with some modifications, in the regulation of BT, with X being set initially at 3. One of the principal changes was to include long distance calls in the priced basket of services. Subsequently it was adopted, again with modifications, for the other regulated industries.

Paradoxically whilst almost everything said in the quotation concerning the burden of regulation has proved to be false in practice, the method has survived in some form. Its resilience can be attributed to two considerations, in our view. First the information position in the real world is such that the regulator knows far less than is supposed by any model. Clearly, from the experience of regulation, not merely the regulator but also the principal regulated firm has only a hazy view of the costs of many components of its activities. For example, the original position of post-privatisation British Gas regarding its network transportation costs was substantially different from its current position (e.g. as regards transport costs for interruptible gas, which it took to be negative). In such a situation, only ad hoc controls are feasible.

Second, but probably somewhat linked, structural regulation may be feasible or desirable, but the extent to which this can sensibly be pursued is often unclear. Most optimality approaches implicitly assume the structure is given so the focus is on conduct regulation. But Littlechild, in his original report on BT in fact made a number of recommendation regarding structural modifications to the industry, many of which were not adopted.

Whilst simplicity explains the use of ad hoc frameworks, one can also note the dangers in the absence of a clear conceptual base. This leads us to consider the main theoretical issues and the problems in their implementation. We first describe price regulation as practised in the UK, focusing on changes in the light of experience and interpretation in terms of simple models. We then go on to cover the structural issues in more detail, including matters concerning the identification of natural monopoly and competitive issues. Finally, we move to some less-often aired questions of the nature of procedure and of type of agency in regulation.

But first a few words about context. In 1979, when the Conservatives came into power in the UK, a position they have enjoyed ever since, the state-owned sector of the industrial economy was substantial, accounting for over 10% of GDP, and 8% of the workforce. Some of the main companies/sectors involved are listed in the table in the Appendix. The progress of privatisation could be thought of in two main, and somewhat overlapping, phases. The first phase consists of those companies in government hands which are clearly not in the category of natural monopolies. These are not our concern.

The second phase is of those firms where there were considerable elements of actual and natural monopoly, and many of the products are essential to civilised life. A substantial proportion of some consumers' budgets would be used in purchasing their products. Hence they are involved to some extent with regulation and the development of regulatory offices. These include BT (1984 and later), British Gas (1986/7) the Water industry (1989), the Electricity industry (1990/1) as well as the British Airports Authority (1986), a slightly special case.

Some are still on the agenda for privatisation. These include British Rail (where the first privatisation is planned for 1996) and possibly the Post Office. They will also involve regulatory offices.

This programme has been going on in the context of sale of various other governmental agencies, for instance the Property Services Agency, which supplies office facilities for civil servants, also enforced "contracting out" of a range of local authority operations (cleaning, refuse collection, maintenance etc.) "reforms" to bring market mechanisms into the National Health Service as well as other similar (sometimes contradictory) programmes in schools, universities, social services and so on.

The objectives of this vast programme are largely implicit rather than explicit. Amongst them were desires to widen the constituency of share-owners, to reduce union power, to increase the efficiency with which these industries operated, to introduce competition and to benefit the exchequer.

Taken one by one, none of these objectives is completely convincing when compared with policy as followed. For example, a greater increase in share ownership could have been engineered by giving shares away to the public. Benefits to the exchequer largely result from an accounting convention. Moreover the objectives are in some respects achievable by other means - for example large improvements in efficiency have occurred in several of the concerns under state ownership (Kay 1987; Kay and Thompson 1986). Yet they carried sufficient political momentum to push the programme forward.

In the sections below we discuss price regulation and its development over time, the concept and application of "regulation for competition", and the design of regulatory institutions. In each case, theoretical analyses and practical developments are both stressed.

2. DEVELOPMENTS IN THEORY AND PRICE CAP REGULATION

The basic logic behind price cap regulation is very simple. The regulator sets a price, called the price cap (which is an average of prices in the case of multi-product firms) and the regulated firm is allowed to retain whatever profits it earns, provided that the price it charges is below or equal to this cap. The price cap is adjusted over time by a supposedly exogenous factor (X) and at longer intervals is reviewed by the regulator. Recent achievements of an extensive literature on optimal regulatory theory have so far had only a very limited influence on policy making in the UK. Yet theory provides frameworks within which, in principle, the regulator could practice optimal governance of the industry, subject to some reasonable constraints.

Thus we discuss both theoretical and practical approaches starting from the main theoretical issues, but not neglecting the problem of their implementation. Specifically, in what follows, before highlighting some of the differences between price cap schemes, we address the most relevant problems arising from the incentive theory perspective, such as: i) the convergence of price adjustments towards socially optimal pricing and ii) the trade-off between incentives to efficiency and rent extraction.

2.1 General Theoretical Issues

The economic modelling of regulatory mechanisms started from the analysis of rate of return regulation (henceforth ROR) according to which prices are set so that the firm could cover variable cost and a fair return on its assets. A large part of the literature following the contribution by Averch and Johnson (1962) suggested that ROR could lead to inefficient input choices and output price distortion. ROR has also being often criticised for compensating a firm for its expenditures rather than for its performance. The price cap approach, introduced in the UK by Littlechild (1983), has been analysed by Bradley and Price (1988), Vickers and Yarrow (1988) and Waterson (1988) and (1992) among others.[2]

Claims for the superior efficiency of price cap regulation over ROR stem from the notion that ROR, being a cost driven scheme, provides no incentive to minimise costs. Namely, price caps are high powered contracts (providing best incentives for cost reductions), whilst ROR represents a low powered scheme (ideal for rent extraction). In fact, from the following general form of price controls:

$$p = c + \alpha(c^* - c) = (1 - \alpha)c + \alpha c^* \qquad \text{with } 0 \le \alpha \le 1 \qquad (1)$$

where p denotes the price level, c the unit realised cost and c* its efficient level, price cap and ROR can be derived by setting α (the power of the firm's incentive to reduce costs) equal to one or zero respectively.

Before considering the trade-off between efficiency and rent extraction, let us first explore the following preliminary question: which type of regulation should be adopted in order to implement socially optimal pricing (or at least efficient pricing) when the authority is uninformed on firms' characteristics?

In a first best setting Loeb and Magat (1979) developed an optimal incentive regulatory mechanism implementable when the regulator can subsidise the regulated firm with a generous bribe (which amounts to the total net consumers' surplus).[3]

In the absence of incentive transfers, when only the manager knows costs and demand functions, Vogelsang and Finsinger (V-F) in 1979 propose a simple price adjustment process that leads to Ramsey pricing (which is socially optimal, given a break-even constraint). Specifically, as only past values of prices and quantities and costs are known by the regulator, the actions of the firm in one period determine the options that the regulator allows in the following period. The regulator, not knowing what Ramsey prices are, simply uses the information on last period's outputs and costs. She sets current prices so that they do not result in positive profits applying to last period's outputs and costs.

Basically, price regulation may lead to efficiency in the short run and may eventually converge to socially optimal pricing. However, it should be borne in mind that the adjustment process may take many periods or may not converge, due to strategic behaviour as envisaged by Sappington.[4]

Thus more information or an incentive scheme for efficient pricing based on observed past values of prices and quantities may be needed. Finsinger and Vogelsang (1981) proposed to add a transitory subsidy approximating the social surplus change in each year and Vogelsang (1989) to substitute it through the fixed part of a two part tariff. Hagerman (1990) modified the V-F scheme introducing a franchise transfer (based on past observations) to take into account the maximisation of the present value of all future profits.

However, so far we have considered short term efficiency in a stationary environment; capacity being given, cost and demand being stable over time. Things become more complex when changes in cost and demand functions interfere with the convergence process.

Ramsey-pricing can be reached immediately when an incremental surplus subsidy (hereafter ISS) is given to the firm, as shown by Sappington and Sibley (1988). Specifically, the ISS given to the firm in each period is set equal to the consumers' surplus change minus the level of last period profits. Eventually, subsidies can be avoided using two-part tariffs, as suggested by Sibley (1989). In this setting the firm can offer any tariff, but customers may opt for a mandatory tariff (characterised by last period prices as variable fee and minus per customer profit as a fixed fee) so that prices can be set equal to marginal costs, as under ISS. Only these mechanisms, in which convergence takes place in one period, are not directly affected by changes in the environment and in the opportunity set.

Such factors can be seen as dealt with in practice through a price cap mechanism incorporating them through the X factor. Apparently, given the periodical adjustment, price caps can adapt to a changing environment. The X factor is meant to take into account the real reduction of costs due to the increase in productivity, technological innovation and eventual variations in the unitary costs (due to the presence of economies or diseconomies of scale). The periodic review remains however at the heart of the issues related to price caps. Its existence introduces the possibility of *strategic behaviour* by the firm, which could prevent the achievement of cost reductions. This suggests that the price cap mechanism may be usefully supplemented by an ISS or optional two-part tariffs as suggested by Vogelsang (1990). The firm can use discriminating fixed fees to finance marginal cost pricing and customers are not worse off, since they may opt for capped prices.

Expectations, which play a crucial role in the periodical adjustment, represent a link with the Bayesian regulatory approach and lead us to examine a particularly relevant question: given some prior knowledge, can we expect price cap regulation to attain optimal price, output and input levels or to be preferable to alternative schemes (e.g. ROR)?

Clearly the regulator can maximise the expected value of her objective function (usually a social welfare function) taking advantage of her knowledge of the prior probabilities on the relevant parameters of firm's cost and market demand (even if unlike the regulated firm she cannot correctly observe their current realisations).[5]

The objective function choice is the source of the basic trade off between providing incentives for efficiency and minimising the rent enjoyed by the regulated firm, because of asymmetric information.[6] Such a trade off arises putting more weight on consumers' surplus, as in Baron and Myerson (1982), or considering the *cost of public funds*, due to distortionary taxation, as done notably in Laffont and Tirole (1986). Moreover, the last approach introduces a moral hazard problem (due to the presence of an effort parameter). However, the introduction of this new problem does not change the basic outcomes, as both the regulator and the firm's manager are risk neutral.[7] In fact, the fundamental result established for asymmetric information on the cost side, remains exactly the same: given a range of potential efficiency levels for the regulated firm, the regulator should induce the price in the case of low efficiency types above the (unknown) intrinsic marginal cost (even if no rent is allowed) in order to limit the informational rent in the case of highly efficient types.

In this setting, as Laffont and Tirole (1993) show, we can improve price caps by lowering the power of the incentive to reduce costs (α) for less efficient firms and consequently increasing expected social welfare through the reduction of informational rents at the expenses of allocative efficiency. In practice, what theory suggests is to incorporate profit sharing into price caps, offering a menu of contracts, in order to achieve better results. Some recent incentive schemes have tried to go into this direction; e.g. according to the price regulation introduced in California in 1990 earnings in excess to a benchmark rate of return of 13% are shared equally up to 18%, whereas earnings above 18% benefit only consumers.

Bayesian regulatory mechanisms crucially depend on the subjective assessment by the regulator (of priors) and are implementable only if the available information is fairly precise and demand and cost functions are simple enough. The amount of private information built into the models is very limited: there is no reason why the regulator should be merely uncertain about the level of the cost function and not about its shape, or the demand condition of the industry as in Lewis and Sappington (1989).[8] Thus normative models should be regarded just as sources of insights rather than solutions to actual regulatory problems.

Many complex features of the real word, such as the repeated strategic relationship between the regulator and the firm are not captured by previous models. This consideration takes us back to the periodic review in price cap schemes, which is probably the major source of strategic behaviour by the firm and the regulator and leads us to address an additional question: under price cap adjustments, can the regulated firm recoup investment costs through the present value of future earnings on the convergence path toward a new equilibrium?

We still have to explore this matter in detail and see how a partial recourse to a profit sharing scheme can alleviate the long run problem. While the cost plus characteristic of ROR makes its performance poor with respect to short run efficiency it may make it more adequate than price cap in preventing opportunistic behaviour and in supporting an optimal investment path. Alternatively with longer adjustment periods (i.e. decelerating the convergence toward a new optimal price) regulated firms become able to recoup investment costs through the present value of future earnings. However, this is socially costly because it reduces short run allocative efficiency.

In the medium and long run, both parties must rely on reputation and credible threats. In fact it is difficult to sustain efficient investment through the provision of a binding contract and to verify in court the essential parameters of that contract. Hence, the regulator's discretion in setting price caps is a crucial issue, which will be considered in section 4.[9]

Here we merely point out how the apparent flexibility provided by price regulation may not always be an improvement over the used and useful rate of return regulation.

Let us now turn to more practical issues in the development of price cap schemes. Nowadays price cap regulation has been operating for some time, so that there is no longer a single approach, if this were indeed ever true. Specifically, a number of distinctions can be drawn, some of which will be examined at some length in what follows.

2.2   Form of the Price Index

One, seemingly trivial, issue which occurs when setting a price cap is how to combine or account for the various prices for the range of goods which is being regulated. An obvious solution is to use a price index, and BT's prices are subject to a Laspeyres (base-weighted) index. This has the very desirable feature of ensuring that, if the index falls in real terms, consumers as a group are better off. But it has the disadvantage that the company has an incentive to develop new goods or manoeuvre old ones outside the group in such a way as to minimise the constraint. (There is a previous example - contraceptive sheaths, for which the Monopolies and Mergers Commission (1982) devised an index which was thus afflicted).

An alternative is to impose average revenue regulation. This does not suffer from the same problem because it relates to a set of goods rather than pre-defined specifics. However, it turns out to have some peculiar features.

Suppose two markets are the focus of regulation. They are identical in terms of demand conditions, but costs of supply differ. Then it is (privately) optimal for the market which is more expensive to serve to have the higher markup. This reduces sales units to the market so the average price is more influenced by the lower cost market. More generally, an average revenue constraint can lead to a markup higher than would be set by an unconstrained monopolist (see Waterson, 1992). In consequence, the welfare effects of average revenue regulation can be adverse; for example, tightening the constraint can reduce consumer surplus (Law, 1995). Further problems, which do arise in the presence of competition, will be shown in the next section.

Nevertheless (either because these problems are not deemed serious or can be counteracted or because they have not been recognised) average revenue regulation has became the popular approach in the UK.

2.3   Cost Passthrough

One of the first major changes to the envisaged price regulatory framework was the development of the "cost passthrough". All the UK's regulated industries except BT and, essentially, the BAA have formulae which allow certain costs to be passed on in full (or virtually so) presumably because these costs are believed to contain idiosyncratic elements. This gives rise to several very substantial changes in the operation. It is easiest to illustrate these by reference to the first formula for units of gas sold to private customers by British Gas (employed from April 1987), then to explain subsequent development. This is:

$$P_t = \left(1 + \frac{RPI - X}{100}\right)N_{t-1} + G_t - K_t$$

where P is the maximum average price per therm, N is the non gas costs per therm and G is the gas costs per therm.

Some values are the subject of prediction and subsequent adjustment through K. Ignoring this for simplicity, means we can write:

$$PQ \leq nU + gI \tag{2}$$

where Q is the number of therms, n is allowed price for non-gas input units of U and g is the price of gas input of I.

This leads us to two issues. First, (2) can be seen as a constraint in the regulated firm's maximisation of profit:

$$Max\Pi = PQ - wU - gI$$

The implication is that in the longer term, if w > n, there will be incentives to relative overuse of the gas input, or too little economising on the non-gas input through what is in effect the Averch-Johnson effect. How might this manifest itself?

- Storage facilities and network could have relatively little investment given insufficient pressure to economise on gas input.

- This would be particularly true if the producer owns some of the input (as British Gas does). On this see also Helm and Yarrow (1988, Appendix).

Second, the regulator inevitably has to know something about the cost side including allocation of costs between activities. This is particularly true if the firm sells input to itself, or if he/she is only regulating a part of the firm's activity.

In more recent developments of the formulae, it has been recognised that even idiosyncratic costs should not be passed on in full. So for example the gas formula has been changed from 1992 in respect of the gas price to

$$\frac{G - 100(1.01^N - 1)}{100} \text{ x original price}$$

(N being the number of years elapsing since the formula was first applied). There is also an element E_t representing allowable energy efficiency cost/therm, which can be added to the formula to encourage efficiency savings.

2.4   Quality, Information and Accounting

There is a clear need for the regulator to receive information about quality of performance where relevant. But there are some less obvious information gathering activities or implications as well. First, in businesses which are substantially restructured, the flow of financial information has to be radically altered. Revenues from particular aspects of the business which may not have been measured separately prior to privatisation can take on substantial significance in a post-privatisation era and need unbundling. One example, which makes the point simply, refers to a case from time to time on the privatisation agenda: the Post Office. This has been split up into three divisions: Post Office Counters, which sells stamps among other things,

Royal Mail, concerned with letters, and Parcelforce, which deals with parcels. But stamps can be used on either division's services. It has transpired after separation that the method by which postage stamp revenues were divided between letters and parcels was rather arbitrary and favoured Parcelforce, a point with obvious implications for the divisions, and less obvious ones for any regulator.

Second, once businesses are privatised, management objectives and ethos can change. BT had traditionally published quality indices, but gave this up on privatisation, claiming commercial confidentiality. Oftel was therefore forced to develop its own procedures, which indicated that BT's quality has been broadly unchanged between 1984 and 1986. BT having failed (or delayed) publishing its own index in 1987 in response to Oftel pressure, Oftel published figures in July 1987 and BT resumed publication in September. The figures showed a fall in the quality, and Oftel became concerned. Subsequently, Oftel has extended its own series of data on this and other matters.

Rebalancing was another early issue of concern. One beauty of Littlechild's formula was that BT could move prices into line with relative costs, as long as it kept within its (original) formula RPI-3% and an additional (informal) agreement not to raise line rentals by more that RPI+2%. But rebalancing (and perhaps competitive strategy against Mercury) tended to favour long distance and peak services, thereby business users against private consumers. Thus domestic customers' bills could easily rise in real terms. In the face of public concern, Oftel investigated the rebalancing and found it justified, but suggested there was no need for significant further relative price changes after 1986 between local and long distance calls. Subsequently a further constraint, that the median consumer's bill should not rise in real terms. was implemented.

Most importantly, regulators do have to get substantially involved in issues regarding costs of capital, rates of return and allocations of costs. Cost of capital becomes relevant when revisions to the formulas are being developed. Cost allocation is important in determining interconnection issues, which are discussed later.

It was recognised early on in the regulatory process that cost of capital would play an important part (Vickers and Yarrow, 1988). Once regulatory formulae come up for revision, the questions of whether they have been too generous arises. A straightforward way to evaluate this is to compare the return earned on capital with what would have been appropriate for an otherwise similar industry in a substantially competitive setting. This then turns on what the cost of sourcing capital for new projects or replacement cost of existing assets in the industry would be. With a given replacement cost of capital (assuming an efficient asset base), the required return on this can be calculated and, with demand and other costs given or assumed, the average revenue required may be predicted for the new period. Hence the formula may be determined. But since there is doubt over a number of the necessary assumptions, and since in particular a single percentage point variation in reasonable rate of return can relate to a substantial amount of profit, a great deal is at stake. Significant debate has been engendered by, for example, Ofwat's calculations of Water companies' cost of capital in 1991. (See eg Cowan (1994), Grout (1995)). At a conceptual level, there is also a question of how different this is from rate of return regulation, with a rather long lag. In order to deal with this question we need to deal with a dynamic framework, as in section 4.

3.   REGULATION FOR COMPETITION

Regulation has often been regarded as the antithesis of competition. This may be true in some circumstances; however, in several cases regulation has a positive role in promoting, preserving and extending the competitive process. In this section we will sketch some of the most relevant links between competition and regulation (especially under price cap schemes). We start discussing theoretical issues, but our attention is mainly related to their practical relevance. The final part is devoted to the problem of access pricing, whose solution is of the most concern.

3.1   Theoretical Analysis and Practical Issues

There is now a substantial theoretical literature on the interactions between competition and regulation.[10] In what follows we will focus on the possible benefits (and drawbacks) deriving from the introduction of competitors in a regulated setting. First, we find it useful to distinguish competition *for* the market (bidding for a natural monopoly) and competition *in* the market, i.e. product market competition.

Let us first consider whether competition through auction may prevent the regulated firm from setting its price too far above cost and may encourage cost reducing activities. In a *static* context, as shown by Laffont and Tirole (1987), competition cannot substitute for regulation. The best that can be done is just to auction a regulatory incentive contract able to achieve the second best level of effort. Competition in the auction just reduces the interval of the possible intrinsic costs.[11] This limits the information rent, because now it is the second lowest bid that has a zero rent ensuring *asymptotic efficiency*. Decreasing the basic regulatory trade off analysed in section 2 it moves the optimal incentive scheme toward fixed price contracts (as with price caps). However, in theoretical models the benefits of selecting the most efficient firm are emphasised while the costs associated with the auction tend to be neglected.

Another reason why regulation cannot substitute for competition is that the selection of the producer (through competition) is just the first step in the organisation of a natural monopoly. It should be followed by the determination of the production level and of the firm's rent and the further stages of the monitoring and enforcement of the contract, in which potential (by re-auctioning or yardstick competition) may play a role, at least mimicking the audit process.[12]

Competition may be helpful also in a *dynamic* context, by providing incentives for investment or innovation, even if in this case important factors may limit its efficacy. Specifically the incumbent usually enjoys a big advantage (due for example to investments in R&D). Thus, there is a possibility that somehow weakening the monopolist may be desirable.

Analysing a sequential model for the acquisition of a newly developed product, Anton and Yao (1987) show how the existence of a less efficient alternative system (never used with full information) may be useful because it establishes the price when the auction is used and it creates the possibility to cut-off the new system, taking as given the cost of the technology transfer. Re-auctioning is examined by Rob (1986) who explicitly derives the R&D process thereby dealing simultaneously with the choice of the most efficient developer and of the incentives needed to induce him to pursue a socially desirable R&D strategy.

However, for long term activities (such as utility industries) the added value generated by investment may be expropriated leading to under-investment in specific assets. Laffont and Tirole (1988) show how the underinvestment problem can be mitigated, if (i) the optimal incentive scheme in period 1 relative to period 2 is low-powered, in order to reduce investment cost in the first period and to favour the capture of its benefits in the second one, through greater rents, (ii) the incumbent is favoured in the re-auctioning.[13]

The general conclusion is that regulation cannot be reduced to a once for all auction.

Competition in the market (even if potential) may be used in order to reduce asymmetric information since it provides valuable information about the firm's performance. In fact, more precise information about the technology of the regulated firm can be collected through the comparison with other firms, i.e. "yardstick competition". Shleifer's conclusions, generalised in the ambit of incentive theory, lead to a very strong result: under the hypotheses of *risk neutrality, no bankruptcy problems* and (appropriately) *correlated information,* extracting the firm's rent is costless, so that fixed price contracts are optimal.[14]

The mere threat of entry is a sort of endogenous regulatory mechanism. In fact, the presence of an uncontrolled competitive fringe has a influence both within the range of regulation and outside it (leading to the shutdown of the regulated firm), as shown by Caillaud (1990).

Competition does not always reduce the regulator's tasks. In the case in which a regulator is uncertain about the demand condition of the industry Biglaiser and Ma (1995) (introducing competition in the form of a Stackelberg follower) isolate a trade off between the efficient distribution of consumers across firms and the excess profit (present even under complete information) which constrains regulation, so that the pricing decision can no longer be delegated to the firm. In a *dynamic* context, with the introduction of the ratchet effect (a kind of implicit incentive) yardstick competition can be undesirable. Meyer and Vickers (1995) discuss this question, showing the importance of the informational structure of the model.

Competition can be undesirable, as Mankiw and Whinston (1986) pointed out, when part of the profits of entry comes not from the generation of additional consumers' surplus, but from the opportunity to steal profits from one's competitors. A second source of inefficiency occurs when entry reallocates output from a low marginal cost incumbent to a high marginal cost entrant. Brennan (1991) showed how a similar reasoning applies when a regulated firm faces competition from firms offering differentiated products.[15]

There is often concern about "cream skimming" in which competition focuses on the most profitable part of the demand market served by a regulated firm engaged in price discrimination.[16] Where competitors are successful high-demand consumers bypass the regulated monopoly, which is left with the less lucrative part of the market ("skimmed milk").[17] However, even the mere threat of cream skimming competition interferes with the pricing policy of the monopolist (in the context of second or third degree price discrimination and pricing below marginal cost may emerge). Hence, there is a role for a restrictive policy toward such aggressive competition that serves the low-cost and high-return part of the market.

Price cap regulation can itself have effects on competition. An average revenue constraint can induce the incumbent to set price below marginal cost, with unintended negative effects on potential competition or in response to entry. For simplicity's sake, suppose that the regulated incumbent operates in two markets, one of which is potentially open to competition. If the prices are required to be equal and are restricted from above by the upper bound given by the regulated price cap, the firm has no incentive to engage in pricing predatory behaviour, since whenever it reduces the price in the competitive market it automatically does so in the other market, losing profits. The incumbent's response to entry is likely to be more aggressive if price discrimination is allowed with a resultant effect on entry. In particular, the larger the scale of entry, the lower (higher) is the price in the competitive (captive) market; even pricing below marginal costs may become profitable. Armstrong and Vickers (1991) argue that the presence of this kind of predatory behaviour provides a strong case against regulated incumbents' freedom to price discriminate. Separate price caps on each market can therefore be an important element of policy to promote competition.[18]

However, welfare consequences of price discrimination are ambiguous: the incumbent benefits from the possibility to reduce price in the competitive market (as consumers) and to increase it in the captive one, but competitors (and consumers in the captive market) are worse off.

3.2 The Identification of Natural Monopoly, Competitive Components and Access Pricing

As noted in the introduction, industry regulators in the UK were faced with an initial industry structure which had as much to do with political exigencies as with economic logic. In some cases, particularly the later ones, significant structural modification had occurred, in others not. But as Baumol et al. (1982) have noted, determining what constitutes a natural monopoly is not straightforward, and in general requires knowledge of the whole cost function. Moreover market mechanisms can lead to industries remaining in the hands of a monopoly when not a natural monopoly (as a result, eg of barriers to entry) or (less familiarly) entry occurring which is inefficient. Thus in the absence of price regulation, we are not assured that the structure is ideal. However the Weak Invisible Hand Theorem states that if cost conditions are right, and prices are Ramsey-optimal then the natural monopoly structure will be sustainable. This is of some interest since we might expect over time that price regulation will lead towards Ramsey-optimal prices, but it does assume the correct <u>set</u> of prices is being regulated, so there is an element of circularity. Also, particularly in some industries, the world is too dynamic to fit in with the static Baumol et al. frame of reference.

All this is by way of an introduction to the point that regulators can and possibly should attempt to identify those aspects of their industry which could be made or encouraged to be more competitive and those which should not be. It is evident from their annual reports that all feel some duty (sometimes enshrined in statute) to allow or develop competition where possible.

Markets do not develop unaided. One step further down the track from regulated interconnection charges is the explicit development of a market, through which such transactions take place. The function of the market is to act as the conduit and middleman, to arrange appropriate protocols, act as a certification agent, to provide storage, or a market for storage (not relevant for electricity), and confidence that the institution will not collapse. All these activities need some organisation, and are costly to provide. One important factor is that the physical conduit in electricity and gas is a multi-billion pound asset and is essentially nonseparable. Its owner, whoever that may be, has an important and continuing source of monopoly power. The monopoly is not absolute; should its charges be high there will be some customers who will bypass the network in favour of a direct link between generation and consumption, but who may not do so if the charges are low. Assuming the monopoly is a natural one, the fact that bypass occurs itself raises costs to other participants. Because of the importance (size) of the market, continuing regulation is likely to provide a cost-effective means of ameliorating these problems even when the market has developed.

It has been claimed in favour of price cap regulation that it would naturally "wither away" as competition developed and the market took over. So far it seems instead that more regulation is actually required when competition first emerges, a "paradox of regulation". The experience of electricity generation shows how injecting a market and competition into a previously monopolistic framework is much trickier than it may appear at first sight. The model with which the framers of the structure in electricity in the UK were working appears implicitly to have incorporated Bertrand-type pricing assumptions on generating supply. In fact, the pricing mechanism they designed arguably corresponds more closely to supply function equilibria (Green and Newbery, 1992). Moreover there are constraints on the system, the reason being that power has traditionally been exported from the Yorkshire and Nottinghamshire coal mining areas to the heavily demanding South of England. At times of peak demand, substantial system losses in transmission are created. Knowing this is likely to happen, these stations can be bid in only at very high prices, creating a system cost known as uplift. Moreover, the simultaneous presence of the contract market changes incentives, though the precise impact is controversial.

Amongst other things, potential inputters into the system and extractors from it require regulatory surveillance at least at the point when they enter the market. Protocols apply not just to the network itself but also to these agents, who may otherwise impose significant externalities on other players. For example an independent gas supplier must take instructions as to when and how it puts gas into and out of the system, but if the network provider writes these instructions they may be given in such a way as to limit competition. Therefore the regulator needs to be involved.

Broadly speaking, since regulators have identified "the (transport/distribution) network" as the natural monopoly element, and what remains as being potentially competitive regulation might be expected eventually to reduce in its scope. Clearly, as more is discovered about the true extent of natural monopoly, regulation will be refocussed. Attention is already switching in this way, towards access or interconnection pricing and away from final price.

Regulatory authorities should consider questions about *structure* (i.e. mergers and vertical integration, and the possibility of divestiture) and *conduct* (e.g. possible predatory behaviour). Economies of scale provide a case for limiting competition in the network provision but competition may be beneficial (inducing, for instance, greater efficiency levels). It is crucial to decide whether this trade-off should be solved by the market forces or by regulation (e.g. by licensing a few competitors). The radical solution implies the *divestiture* of the integrated firm in order to avoid favourable treatment of internal consumers.

In most cases, the development of a reasonable framework of interconnection charges has required vertical separation of businesses, or at least of accounting transactions. For example BT (a still-integrated business) has since April 1995 produced "network" accounts and been forced to charge itself the same amount as competitors for access to core facilities. After some prevarication on the part of Government, British Gas now has a separate division (Transco) which runs the pipeline network and whose tariffs are being regulated. National Grid runs electricity (high voltage) transmission and the regional electricity companies have separate tariffs for distribution and supply. Both transmission and distribution tariffs are regulated. The plan is to allow all consumers to choose their supplier of gas and of electricity from 1998; currently only the larger ones may do so. Since both these products are essentially homogeneous, if access to supply is easy and interconnection prices are fair, substantial competition may be expected.

A reasonable menu of interconnection prices relies for its basis on access costs; after all, it is towards efficient cost levels that one desires price regulation ultimately to push prices. However, in separating out an integrated business, it may not be possible to attribute all costs clearly to one activity or another, and in any case established thought processes and business structures will need to undergo substantial change. There appears to be a natural tendency to retain implicit assumptions which may no longer be appropriate, and therefore to consider a wide range of costs to be fixed. Often the problem is not that costs are fixed but rather that output is not an important driver of cost. Thus in those cases where the methodology is best developed, for example telephones and gas, a substantial dialogue between regulator and network owner on costing has been required.

Difficult questions on access, storage, protocols, and thus a charging methodology for transport on the gas transmission network are being debated by the regulator Ofgas at the time of writing. Clearly access charging methodologies are of considerable interest to the providers of the network. Amongst other things they do not want to be left with stranded assets. But equally, without a reasonable regime of access charges the market cannot be created. For instance, British Gas's competitors need to have access to British Gas's distribution network in order to operate in the market.

3.3   The Baumol-Willig Rule and other Developments

The regulator's task of promoting efficiency is therefore moving towards a focus on the terms of the interconnections between the regulated firm and competitors.

Laffont and Tirole (1994a) compute pricing rules, using the standard Ramsey principles, interpreting the intermediate and the final output as substitutes.[19] If there is no need to create new infrastructure or facilities to connect the competitors with the existing network, the regulated firm cannot falsely claim a higher access price, without being hurt in the final goods market. In this case, even with full information the input price exceeds the marginal cost of providing access and with asymmetric information it is optimal to increase access price further, due to the incentive correction associated with the network activity.[20]

Introducing discrimination through non-linear pricing (for final and intermediate goods) in this framework, cream skimming becomes the only type of competition allowed by the incumbent, and probably by a welfare maximising regulator. In particular, when the incumbent is a monopolist and the entrant comes in at only one vertical level (a common event in network industries) Vagliasindi and Waterson (1995b) provide a rationale for entry concentrating on high-demand consumers. In this framework they also consider the relevance of the Baumol-Willig rule - introduced by Willig (1979) and Baumol (1983) - as an efficiency reference point (according to which entry should be allowed if the opportunity cost of entry for the incumbent can be paid by entrants).

Recently, the Baumol-Willig rule has been reconsidered in potential applications in the case of New Zealand by Baumol and Sidak (1994). Abstracting from information and incentive problems in a model in which both prices and output are exogenously given, Armstrong, Doyle and Vickers (1996) define the concept of opportunity costs of entry under different assumptions about supply conditions, bypass and possibility of substitution, showing that they are often lower than those implied by the application of a simple price margin rule. Laffont and Tirole (1994b), instead, criticise the use of a partial price cap together with the efficient component pricing rule, since it provides a form of subsidy to non-competitive segments (in the sense that access charges are considered too high). They recognise the demanding requirements of the Ramsey approach, but at the same time they show how Ramsey pricing can be obtained by imposing a global price cap -including access as a final good- on the incumbent, with weights exogenously determined and proportional to the goods' forecasted quantities.

As an illustration, consider telecommunications. In 1990, at the beginning of the Duopoly Review for telecommunications the terms on which rivals -Mercury (MCL) and others- should gain *access* to British Telecom's local networks and the wider issue of British Telecom's *vertical structure* were discussed. The Office of Telecommunications (Oftel) decided that a potential existed for competition at a local level, the benefits of competition being considered to outweigh the losses of economies of scale. Although BT was contributing to some of the costs of its local network through the prices for long distance calls, MCL was allowed to interconnect with BT's network without making an equivalent contribution to BT's local costs. This advantage helped MCL to offset disadvantages from its lack of economies of scale in pricing its long distance calls. Furthermore, as BT was practically constrained to charge uniform tariffs, MCL could concentrate its effort on the densest telephone traffic, with a limited ability of BT to respond.

More recently, in Autumn 1993 Oftel published the determination of interconnection charges between BT and MCL and indicated how to deal with the Access Deficit Contribution (ADC) waivers. The ADC system aims to compensate BT. With linear prices on long distance calls (regulated by a price cap) Oftel imposes on Mercury a per call tax proportional to the profitability of that call for British Telecom (defined as the ratio between the variable profits in the local network and the total variable profits, including access charges). Notice how, in principle, if the price cap is successful in keeping the budget in balance the Oftel rule collapses to the Baumol Willig one. This shows how one of the main purposes of ADC was indeed to discourage inefficient entry.

Since mid 1993 competition has come to all market segments.[21] The Oftel rule has been applied to multiple competitive segments (and therefore access charges) including mobile services. An interesting feature of these developments is that they entail competition between technologies with different cost structures. Intuition would suggest that customers will segment themselves according to the cost structures of the operators, which would also be reflected in their tariffs. For instance, a wire based technology characterised by substantial access costs and low usage costs appeals to high users, whilst wireless technologies with low access costs but high usage charges would favour low users.[22]

4.   THE DESIGN OF REGULATORY INSTITUTIONS

4.1   The Relevance of Regulatory Commitment

It is a fundamental ingredient of the basic theory of regulation (more generally, of principal-agent models) that regulators can commit fully. This is perhaps one of the main drawbacks of current regulatory practices.

Within a static principal-agent setting the regulator has no bargaining power to renegotiate the contract. This arises because any expectation of renegotiation destroys the incentive compatibility property of the solution. Since pricing (and effort levels) are socially suboptimal as regards less efficient firms in the static solution, renegotiation may improve efficiency by reducing prices (and actual costs) without increasing rents. However, more efficient firms will anticipate this modification of less efficient firms' contracts and will not reveal their true efficiency level, since their incentive compatibility constraint is no longer satisfied. Hence, the presence of regulatory discretion to renegotiate is ex ante detrimental, even if it would be socially optimal ex post (because it can eliminate the trade off between incentives to efficiency and rent extraction).

In a *dynamic* context (and multiperiod models) matters become more complicated because of the presence of the *ratchet* effect -a kind of *implicit* incentive, which implies the dampening of a firm's incentive to reduce costs, because of the anticipation of future price reductions. Basically, the larger is the regulator's bargaining power in following periods the stronger is the ratchet effect.

The practical relevance of these issues emerges from the following. As we have seen, the price cap is adjusted over time by an exogenous factor and discretionary decisions usually take place each five years at the review. This limits the relevance of the ratchet effect, since profits can be kept till the next review takes place. However, regulators have had a good deal of discretion in the UK experience, especially in performing their periodic review task (e.g. setting the efficiency target of cost-reductions and the "normal" rate of return and extracting rents due unanticipated cost reductions). This in general weakens incentives and in particular may cause distortions in effort and investment towards the end of each cycle. In general the greater is the proportion of unanticipated cost savings being kept by the regulated firm the greater is the incentive to make cost reductions and consequently the lower is the relevance of the ratchet effect.

Such considerations may also lead to the problem of long run under-investment in specific assets, because the added value, generated by the investment, may be expropriated during the subsequent bargaining processes. Valuable improvements could be made by specifying the regulators' review process for instance through public schemes which fairly remove unanticipated rents or take into account sunk investment costs. In fact, this may significantly enhance incentives to engage in cost reduction activities and make long run investments, especially if firms are risk averse, by reducing uncertainty and regulators' discretion. Alternatively, current schemes would be improved and the ratchet effect ameliorated if the regulator could commit for longer periods.

Unfortunately, for long term activities (such as utility industries) a perpetual automatic price cap scheme has serious drawbacks as a rent extraction mechanism - complete contracts with commitment are inconceivable. As we have already seen, the benefits from potential or actual competition may be reduced in this case. However, let us briefly consider if the rent extraction problem, tied to a permanent bargaining processes, can be somehow alleviated by the presence of competition.

Anton and Yao (1987) examine a similar problem. In practice, incentive contract designs that induce revelation if regulators are committed to use only reprocurement auctions (or second sourcing) in order to reduce informational rents, and not to exploit cost information revealed by the incumbent, may be available. Hence, it is the very absence of discretion or the "auction commitment" which, by limiting the ability of the regulator to dictate the terms of reprocurement (using the cost information revealed by the firm during the initial stage) which matters and allows competition to play a useful role. Unfortunately, the experience advantage of the incumbent over competitors (which simply consists in lower production cost of additional units) greatly reduces the potential benefits of competitive bidding.

Substantial developments in the field of principal-agent models of regulation have been achieved also in a dynamic framework. The consequences of regulatory *commitment* have been considered in two period models.[23] In these models the regulator would find it optimal to commit to play the optimal static game twice. However, this optimal incentive scheme is clearly not *renegotiation-proof*.

Put simply, the fact that the firm is concerned about the expropriation of its informational rent in the second period makes separation of types costly.

An inefficient type may adopt the take the money and run strategy. To induce an efficient type to provide some information in the first period, the first period contract must offer him a deal that would make it optimal for an inefficient type to mimic the efficient type and quit the relationship in the second period.

The common feature of renegotiation-proof contracts is that the efficient type produces at its socially optimal cost level. The inefficient type's production cost, instead, lies in between the socially optimal cost and the optimal static contract conditional on the regulator's posterior beliefs and this explains why we speak in terms of *rent constrained* contracts. The two extreme cases of optimal contracts are a *price cap* scheme in which the inefficient type also produces at its socially optimal cost level and a *conditionally optimal* contract (given the regulator's posterior beliefs about the firm's type. Intuitively, the regulator faces a trade off between lowering the efficient type's rent and bringing the other type's efficiency closer to the optimal one.

The main insight we can draw from this literature is that high powered incentive schemes yielding efficient production are less subject to renegotiation than low powered schemes, which are designed to limit the firm's rent. This result contrasts with the conventional wisdom that price caps are likely to be renegotiated.

However, ex post uncertainty and bankruptcy or political reasons may well change the results. Moreover we have not dealt with the long run investment problem and we have implicitly embraced the "public interest" paradigm, which consider the regulator to be a benevolent maximiser of social welfare. In both cases a (sometimes implicit) fundamental element, i.e. the strategic aspects of the repeated relationship between the regulator and the firm, has been neglected.

Let us first refer to the *hold up* problem. An investment which is ex ante efficient won't be ex post efficient, unless specific guarantees are given that the regulator will not act opportunistically against the firm. If the regulator lacks the ability to commit to future prices the concern arises that, after the firm has made sunk cost investment expenditure, regulatory policy will be tightened, with the result that the firm does not recover its cost of capital. Once the firm anticipates this they will adopt a risk premium for regulatory risk, and in some circumstances may be deterred from investing efficiently.

Hence serious danger of underinvestment arises, especially in utilities where sunk costs are relevant. This is the reverse of the Averch Johnson overinvestment result. In fact, we know that a commitment to a fair return on investment characterises ROR. However, in practice this commitment cannot be absolute. Since the mid 1970s the rates of return achieved by a number of US utilities have been eroded as a result of inflation, regulatory lags in adjusting nominal prices, and regulatory decisions not to include some assets in the rate base.

Another important problem is that the regulator may engage in strategic behaviour with respect to sunk investment, perhaps because the regulator wants to redistribute income from the utility to consumers. In practice, he cannot resist the political pressure from consumers' interest groups. Recently Gilbert and Newbery (1994) have modelled regulation as a repeated game between a firm facing a stochastic demand and a regulator tempted to disregard past investments. They assume that capital completely depreciates in one period and investment is decided before the state of the demand (high or low) is realised. There is a technology with fixed coefficients to avoid short run efficiency issues. They also argue that in the practice with what they call UUROR (used and useful rate of return regulation) the regulatory conflict has been on the assets that should be included in the rate base. In this assessment problem the regulator considers if the management followed norm of prudent business behaviour and whether there was an economic need for the capacity that was built.

Gilbert and Newbery show how UUROR (with a commitment to an adequate rate of return on useful and used capital, i.e. prudently invested) support an efficient investment programme for a larger set of parameter values than price regulation (when the regulator is unable to make state-contingent transfer payments). The reason is that price regulation requires a high price in a state of high demand to encourage the firm to invest. This high price gives the regulator (who is interested primarily in consumers' surplus) a large incentive to deviate from her announced policy.

In particular under price regulation carefully designed responses to deviation and state contingent transfer payments to compensate the firm may be needed in <u>both</u> states of demand, increasing the regulator temptation to cheat on her announced rewards.

Reality seems compatible with this underinvestment equilibrium. In fact the reduction in capital intensity may be the consequence of utilities' strategy to avoid sunk costs expropriation, building only for a low level of demand and relying on smaller (higher operating cost) plants when facing high demand.

It seems more difficult to take action that makes direct expropriation less likely. We have seen how the firm may choose a less capital intensive technique with higher operating costs. Yet this seems to be a problem we want to avoid. Williamson (1985) suggested that the regulator should not protect against the adverse consequence of supply shortages. But this appears a quite unreasonable policy, being necessary to provide some security.

So far we have discussed many drawbacks due to the absence of commitment. However, even in the absence of transaction costs, the ability to commit over the long run may be equally or even more dangerous if the agency is not benevolent, ideologically biased or more simply incompetent. Moreover, once a wrong decision is taken it cannot be reversed and society is forced into a poor outcome over a very long period.

4.2   Institutional Frameworks: Discretion and Collusion of the Regulatory Agencies

Regulatory agencies may be subject to *capture* (i.e. collusion between regulator and firm or other interest groups). This is likely to frustrate the government in achieving its objectives. Laffont and Tirole (1993) believe that there is a crucial principal-agent relation between politicians and bureaucrats and only agency-theoretic models can explain why regulators have discretion, interest groups have power (and enjoy rents) and how they try to capture parliamentary and government resolution, influencing decision makers through collusive activities. It might be the case that the regulator instead of promoting competition actually prevents new entry, maintaining monopoly power.

This point leads us to explore more general problems of *institutional design*. One may notice the difference in regulatory procedure adopted in the UK and USA. UK privatised utilities industries typically involve a Regulatory Office, whose role is mainly to administer a price-based formula imposed on the major products, with a regulatory process not open to public scrutiny. The regulator need not justify her decisions, to show their internal consistency, nor publish the evidence on which they are based. By contrast, the particular feature of the US system is the openness of the Regulatory Commissions, charged with setting prices, establishing service quality standards, monitoring performance and assisting investment programmes. McCubbins et al. (1987) shows how administrative procedures such as hearings are ways to control agency. The utility has a relevant incentive to reveal information in order to get what it wants. Users would get an opportunity to raise important issues, such as the environmental impact.

Moreover, the openness of the process is important since a close scrutiny of cost is essential, if prices are related to costs. Under price regulation the regulatory body may be more subject to *capture* during the review process when costs do enter in the picture. Yet there is little evidence that regulators have been subject to capture in the UK. On the other hand, there are potential relative disadvantages of the openness of Regulatory Commission; e.g. its cost in comparison to the one involved in the Regulatory Office approach. Moreover, the presence of competition may jeopardise the public availability of detailed information. Under certain circumstances these disadvantages may be severe. Hence, different industries may use different forms of regulation.[24]

Laffont and Tirole (1993) embrace the idea that institutions should be viewed as incomplete social contracts (since the legislator who wrote them cannot foresee all future contingencies and describe them appropriately). They evaluate them taking into account also incentives given to self interested regulators who execute these contracts not to collude with interest groups (but to accomplish the legislator's intent). The social contract distributes the authority over economic transactions to be regulated and it may restrict ex ante the extent of possible resolutions and the possible use of policy instruments, creating a viable system of checks and balances. In this way it aims to prevent abuses of the authority and the realisation of interest groups' objectives. It is the possibility of collusion that justifies limitations on the extent of powers the regulator is allowed by law. In comparing two standard institutions - average and marginal cost pricing rules for natural monopolies - Laffont and Tirole find a rationale for the absence of transfers. In particular, they show how a suboptimal mechanism such as the average cost pricing rule may dominate, due to its relative robustness to collusive activities.

Following Brennan and Buchanan (1991) one can argue that, once established, the authority becomes largely "uncontrollable". The US Congress usually reacts only to evidence brought by other parties. This may in part confirm the validity of Laffont and Tirole's model.

In this model however we have just a single autonomous regulatory agency and a unique watchdog representing consumers. In many European realities consumers are not well organised to perform the role of a powerful interest group. Moreover, when there are several distinct institutions involved in regulating the behaviour of a single utility industry and many agents with somewhat divergent interests playing a monitoring role, the efficiency of the monitoring activity could be reduced instead of being enhanced.

4.3   Practical Issues concerning the Organisation and Design of Regulation

It seems important at this point to get some feel for the financial magnitudes involved. The Office of Electricity Regulation (Offer), whose running costs in 1993/4 were £9.3m, is funded through a levy on those it regulates on the basis of their megawatt hours of throughput. Since we know roughly the variable cost of producing and delivering a megawatt hour of electricity ($\geq$£3, say), we can calculate an upper band for the fraction of revenue used up in regulation by the regulator. It is less than one thirtieth of one percent, a figure with which Harberger (1954) would probably be happy. The cost of Oftel is a similar fraction of relevant revenue in Telecoms.

Intermediate cases are somewhat trickier to determine. The decisions about whether to have specific agencies for the rail industry and the bus industry could be argued to be wrong, in either direction. In the case of rail, the raison d'etre of the agency seems to be to create contractual conditions between parts of a previously holistic industry, that is to oversee a vertical disintegration of dubious merit rather than to act as consumer champions. It is difficult to pretend this is anything but a costly exercise entered into in the hope of bringing reluctant competitors into a part of the industry of which they are relatively unignorant.

An almost opposite view has been taken of the bus (stage carriage) industry. It is supposed to be a largely non-network, essentially competitive industry. Therefore it is overseen by the normal competition agencies, mainly the Office of Fair Trading (OFT) and the Monopolies and Mergers Commission (MMC). For a supposedly competitive industry it has kept them remarkably busy! Over a period of around eight years at least eight separate anticompetitive actions have been reported on by the Director General of Fair Trading, several of which have proceeded to the MMC, following failure to agree. In addition, nine bus mergers have been referred to the MMC. And following OFT investigations the Restrictive Practices Court has had to strike down two separate agreements on prices and market sharing. This volume of activity is considerable for a relatively small industry. What appears to be happening is a very substantial concentration of bus transport activities in the hands of a small number of acquisitive, abrasive but probably efficient, operators.

It would be plausible to argue that there is sufficient activity in bus transport for a specialised agency to handle it, and indeed that some investigations which might be thought marginal would be less so in a specialised agency. But then there is a question about whether an agency to cover rail, but and coach transport would be desirable. To date, regulatory economics has had little to contribute to such questions.

In order to identify the extent of expenditure desirable on regulation, it is important to attempt an evaluation of the costs and <u>benefits</u>. The direct cost of regulation is relatively clear, being the cost of running the agency. But there are of course indirect costs. The companies being regulated have to spend money and divert human resources themselves in order to respond to the regulator. Judging merely by the quantity of paper produced by each side, the regulated firms' costs are roughly equivalent to the regulator's. Very roughly then, we have an evaluation of the costs; what of the benefits?

Clearly, amongst the benefits of regulation are prices which are lower than those absent regulation. We suggested earlier that, so long as monopoly remains at a vital stage in the chain of supply, such a monopolist can capture for itself the whole of the monopoly profit available (Vagliasindi and Waterson, 1995b). Therefore a regulator who brings prices down near to a competitive level performs a continuing service, although the marginal benefit may decrease over time. Roughly, calculations in Green (1996) suggest that a single action by the regulator (forcing divestiture of 15% of generating capacity) would produce benefits (a reduction in deadweight loss) many times the operating cost of Offer.

However, it is a mistake to believe that the only benefits (or costs) of a regulation arise through effects on pricing. Regulation is, in addition, about the identification, preservation and development of natural monopoly.

We have already discussed identification - the task of the regulator is isolating the network activities of integrated firms and providing reasonable access to them for those engaged in competitive aspects of service provision.

Preservation of a natural monopoly is about determining how to prevent such activities as inefficient bypass of the network, namely privately desirable but socially undesirable destruction of the network properties. In part this relates to keeping the network component efficient - a task with which Offer has been engaged with respect to the National Grid (concerning matters such as "uplift"). More problematic is the role of the rail regulator (and a bus regulator, if there were one) in preserving network elements of transport interconnection, both inter and intramodal. This is particularly acute because competition can be inimical to cooperation in the service of the passenger (as seen at Piraeus, regarding transport to the Greek islands, for example). Through tickets sit somewhat awkwardly with competition in price, but they are certainly convenient. And many transport, particularly bus, operators for reasons best known to themselves, provide remarkably little information about their services, seeming to rely on word of mouth or habit amongst intending passengers.

Yet of course the network itself should not be set in aspic, unresponsive to change. Demand and supply elements modify over time, requiring a response. Examples can be found in both gas and electricity industries. In gas, a new high pressure pipeline system based upon transporting natural gas from east coast terminals to centres of demand was developed efficiently, largely in ten to twelve years starting in 1966. In electricity, significant changes in the generation fuels mix will demand modifications to the national grid network. The former was developed within a holistic publicly-owned firm. The latter requires regulatory input since signals distorting relative transmission prices will distort development of the network and lead to inefficiency. The lesson of early experiments on entry into gas and electricity is that without a range of preconditions entry will not occur. Clearly a network developed with the central aim of security supply under monopoly (as in the case for the gas and electricity transmission networks) is not necessarily appropriate in structure for common carriage under competition.

It has to be said that the initial development of networks is something in which the market process unaided has not performed well, at least in the UK in the past. There are examples (rail) where the privately-constructed network contained significant redundancy. But in electricity, the history of the first two decades of this century is one where a clear perceived need and desire of network benefits nevertheless led to substantial conflict and a state of impasse, until the Central Electricity Board stepped in to oversee the development (Hannah, 1979). It is notable how much less extensive the onshore oil pipeline network is than the gas pipeline network in Britain, and some of that is Government-developed.

5.   CONCLUDING REMARKS

We introduced this paper by noting the somewhat rushed early development of regulatory framework for UK industries. At the same time, quite pathbreaking decisions were being made concerning the nature of regulation and the specific form it should take. Much of the theoretical development therefore came later, and considerable changes have been made to the nature of the regulation. Many mistakes were, and probably are, being made. Undoubtedly though the experience is a positive one for observers from outside the UK!

No one has attempted a serious answer to the obvious but difficult question of whether the form of regulation adopted in the UK has been better than a feasible alternative. There are several problems involved in doing so. The general presumption might be that UK regulation has been a success. Yet we would have expected, in telecoms at least, rapid technological change whatever the regime. We had already become accustomed to falling real gas prices. Given falling fuel input prices, we would have expected electricity to become cheaper (perhaps more rapidly than it in fact has - see Yarrow, 1992). And real prices of water services of have of course been rising, to pay for quality improvements. Real prices will also rise in rail services, it is anticipated. Therefore the answer is not obvious, though the system clearly has strengths.

We do not think it feasible that regulation of the network industries will wither away, because the network itself will remain in existence, albeit changing over time in form and (possibly as in telecoms) in importance. But the extent of regulation will, hopefully, not grow, and in itself must change in form in ways yet to be determined.

It is natural to think that we are wiser now than we were, and are now able to devise systems which are superior to those we once had. Thus the price cap system was seen as superior to rate of return regulation, yet in some ways it is merely a modified version of the same thing.

The use of regulation as a means to develop competition and the proposed use of information revelation mechanisms may have better claims to originality. Yet surprisingly sophisticated schemes are thrown up by the experience of the past. Foster (1992) catalogues how, in the run up to Gladstone's Railway Bill (which led after some substantial changes to the Railway Act 1844) some very farsighted views on regulation were expressed by Morrison and the Select Committee members. The problems of uncertainly, fixed costs, technical change in the industry and induced technical change in the industries it served, but the necessity for some control over rates for carriage were all debated. The difficulties of setting specific rates, but the equal difficulties of setting rates of return, problems of hiding profits and of cutting quality were covered. But the most remarkable element was the perceived requirement for an ultimate sanction which as proposed in the first draft of the Bill, was nationalisation! Naturally, since powerful railway interests were well-represented in Parliament, the Bill was emasculated by the time it became an Act. Yet the remarkable prescience revealed by many of those involved is rather humbling.

APPENDIX

Table 1: The major public enterprises in 1979

	Turnover (£ million) 1978/79	Employment (thousands) 1978/89	First Substantial Privatisation
Electricity Council	5,445	160	1990
Post Office[1]	4,619	411	BT 1984 PO ?
National Enterprise Board	4,158	279	[3]
British Steel	3,288	190	1988
National Coal Board	2,989	300	1994
British Gas	2,972	102	1986
British Rail	1,979	243	1996
British Airways	1,640	58	1987
British Aerospace	894	72	1981
British Shipbuilders	731	87	1988
South of Scotland Electricity Board	463	14	1991
National Bus	437	64	1986
British National Oil Corporation	432	1	1982
National Freight	394	40	1982
North of Scotland Hydro-Electricity Board	173	4	1991
British Airports Authority	162	7	1986
Water Industry[2]	-	-	1989

Source: Based on Vickers and Yarrow (1988 Table 5.3) with additions and deletions. All Figures are rounded to the nearest integer.

[1]   Separated into telecommunications (BT) and postal operations in 1981.

[2]   Not a unified industry (nor entirely public) prior to 1979.

[3]   A holding company, whose shareholdings were gradually liquidated.

NOTES

[*]   Although the whole structure of the paper has been discussed jointly, Michael Waterson has written sections 1, 2.2, 2.3, 2.4, 3.2, 4.3 and 5, while Maria Vagliasindi wrote the remaining sections.

1   "Prospects for the industry" include proceeds from sale; this inevitably conflicts with "protection against monopoly" as has been borne out in practice.

2   These approaches can be criticised as "ad hoc", however, they are useful complements to optimal regulation. Essentially, the same conditions for efficient regulation are required, the reason being that without truthful revelation and commitment by the regulator neither of them is efficient.

3   A first best solution is reached instantaneously since firms use marginal pricing. But such a transfer, which can be determined only if the regulator knows market demand, may not be politically feasible. In practice, even second best Ramsey pricing (which results from the maximisation of consumers' plus producer's surplus subject to the break-even constraint) is seldom feasible, because of the huge amount of information required on the demand and cost side. These problems cannot always be avoided with franchise-bidding (without a big number of well informed bidders or transferable firm's assets), as we will see in section 3.

4   In fact, the firm may have a weak incentive to reduce costs on the way to the optimum. Moreover, once the hypothesis of a single period profit maximisation is relaxed, as well as the assumption of decreasing average ray costs, the V-F process is no longer implementable. Sappington (1980) showed that there is a relevant incentive to behave strategically (being intentionally inefficient) in order to manipulate the process relaxing the regulatory constraint and increasing profits in subsequent periods. In the absence of detailed cost studies, it may be in the firm's interest to pretend not to have decreasing average ray costs, by incurring losses in order to induce the regulator to modify the scheme in a desirable way.

5   The solution must also satisfy the firms' participation and incentive-compatibility constraints. The first one ensures that the firm can break even in the worst state of the world and will always participate, while the second is meant only to satisfy the firm's profit maximisation (in practice the firm is bribed to reveal the true parameters).

6   No trade off would emerge as long as the regulator's objective is defined as the unweighted sum of consumers' and producer's net surplus, abstracting from *distributional considerations* and costs associated with monetary transfers, as in Loeb and Magat (1979).

7   Vagliasindi and Waterson (1995a) show how their model can be reduced to a pure adverse selection problem with no loss of economic insight. In practice, managerial disutility is ex post observable, once the adverse selection parameter is observed.

8   Optimal regulatory policy drastically changes in this alternative scenario. When marginal production costs increase price decisions can be delegated to the firm, which set efficient prices (enjoying no rent from its superior knowledge). On the other hand when marginal costs decrease with output the optimal policy involves a single price invariant to demand. Informational rents are enjoyed by the firm only for intermediate demand levels (rather than in extreme cases as it occurs in the case of cost uncertainty).

9   Despite the relevance of the repeated strategic relationship regulator/firm, there has been very little work in this area. What has been more extensively analysed are the consequences of regulatory commitment within two period models. Gilbert and Newbery (1994) fear the danger that regulators may engage in strategic behaviour with respect to sunk investment. Specifically, they argue that the recent sharp reduction in capital

intensity of price cap regulated utilities may be due to the fact that firms are following a risk-minimising approach in building plants (relying on less capital intensive and smaller plants) offering the regulator less incentive to expropriate sunk costs.

[10] A number of extensions of the standard monopoly analysis has been proposed (also on access pricing) by the "new economics of regulation". In particular, several extensions of the basic approach introduced by Laffont and Tirole (1986) have been collected together (1993). For instance they consider competitor with 'market power' and subsidised competitors.

[11] Essentially, with a second-price auction (or Vickrey auction) we are back to the standard optimal monopoly contract problem with a *random upward truncation point*, given by the intrinsic cost revealed by the second lowest bid. Competition through auction *benefits* the regulator, as shown by Riordan and Sappington (1987) because the winner's rent is also a nonincreasing function of the number of bidders.

[12] In the absence of investments, Demski et al. (1987) show that it may be useful to make a regulated monopoly incumbent subject to the threat of break-out in favour of a second source. This threat may alleviate the incentive constraint and reduce the rent of efficient firms. The second supplier may also be used to monitor the incumbent's cost, however the desirability of entry is a necessary but not sufficient condition for an audit (of incumbent's cost report).

[13] However, if the investment is specific, the unobservability of non-transferable investment imposes no cost and the slope of incentive schedule is time invariant and it is optimal to bias the break-out rule in favour of the entrant.

[14] One possible way to escape from this extreme result is to assume the presence of two kinds of shocks, an aggregate and an idiosyncratic one (whose sum constitutes the technological parameter of each firm). In this framework it is the aggregate shock that can be treated as the common knowledge's factor, and can therefore be elicited costlessly by the regulator, as in Auriol and Laffont (1992).

[15] To understand his reasoning consider the following example. Suppose we have an incumbent who initially serves two types of customers, earning zero profits (as the revenues simply cover his costs). Assume now that competitive entry occurs in one of the markets driving the price down to the entrant's marginal cost. The incumbent no longer finds it profitable to stay in, causing a welfare loss in the other market. Under these circumstances, entry will reduce social welfare in an unregulated setting if the consumers' gain from the market in which entry occurred is less than the consumers' loss in the other market. In multiproduct regulated markets, if the entrant's cost of serving the market exceeds the incremental cost to the regulated firm, entry is inefficient and is induced only by the price structure. There may be welfare losses even without recourse to distributional consideration (or favouring certain types of customers). Such losses can simply derived from the requirement that only the regulated firm's customers are expected to contribute to fixed costs. Hence, entry in regulated markets shrinks the set of markets from which cost recovery can be generated.

[16] In the pure monopoly case (without regulation) it is well known that price discrimination has an ambiguous welfare effect, which can be positive only when there is an increase in *total output* (the negative consequence of price discrimination is that it induces marginal

utilities to differ; we will refer to this phenomenon as the *inequality* effect). On price discrimination see Phlips (1983), Tirole (1988) and Varian (1989).

[17] As Laffont and Tirole argue, the presence of asymmetric information between the regulator and the firm, rising the actual cost, increases the probability of bypass in comparison with the optimal complete information level.

[18] The previous result does not necessarily hold when the scale of entry is endogenised (in fact, price discrimination may promote entry). While in Laffont and Tirole (1990) with second degree price discrimination the incumbent's predatory behaviour arises in order to avoid the potential danger of cream skimming by inefficient competitors, in Armstrong and Vickers (1993) even more efficient competitors may be thwarted, due to the presence of average price regulation. This anticompetitive strategy chosen by the incumbent would not be optimal without regulation or with separate price caps.

[19] This interpretation can be justified since the fringe makes no profit (so that the shadow social cost attached to their profit is irrelevant). The access price is not only greater than the marginal cost, but also than the one provided by the application of the Ramsey rule.

[20] In the *network expansion* case, instead, less access is given than under the full information benchmark, a result (*too little* competition) that seems to clash with the one obtained in the analysis of the optimal bypass (*excessive* competition), already discussed in section 3.1. However, the difference in these results is easily explained: here, the rise in the cost of the intermediate good (due to incentive issues) hurts competitors, whereas, in the bypass problem, it is directly transferred to the consumers, through higher prices in the final output, which in turn favour competitors.

[21] Subscribers to telephony provided by cable television operators have developed and radio-based technologies penetrated into the local loops providing both fixed services such as Ionica and mobile services as Mercury One to One and Euro Digital.

[22] This intuition seems to be supported by the outcomes of theoretical models; in particular endogenising the choices of the customers' type for the competitor, Vagliasindi (1995) gets similar results.

[23] See for instance Baron and Besanko (1987) and more recently in Lewis and Sappington (1991) and Besanko and Spulber (1992).

[24] For a discussion of such issues, see Waterson (1990).

REFERENCES

Anton, J. and D. Yao, 1987, 'Second Sourcing and the Experience Curve: price competition in defense procurement', *Rand Journal of Economics*, 18, 57-76.

Armstrong, M.; Cowan, S. and J. Vickers, 1994, *Regulatory Reform - economic analysis and british experience*, Cambridge, MIT Press.

Armstrong, M.; Doyle, C. and J. Vickers, 1996, 'The Access Pricing Problem: a Synthesis', *Journal of Industrial Economics*.

Armstrong, M. and J. Vickers, 1991, 'Welfare Effects of Price Discrimination by a Regulated Monopolist', *Rand Journal of Economics*, 22, 571-80.

Armstrong, M. and J. Vickers, 1993, 'Price Discrimination, Competition and Regulation', *Journal of Industrial Economics*, 4, 335-59.

Auriol, E. and J. Laffont,1992, 'Regulation by Duopoly' *Journal of Economics and Management Strategy*, 1, 507-33.

Averch, H. and L. Johnson, 1962, 'Behavior of the Firm under Regulatory Constraint', *American Economic Review*, 52, 1053-69.

Baumol, W., 1983, 'Some Subtle Issues in Railroad Regulation', *International Journal of Transport Economics*, 10, 341-355.

Baron, D. and D. Besanko, 1987, 'Commitment and Fairness in a Dynamic Regulatory Relationship', *Review of Economic Studies*, 54, 423-36.

Baron, D. and R. Myerson, 1982, 'Regulating a Monopolist with Unknown Costs', *Econometrica*, 50, 911-30.

Baumol, W., Panzar, J. and Willig, R., 1982,, *Contestable Markets and the Theory of Industry Structure*, San Diego CA: Harcourt, Brace, Jovanorich.

Baumol, W. and G. Sidak, 1994, *Toward Competition in Local Telephony*, Cambridge, MIT Press.

Besanko, D. and D. Spulber, 1992, 'Sequential-equilibrium Investment by Regulated Firms', *Rand Journal of Economics*, 23, 153-170.

Biglaiser, G and Ma, C., 1995, 'Regulating a Dominant Firm: unknown demand and industry structure', *Rand Journal of Economics*, 26, 1-19.

Bradley, I. and C. Price, 1988, 'The Economic Regulation of Private Industries by Price Constraint', *Journal of Industrial Economics*, 37, 99-106.

Brennan, T., 1991, 'Entry and Welfare Loss in Regulated Industries' in Crew, M. ,(ed) *Competition and the Regulation of Utilities*, Boston, Kluwer, 141-156.

Brennan, G. and J. Buchanan, 1991, 'Towards a tax constitution for Leviathan', *Journal of Public Economics*, 8, 255-273.

Caillaud, B., 1990, 'Regulation, Competition and Asymmetric Information', *Journal of Economic Theory*, 52, 87-110.

Cowan, S., 1984, 'Privatisation and Regulation of the Water Industry in England and Wales' in M. Bishop, J. Kay and C. Mayer , (eds) *Privatization and Economic Performance*, Oxford University Press.

Demski, J.; Sappington, D. and P. Spiller, 1987, 'Managing Supplier Switching', *Rand Journal of Economics*, 18, 77-97.

Finsinger, J. and I. Vogelsang, 1981, 'Alternative Institutional Frameworks for Price Incentive Mechanisms', *Kyklos*, 34, 388-404.

Foster, C., 1992,, *Privatisation, Public Ownership and the Regulation of Natural Monopoly*, Oxford: Blackwell.

Gilbert R. and D. Newbery, 1994, 'The Dynamic Efficiency of Regulatory Constitutions', *Rand Journal of Economics* , 538-54

Gray, P.; Helm, D. and Powell, A., 1995, 'The Experiment of Competition in British Electricity Generation: an interim appraisal', Mimeo, Oxford.

Green, R., 1992,, 'Contracts and the Pool: the British Electricity Market', Mimeo, Department of Applied Economics, Cambridge.

Green, R., 1996, 'Increasing Competition in the British Electricity Spot Market', *Journal of Industrial Economics*, forthcoming.

Grout, P., 1995, The Cost of Capital in Regulated Industries' in M. Bishop, I. Kay and C. Mayer , (eds) *The Regulatory Challenge*, Oxford University Press.

Hagerman, J., 1990, 'Regulation by Price Adjustment', *Rand Journal of Economics*, 21, 72-82.

Hannah, L., 1979, *Electricity before Nationalisation*, London: Macmillan.

Harberger, A., 1954, 'Monopoly and Resource Allocation', *American Economic Review*, 44, 77-87.

Helm, D. and G. Yarrow, 1988, 'The Assessment: the Regulation of Utilities', *Oxford Review of Economic Policy*, 4, i-xxxi.

Kay, J., 1987, *The State and the Market: The UK Experience of Privatization.* Group of Thirty, London.

Kay, J. and Thompson, 1986, 'Privatization: a policy in search of a rationale', *Economic Journal*, 96, 18-32.

Laffont, J. and J. Tirole, 1986, 'Using Cost Observation to Regulate Firms', *Journal of Political Economy*, 94, 614-41.

Laffont, J. and J. Tirole, 1987, 'Auctioning Incentive Contracts', *Journal of Political Economy*, 95, 921-37.

Laffont, J. and J. Tirole, 1988, 'Repeated Auctions of Incentive Contracts, Investment, and Bidding Parity with an Application to Takeovers', *Rand Journal of Economics*, 19, 516-37.

Laffont, J. and J. Tirole, 1990, 'Optimal Bypass and Creamskimming', *American Economic Review*, 80, 1042-1061.

Laffont, J. and J. Tirole, 1993, *A Theory of Incentives in Procurement and Regulation*, Cambridge, MIT Press.

Laffont, J. and J. Tirole, 1994a, 'Access Pricing and Competition', *European Economic Review*, 38, 1673-1710.

Laffont, J. and J. Tirole, 1994b, 'Creating Competition through Interconnection: theory and practice', paper presented at the conference on "New developments in access pricing for network utilities", London, May 24, 1995.

Law, P., 1995, 'Tighter Average Revenue Regulation Can Reduce Consumer Welfare', *The Journal of Industrial Economics,* 43, 399-404.

Lewis, T. and D. Sappington, 1988, 'Regulating a Monopolist with Unknown Demand', *American Economic Review*, 78, 986-998.

Lewis, T. and D. Sappington, 1991, 'Oversight of Long Term Investment by Short-lived Regulators', *International Economic Review*, 32, 579-600.

Loeb, M. and W. Magat, 1979, 'A Decentralized Method of Utility Regulation', *Journal of Law and Economics*, 22, 399-404.

Littlechild, S., 1983, *Regulation of British Telecommunications Profitability*, Department of Industry, London.

Mankiw, G. and M. Whinston, 1986, 'Free Entry and Social Inefficiency', *Rand Journal of Economics*, 17, 48-58.

McCubbins, M., Noll, R. and B. Weingast, 1987, 'Administrative Procedures as Instruments of Political Control', *Journal of Law, Economics and Organization*, 3, 243-277.

Meyer, M. and J. Vickers, 1995, 'Performance Comparisons and Dynamic Incentives', CEPR, Discussion Paper n. 1107.

Monopolies and Mergers Commission, 1982,, *'Contraceptive Sheaths' ,2)*, Cmn 8689, London: HMSO.

Oftel, 1993, *Interconnection and Accounting Separation*, Oftel, London.

Phlips, L., 1983, *The Economics of Price Discrimination*, Cambridge University Press, Cambridge.

Riordan, M. and D. Sappington, 1987, 'Awarding Monopoly Franchises', *American Economic Review*, 77, 375-87.

Rob, R., 1986, 'The Design of Procurement Contracts', *American Economic Review*, 76, 378-89.

Sappington, D., 1980, 'Strategic Firm Behavior under a Dynamic Regulator Adjustment Process', *Bell Journal of Economics*, 11, 360-72.

Sibley, D., 1989, 'Asymmetric Information, Incentives and Price Cap Regulation', *Rand Journal of Economics*, 20, 392-404.

Sappington, D. and D. Sibley, 1988, 'Regulating without Cost Information. The Incremental Surplus Subsidy Scheme', *International Economic Review*, 29, 297-306

Tirole, J., 1988, *The Theory of Industrial Organization*, Cambridge, MIT Press.

Vagliasindi, M., 1995, 'The Cream Skimming Paradigm', mimeo, University of Warwick.

Vagliasindi, M. and M. Waterson, 1995a, 'Access and Cream Skimming in Network Industries. A Note on Agency Problems and Competitive Issues in the Theory of Regulation', Warwick Economic Discussion Paper, 9508.

Vagliasindi, M. and M. Waterson, 1995b, 'New insights on the Interactions between Regulation and Competition in Vertically Related Markets', Warwick Economic Research Paper, University of Warwick, 438.

Varian, H., 1989, 'Price Discrimination' in Schmalensee, R. and R. Willig ,(eds.) *Handbook of Industrial Organization*, Amsterdam, North Holland.

Vickers, J and Yarrow, G., 1988, *Privatization: an economic analysis*, London: MIT Press.

Vogelsang, I., 1989, Two Part Tariffs as Regulatory Constraints', *Journal of Public Economics*, 39, 45-66.

Vogelsang, I., 1990, 'Optional Two Part Tariffs Constrained by Price Cap', *Economic Letters*, 33, 287-92.

Vogelsang, I. and J. Finsinger, 1979, 'A Regulatory Adjustment Process for Optimal Pricing by Multiproduct Monopoly" *Bell Journal of Economics*, 10, 157-71

Waterson, M., 1988, *Regulation of the Firm and Natural Monopoly*, Basil Blackwell, Oxford.

Waterson, M., 1990, 'The major Utilities: Ownership, Regulation and Energy Usage' in Cowling, K and R. Sugden ,eds) *A New Economic Policy for Britain*, Manchester, Manchester University Press, 174-191.

Waterson, M.., 1992,, 'A Comparative Analysis of Methods for Regulating Public Utilities', *Metroeconomica,* 43, 205-226.

Williamson, O., 1985, *The Economic Institutions of Capitalism*, New York, The Free Press.

Willig, R., 1979, 'The Theory of Network Access Pricing' in Trebing, H. (ed) *Issues in Public Utility Regulation*, Michigan State University, East Lansing.

Chapter 6

PUBLIC PROCUREMENT IN THE EU

Ilde Rizzo
University of Catania, Italy

1.   INTRODUCTION

In this paper the issue of public procurement in the European Union (EU) will be addressed as a special case study, in order to investigate whether competition matters in practice as it has been claimed in the literature.

In the EU a widely debated issue is that, notwithstanding the extensive European legislation as well as the relevant amount of resources invested to open-up public markets, such an effort has not been successful. In fact, a common feature of EU Member States' purchasing policies still seems to be that of favouring domestic suppliers.

With respect to such an issue, the scope of this paper is to investigate, in the light of the political economy approach, what problems such a programme has encountered so far. Theory and practice will be compared in order to argue that, perhaps, sometimes in theory too much emphasis is put on issues, such as competition, which, in practice, seems to appear more controversial. The analysis goes as follows. In section 2, the main features of government purchasing in the EU, what it is and why it is important, will be presented. EU procurement rules and the problems of their implementation will be reviewed in section 3. Some concluding remarks will be offered in section 4.

The tentative argument that emerges from the paper is that heavy regulation in procurement, aimed at ensuring competition anyway, might not necessarily be effective in a domestic as well as EU context.

2.   EU PROCUREMENT AND DOMESTIC PREFERENCES

In most EU countries, government is the largest purchaser of a wide array of goods and services, ranging from standard items (cars, office equipment and so on), to complex products and services (motorways, defence equipment, engineering, etc.). Purchasing by government and other public bodies in the EU accounts for about 14% of its gross domestic product and, as a consequence, exerts a relevant economic impact on the EU economy.

The goals of public purchasing are usually described in terms of <u>value for money</u>, i.e., «obtaining the right product at the right time and at a satisfactory price»[1] . However, from the fact that government purchasing may be so influential on industry it follows that wider policy objectives - such as supporting employment, promoting high technology, reducing regional disparities and so on - are likely to be pursued other than only cost-effectiveness in spending.

An extensive literature on procurement, adopting cost-effectiveness in spending as an objective, identifies the award criterion as well as the type of contract and the procedures to be followed[2] which are suitable to the different types of goods or services to be purchased. In the choice of the award procedure, it is widely accepted that, whenever possible, competition should be the leading rule in bidding.

Entering the details of such extensive literature is outside the scope of this paper; our attention will be limited to questioning whether bidding competition really matters in practice as much as it has been claimed to do in the literature[3] , using EU procurement as a case study.

According to official figures, (Commission of the European Communities, 1998) the share of imports for public contracts remains modest: the overall amount of public sector imports (both direct and indirect imports) has risen from 6% in 1987 to 10% nowadays[4] . Moreover, the prices practised in the various Member States do not seem to converge in the same period.

As it has been pointed out (Commission of the European Communities 1996a), "the extent of European public procurement means that buying goods and services by effective purchasing systems can make significant savings for government and thus for taxpayers". The estimates of potential savings, however, as well as those on the overall macro economic impact of the single market, have been extensively debated and vary different numbers have been provided[5] . As Helms (1993) suggests, the margin of error is large and it depends on the responses of European firms and consumers, as well as on the trade effects compared with what would have happened in the absence of the policy. The lack of consensus seems to reflect a more general theoretical disagreement on the nature of economic behaviour.

In the EU procurement, the issue of open competition is usually linked with the existence of discriminatory practices against foreign firms. In theory, discriminatory purchasing policies can mainly take the form of price-preferences[6] and of the exclusion of foreign bidders. These policies exert different effects.

The possibility of using price preference is de facto ruled-out in the EU single market because it is explicitly in contrast to the principles established by the Treaty of Rome (see section 3), and no attention will be paid here to such a form of preferential procurement.

In the EU, domestic preferences, therefore, are exerted through the discrimination of foreign bidders. Such discrimination cannot rely on legislative action – EU membership rules out such a possibility – but on administrative regulation. The methods are likely to show various degrees of visibility; for instance, they include selective-tender or single-tender bidding schemes, short time limits for the submission of bids and the specification of technical requirements in a way that makes it impossible for a foreign firm to comply. It is this type of discrimination, though in a hidden form, which is at issue in the debate on EU procurement and will be addressed in the following pages.

3.   PROCUREMENT RULES IN THE EU: PROBLEMS OF IMPLEMENTATION AND ENFORCEMENT.

The Treaty of Rome does not lay down any specific ruling related to public procurement, it does, however, establish four fundamental principles which apply to public contracts, whatever their value:

no discrimination on grounds of nationality (Article 7);
free movement of goods and the prohibition of quantitative restrictions on import and export and measures having equivalent effect (Articles 30 et se.);
freedom of establishment (Articles 52 et se.);
freedom to provide services (Articles 59 et se.).

The rules espoused in the Treaty prohibited certain unfair practices, but did not establish any positive obligation ensuring transparency and competition in contract award procedures. Legislative action was thus called for at a Community level.

In 1985 the Commission published a White Paper entitled, «Completing the internal market», aimed at achieving freedom of movement for persons, services, capital and goods. Among other things, the White Paper contained rules requiring the opening-up of public contracts. The White Paper was enshrined in the 1987 Single Act and has been largely transformed in Council decisions: 95% of the proposals based on the White Paper have been adopted. In the sphere of government procurement the whole programme is complete, this statement referring to the Council legislative activity in the public procurement field, i.e. to the fact that all the Directives have been adopted to regulate the relevant areas of public procurement[7]. This statement, however, does not necessarily imply that public contracts are, in practice, opened up. Indeed, as has been pointed out, such a target is far from being reached within the Union.

In the following pages, some comments will be made on the content of the Directives and on the problems related to their enforcement in the light of the political economy approach.

It should be stressed that the aim of the Directives is not to harmonise all national rules on public procurement. It is to co-ordinate national contract award procedures, by introducing a minimum body of common rules for contracts above a given threshold. These common rules are the following:

rules defining the type of procurement agency and the scope of contracts subject to the Directives;

rules defining the type of contract award procedure which procurement agencies should normally use;

rules on technical specifications, whereby preference is to be given to Community standards;

advertising rules, whereby tender notices must be published in the Official Journal of the European Communities, must comply with specific requirements concerning time-limits and must be drawn up in accordance with pre-established models;

common rules on participation, comprising objective criteria for qualitative selection and for the award of contracts (either the lowest price or the most economically advantageous tender, at the contracting authority's choice);

obligations as regards statistical reporting.

Entering into the details of the above Directives is outside the scope of this paper; however, some general comments on the major issues are required.

Award procedures. The public supply, works and services Directives provide for three types of award procedures which contracting authorities can use. The normal award procedures are the open procedure[8] (all interested contractors or suppliers may submit tenders) and the restricted procedure (only those suppliers or contractors invited by the contracting authority may submit tenders)[9].

Under the open and the restricted procedures, no negotiation is allowed between the contracting authority and the tenders on fundamental issues such as price. Only in specific cases, which are listed in each Directive, contracting authorities may use the negotiated procedure, with or without prior publication of a tender notice.

Information. The Directives seek to increase openness of procedures and practices in awarding public supply contracts: a crucial role is assigned to information. The «information policy» develops through three main lines: - ex-ante information on the purchasing programmes of the contracting authority; publication of the invitation to tender in the Official Journal; publication of the main elements of the contract after it has been awarded[10] in the Official Journal.

Selection. The Directives seek to avoid unjustified discrimination of applicants and provide a list of criteria for their selection, such as: professional qualification, financial economic and technical reliability[11].

Award criteria. The Directives provide that the criteria, on which contracting authority shall base the award of contracts subject to Community release, are either the lowest price or the most advantageous tender[12]. When the latter criterion is chosen the contracting authority can take into account «variations» proposed by suppliers, provided they satisfy minimum requirements indicated by contracting authorities themselves.

European legislation in the form of Directives is binding for the Member States. However, each is free to choose the form and methods for implementing each Directive.

The Commission has frequently expressed its continuing concern that the current level of public procurement Directives implementation is inadequate. Public procurement is one of the internal market areas where there are the most severe problems both in terms of communication of the implementing measures and in terms of the quality of implementation. According to official data (Commission of the European Communities 1998), in November 1997 the correct implementation of Council Directives on procurement was not greater than 55.6% and only 5 Member States had fully implemented the Directives.

Moreover, the fact that the Directives have been transposed in national legislation does not guarantee the effective opening-up of public markets. This outcome requiring, in fact:

that the transposition is correct;
that all the provisions are implemented;
that all the citizens of the Union have the means to redress.

Indeed, the Directives have been improperly transposed into national law and there has been a widespread abuse of exception clauses. According to the Commission of the European Communities (1996a), some relevant examples are:

deliberate splitting of contracts;
improper use of negotiated procedures;
failure to supply interested firms with full and accurate information;
inclusion of discriminatory requirements in the contract documents.

Technical, economic as well as political explanations can be identified for the unsatisfactory implementation which the public procurement Directives have received so far.

According to Siedentopf-Hauschild (1988), with respect to the Directives as a whole, transposition is usually carried out in each country adopting national schemes, which differ from one country to the other. Nor has national implementation and administrative monitoring of European legislation, caused relevant changes in the public administration of each Member State. Indeed, administrative style and capability have been identified as relevant factors affecting the correct implementation of Directives. It is argued that the quality and quantity of administrative resources are strategic factors: they vary across the Member States (and within each state among different levels of government) [13].

As Fernandez Martin (1996) also stresses, even in the procurement area, the impact of Directives on national procedures varies according to the legal system operating in each country. While in some Member States implementations were performed through the adoption of legally binding rules creating enforceable rights for individuals, in others they were performed using only administrative action. No relevant differences in performance, however, have been identified.

Indeed, the «philosophy» underlying the Directives on procurement does not always seem to align itself with the economic reality of procurement. First of all, European procurement rules attempt to positively dictate every step, which the contracting authority must follow, and every factor, which it must take into account. Preference is given to those procedures, which, in relation to the circumstances, ensure competition as much as possible. This approach, however, does not necessarily guarantee the achievement of a «good» contract because it underestimates the importance of factors, which might be relevant for the contracting authority[14].

For instance, looking at the supply, works and services Directives, it might be observed that not all the relevant commercial factors of selection are included. Indeed, the Directives seem to establish a rigid framework, which does not allow any flexibility, even when sometimes in contrast with the purchasing authority's interests. According to the Council Directives, in fact, the purchasing authority, when asking a contractor to tender, can rely upon the following considerations: past experience, financial viability, technical ability, previous performance in similar works. On the other hand, the authority cannot base its choice on other relevant considerations such as, previous experience in working with the same authority[15], reputation for excessive claims, trade record in the same or in other authorities. In other words, the subjective judgement of the purchasing officer is left out[16].

There are other sound reasons pointing toward domestic preferences-oriented purchasing practices, which constrain the feasibility of EU procurement. Purchasers might prefer to buy from companies, which have a local-market presence because this would facilitate rapid repairs, and thus reduce reserve capacity and costs. Moreover, purchasers might prefer dealing in one language and with few suppliers since this may foster close co-operation in R&D.

Another concern for the administration refers to the fact that the client-supplier relationship is also, (or should be), based on mutual trust. Whenever a problem arises in such a relationship, as a consequence of an excessively detailed legislation, for instance, the local contractor can be expected to «understand», especially in the light of future contract awards. The foreign contractor is less likely to exhibit such a favourable attitude.

It should not be overlooked that several years of close supplier-customer relationship have resulted in distinctive national design standards. This issue is extremely relevant in utilities; the national network is usually tailored on specific technology, which limits the scope for economies of scale. On the other hand, neither purchasers nor suppliers are interested in devising European standards and, as a consequence, producers who have developed technologies with the network operator are favoured. Purchasing authorities are, however, constrained by domestic legislation.

Moreover, the features of the markets targeted by the procurement Directives have affected the poor performance of the Directives. In the case of the public works market, for instance, tenders for big projects require research and planning on the part of prospective tenders which cannot be carried out from a distance. «A contractor will need a detailed knowledge of the layout and site conditions. It will be necessary to have an understanding of the local labour market. Considerations will need to be given to the linkages that might be developed with local subcontractors, suppliers of construction materials and plant hire firms» (Diggings, 1991, p.34). Competitive advantages, arising from technological breakthroughs is not common, since technological know-how is well spread among top European contractors. Because of the above mentioned problems, it is likely that a firm aimed at entering a foreign procurement market for public works will consider establishing a joint venture, joining a consortium or if the previous alternatives are too costly, acquiring a local firm.

A survey carried out by the Association of Metropolitan Authorities Purchasing and Supply group, shows that the response rate from foreign suppliers to U.K. local authority advertising contracts in the Official Journal of European Communities is negligible. Though, to date a substantial number of contracts still appear in the Official Journal, the response from non-national contractors has been negligible. Nor has the Commission undertaken effective actions to reduce the major barriers, such as, providing the contractors entering non-domestic public markets, with adequate support to reduce the risks of foreign projects. More generally speaking, the reasons for the apparent lack of interest in international bidding may also be found in the low credibility of the market opening. Suppliers are disinclined to waste time and money bidding for foreign contracts, which they are convinced, they would not get[17].

With the main bulk of EU procurement policy placing great emphasis on very detailed rules, what ultimately happens is that with rules remaining fixed through time, they are likely to become out-of-date, or, at least, inadequate in meeting the inevitable changes occurring in the market. The complexity of the decision-making process at European level is such that updating is likely to take place rather slowly, even if it will take place eventually, at different rates in different cultures.

The Commission seems to be aware of the relevance of the above issues. In fact, the necessity for more flexible procurement systems had been stressed: "The Commission acknowledges the complexity of the current legal framework and the rigidity of its procedures. It intends, therefore, to simplify the former and make the latter more flexible» (Commission of the European Communities 1998), and has recently led to the adoption of two proposals for a Directive.[18]

Political reasons may also be used to explain the limited openness of the government purchasing market: «buy national» policies rely on political considerations, among other things.

The theory of the political economy of protection, views trade policy as endogenously determined (Hillman, 1989, p.2); the same point of view can be applied to the subset of domestic preferences in government procurement. It may be viewed as determined jointly by i) the objectives of policy-makers; ii) the influence over policy exerted by the gainers and losers from protectionist proposals; iii) the institutional setting governing the interaction between policy makers and the gainers and losers from protection.

A detailed analysis of the decision-making process underlying the European integration is outside the scope of this paper[19]; it is noteworthy that in the EU context, a principal-agent relationship links the Union and each Member State[20] with diverging interests between policy-makers at domestic and Union level.

Starting from the latter, it is reasonable to assume that it is in the interest of 'eurocrats', i.e. the Commission, to build a strong Union, the stronger it becomes the greater their influence, power and prestige[21] . Acting as guardian of the Treaty, preparing decisions and regulations to implement the policy in the Treaty and monitoring Member countries to ensure they apply them, are some of the functions of the Commission. It can rely upon to act in the Community's interest, as expressed by the potential savings accruing[22] as a consequence of the abolition of any domestic preference in procurement. In other words, the Commission aims to ensure international competition, regardless whether it is, indeed, feasible or not in the procurement case, or whether it is beneficial for the contracting authority[23] , and almost regardless of the distributive consequence of the opening up. To pursue such an objective, a wide array of rules to be followed by contracting authorities are prepared: whether they are enforced or not, whether they are effective is another question.

On the other hand, as Forte (1985, p.152) points out, «political leaders negotiating EU matters, being national leaders, are expected to bring home either the best domestic result compatible with continued EU membership, or the best EU result compatible with some minimum domestic «net gain»[24] . Domestic organised interests press them: as is well known, the more sectorial and concentrated interests are, the greater their strength is. The strengthening of the majority principle (Art 100a Treaty), however, has somehow reduced the pressure of national interests over politicians: the individual member of the Council, in fact, can pretend to have struggled to defend domestic interests and of having been overruled by majority.

Discriminatory policies, thus, are a good example of policies designed to satisfy these kind of interests at a national level and, therefore, are likely, to generate contrasting interests between the EU and Member States[25] . The reasons for such a discrepancy lie in the public good nature of homogenisation. Each Member State may gain if others open the access to their public procurement markets while it does not, because it gains access to other markets while protecting its own position, i.e. the classical free-rider problem arises. The existence of free riding calls for effective enforcement rules to be defined at European level[26] , if Directives have to be effectively applied.

Discriminatory public procurement is usually explained as a result of the operation of the political process. National policy-makers are assumed to be under constant pressure from national interest groups to protect their specific interests. Discrimination of foreign bidders can be considered an answer to such a demand.

Moreover, it is undeniable that the scale of government procurement is such that preferential procurement regulation can be used to achieve political objectives such as, the protection of local industry, the protection of minorities, the supporting of small business and the development of high-unemployment areas. The social group most directly affected by the opening-up of the public markets is the work force of these markets. The claimed beneficial macro-economic effects of EU tendering[27] do not prevent, however, that unemployment is likely to result in some areas, depending on how the costs and benefits will be distributed between groups, firms and regions[28] . Such a situation strongly affects political attitudes toward the opening-up of procurement markets: as Peacock-Rickets (1991 p.75) argue, though voters may have an interest, such as taxpayers, in the minimisation of costs, as producers have much stronger interests: in other words, the effects on jobs are much easier to grasp. «Consequently, vote sensitive governments have to think twice about placing contracts with overseas suppliers[29] .

Indeed, the effects on employment deriving from the exploitation of wage differences between Member States[30] are one of the major unresolved issues[31] in the implementation of EU Directives[32] . The fact that at EU level no clear provision for the unemployment is offered, is likely to undermine the future successful implementation of the above mentioned Directives.

The correct transposition and implementation of the Directives into national laws has not been supported by an effective enforcement system at the European level.

The legal structure governing public purchasing and the remedies against illegal practices vary across countries. For instance, in some countries such as France and Italy, there are administrative laws and courts while in others, such as Britain and Denmark, there are no administrative courts. Without entering the details of each Member State's legal structure, what is important to stress here is that remedies exist in each country but are seldom used. The EU programme, rather than providing a central regulatory regime, seeks to offer equivalent national remedies. The core of the Directives was to require all Member States to offer the following remedies: interim measures to correct infringements[33] , setting aside unlawful decisions and discriminatory technical economic and financial specifications in the invitation to tender.

In practice, the Commission has to carry out a cumbersome monitoring activity. In fact, the amount of national legislation to be controlled is extremely large[34] . Given that the Member States are given discretion in transposing the Directives, the result is a relevant amount of heterogeneous national legislation, reflecting the differences in the national administrative and law systems. Moreover, the number of procurement agencies and the number of contracts awarded are extremely large.

As a consequence, the Commission, rather than detecting directly the violations of the Directives to seek out infringements, heavily relies upon complaints and private action coming from citizens and firms[35] . According to EU procurement rules, any contractor or supplier, who believes that an unlawful decision has been taken by a contracting authority, is free to submit a complaint to the Commission[36]. Such a complaint may be made at the same time as the case is raised before a national court; the two cases are independent.

The perspective of obtaining only limited advantages from formal complaints is likely to reduce the likelihood of this complaint[37]. It is interesting to stress that «to ensure that the Commission's action is effective, complaints should be lodged before the contract is signed» (Commission of European Communities, 1991, p.33). This means that the advantages the contractor may expect to gain from the complaint to the Commission do not allow for changing the decision of the contracting authority and this may limit the convenience for the complaint itself. In other words, the only gain they expect to obtain is the repayment of damages, i.e. the expenses borne for preparing the tender.

Moreover, the fact that the decisions of the national courts are not recognised in other Member States implies that the tender can seek remedies only from national administrative or judicial bodies, bearing the related costs. Such a situation is likely to constitute a further «barrier» preventing the tender from going to court.

Even if this form of indirect control is perceived as potentially threatening, it does not necessarily follow that it will constitute an effective incentive toward compliance at all stages of the procurement procedure. What is the risk borne by the agent (Member State)?

It is interesting to stress that a risk is involved when procurement is financed out of EU "Structural Funds". In 1988 the Commission having observed that procurement rules had not been enforced when public contracts, financed out of Structural Funds had been awarded, decided to introduce a system of compliance with public procurement rules for projects or programmes financed with the assistance of the above mentioned funds. The main idea is that grants for assistance will not be awarded and payment for the on-going projects will be suspended if the principles laid down by the procurement directives are not properly followed[38].

Monitoring the implementation of procurement directives through the "Structural Funds" is likely to be an effective enforcement system but raises questions, i.e. whether a marked diversification may arise between the procurement financed out of the regional policies and the procurement financed by national government. Such a system, in fact, will probably create a disadvantage for the contracting authorities, which are recipients of the "Structural Funds" as compared with those who are not. But they are recipients because they need external support[39], which in such a case might be reduced. The extent of such a problem, however, depends on how successful the implementation of the Remedies Directives will be. Still, the problem of a double treatment remains.

On the other hand, no risk is involved (apart from prestige) for infringements of procurement rules for programmes and projects financed out of national funds. In light of the principal-agent paradigm and recalling the existence of the free-rider problem, the lack of any effective enforcement system is likely to drive Member countries away from the compliance with the Directive.

The Commission is concerned with the improvement of effectiveness of the Remedies Directives. Various alternatives have been proposed to achieve this objective. One possibility would be to assign the Commission more effective investigative powers than it has at the present. Since the Commission has neither the resources nor the information to fulfil such a commitment, it has recently placed emphasis on solutions to be adopted at national level. More precisely, the Commission has invited Member States to consider the establishment or the appointment of independent authorities with the role of improving procurement systems (Commission of the European Communities 1998).

4.   CONCLUSION

In line with the nature of this paper, aimed at raising issues rather than at providing clear-cut answers, this concluding section will only highlight some of the arguments considered earlier to illustrate their relevance for procurement policy in the EU perspective.

The main argument to emerge is that heavy regulation in procurement might reduce the positive effects of competition, usually put forward to recommend contracting out as an efficient alternative to public production.

Indeed, the concept of open competition itself might exhibit some shortcoming in this specific case, in accordance with the nature of the supplier/customer relationship underlying the procurement.

A way of addressing these problems might be to stress the discretionary role of the purchasing officer and, as a consequence, to assign them discretion and at the same time make them liable for the outcome obtained through the procurement process. Of course, such a solution might not always be compatible with the rule of open competition: discretion might imply, for instance, that purchasing officers can offer as an incentive for good performance a promise to award future contracts. At the same time, doubts can be cast on the «philosophy» underlying procurement Directives.

Moreover, the lack of consideration for their distributive impact raises further doubts on the overall effects of the opening-up of public markets. The likely negative impact of procurement market opening-up on employment and on small and medium firms, and the lack of any effective provision at EU level, has probably undermined the political support of national governments to such a process.

Finally, the public good nature of homogenisation should suggest, to those who are seeking its implementation, that effective measures to overcome the free-rider problem are needed. As Meade (1991, p.24) argues, the central authority must have powers and procedures to ensure that these rules are respected by the national authorities; in other words an enforcement system is called for. The conflicting views among the Member States on the objectives to be pursued have prevented the assignment of some discretionary powers to the Commission. As a result, European rules limit national governments but no effective enforcement power does exist at the European level. The tool of national independent authorities could provide fruitful insights to address this issue.

NOTES

[1] As Peacock-Ricketts (1991) point out, such a criterion is empty without defining what «value» means and many problems arise in the attempt to give meaning to such a phrase; in fact, the output may be very difficult to define and, once a suitable definition is found, a conflict of interest may arise concerning the amount of output. These issues, which refer to the broad area of public expenditure decision-making, are not considered in this paper (on these general issues see Peacock (1992).

[2] On these issues, see Laffont-Tirole (1993).

3   The limits of the concept of open competition in procurement have been stressed by Kelman (1990) and Rizzo (1992) and (1994).

4   According to the results of a study on public works contracts reported by Woolcock-Hedges-Screwier (1991), in 1986, only 2% of public procurement contracts in the Union were awarded to firms from a Member State other than the Member State advertising the tender. Differences exist across countries: contractors from other EU countries gained 3.2% of the French market, 2.9% of the German, 1.8% of the British, 1.5% of the Spanish and a negligible share of the Italian contracts.

5   The Cecchini Report had estimated a potential saving of 0.5% of gross domestic product per annum. Such an estimate was carried out over 5 countries (Belgium, Italy, France, Germany and the United Kingdom). The estimated savings depend upon the occurrence of three effects: *static trade effect* (public administrations buy from the lowest cost supplier in the European market), *competition effect* (domestic suppliers are induced to lower their prices because of the external competition), and *restructuring effect* (in the long-term the industry reorganises and obtains relevant economies of scale in the high-tech sectors).

6   The former kind of discrimination implies offering a price preference to domestic suppliers. The economic effects of price-preferences in procurement are controversial. Contrasting the conventional wisdom, McAfee and McMillan (1988) argue, that in some circumstances, government domestic procurement preferences can raise a country's welfare.

7   The Community measures dealing with public supply contracts are the Council Directives 77/62/EEC, 88/295/EEC and 93/36/EEC. The Community measures dealing with public works contracts are the Council Directives 71/305/EEC, 89/440/EEC and 93/37/EEC. The Community measure dealing with remedies for the above sectors is Council Directive 89/665/EEC. The Community measure dealing with public service contracts is Council Directive 93/50/EEC. The latter Directive provides for two-tier application: full application for the «priority services»(these services are listed in the Annex 1A of the Directive) and minimum requirements for the «other services» (these services are listed in the Annex 1B of the Directive). The Community measures dealing with utilities, the so-called «excluded sectors», i.e. water, energy, transport and telecommunications, are Council Directives 90/531/EEC, 93/38/EEC and 92/13/EEC.

8   For supply contracts the open procedure is the rule.

9   When the restricted procedure is used, the contracting authority is required to invite tenders from a sufficient number of candidates <<to ensure genuine competition>>(Turpin, 1989, p.128). The number may vary according to the nature of the works, but it ranges between five and twenty.

10 To improve the dissemination of information, electronic procurement has been identified as a major tool and an initiative has been launched by the Commission in December 1999, calling for "on line government".

11 The Directive on water, energy, transport, and telecommunications leaves more discretion to contracting authorities.

12 The criteria listed in the Directives are: price, date of delivery and technical value. For the services quality, aesthetic and/or functional value and technical assistance are also indicated.

13 The evidence, with respect to the implementation of the overall Internal Market legislation, would suggest that the most critical conditions are in Greece, France, Luxembourg and Portugal (Single Market News, 2000, p.2).

14 An extensive analysis on this issue is provided by Kelman(1990) and Rizzo(1992).

[15] It follows that customers and suppliers cannot enjoy the value deriving from long term, continuing relationships such as those characterising private sector industrial purchasing. The advantages of such a kind of relationship have been stressed by Williamson (1985).

[16] The implications of such an approach have been explored in Rizzo (1992), (1994) and (1998).

[17] A Single Market survey of business leaders in the EU provides information on the perception of suppliers in regard to the public procurement market. The perception is that significant barriers remain: around 35% of respondents feels that the legislation has not yet produced any major change in public procurement (Commission of the European Communities, 1997). On the other hand, information has improved: the number of tenders advertised on the Official Journal has increased from 12,000 in 1987 to 95,000 in 1995 (Commission of the European Communities, 1996b).

[18] Simplification, adaptation and modernisation are the main principles underlying such a "legislative package", aimed at giving a new dynamism to European public procurement policy (the main features are outlined in Single Market News, 2000, I-IV.)

[19] According to Teutemann (1990), in a public choice approach, during the 30 years of European integration the relevant actors were politicians, bureaucrats, producer lobbies and unions at national level, while the most important group at European level were the bureaucrats in the Secretary of Council and in the commission.

[20] The strength of such a relationship is likely to differ, depending on whether the object is only the application of the Directives or whether it is the use of EU resources transferred to Member States (on latter issue, see par.3.9).

[21] The same considerations underlying the formulation of EU trade policy, though in a different context (the implementation of Art, 115, Treaty of Rome) are put forward by Schucknecht (1991).

[22] See above par.2.2.

[23] See above par. 3.6.

[24] Voters are less influential at European level than at national level. The European Parliament is less powerful than its national counterpart and, as a consequence, no control is exerted on the real European government (Council and Commission). With the Single European Act the distribution of responsibilities between Council, Commission and Parliament has gradually changed in favour of the latter.

[25] This is not the case when discriminatory policies refer to non-EU countries.

[26] See below, par. 3.9.

[27] See above, note 5.

[28] These effects are rather unpredictable; they depend, among other things, on how other barriers develop within the Union and on specific features within procurement, for instance, the kind of subcontracting that is used.

[29] Such a method is what in the international relations literature is called a «low», or technical track. As Finger, Hall and Nelson (1982) argue, a technical track is relatively cheap to operate, since it minimises the political cost of the decision. In fact, whenever domestic preferences imply higher costs, government resources are transferred from taxpayers, who ultimately pay for public contracts, to domestic producers benefiting from protection. The best solution is, therefore, to avoid a formal decision; the implementation of a technical procedure makes the above mentioned costs less visible while still making the advantaged groups aware of their benefits

[30] Low-wage countries using social dumping can reduce their unemployment rates in labour intensive sectors, such as road and maritime transport and building; on the other hand,

high wage Member States are concerned with the prospect of losing jobs in favour of Member States with lower labour costs. Moreover, the existing approach toward <<abnormally low tenders>> tends to permit abuses by large firms or even exploitation of labour, given that contracting authorities are required not to discriminate against foreign bidders by taking into account only the conditions on their domestic markets but also considering, among other things, the favourable conditions (for instance, very low labour costs) available to the tenderer for the execution of the work.

[31] According to the amended public work Directive 440/89, it is left to national legislation to provide some protection from the exploitation of the above mentioned wage differences; countries with a more regulated labour market are likely to be more protected than others.

[32] The same argument applies to the impact of EU Directives on the small and medium enterprises.

[33] Initially, the Commission sought power for itself to intervene, in exceptional circumstances, to suspend contract-award procedures; during the procedure underlying the final approval of the Directive the opposition of Member States raised up against such a power and the Member States retained for themselves the discretion not to suspend or take other interim measures, if <<the negative consequences could exceed their benefits>>. The Commission kept only a corrective mechanism.

[34] National legislation referring to the Single market amounts to over 2,000 pieces of legislation in different languages.

[35] The Directives have direct effect once the time limit for their implementation has expired. In other words, all Directives, including those in the public procurement field, are capable of giving rise to rights or obligations which individuals can enforce before Courts even if their government has failed to incorporate or has only partially incorporated, the Directive into domestic law.

[36] A two-stage infringement procedure is carried out by the Commission. Initially, the Commission sends the State a letter of formal notice referring the complaint and requesting the State to send its observations. The Commission then issues a reasoned opinion and the State is asked to conform within a specified time limit. If the State fails to comply with the Commission's opinion, the case is raised before the Court of Justice which conducts a full inquiry into the merit of the case. The European Court of Justice performs a relevant role: in fact, its decisions complete the existing rules on procurement and clarify specific provisions contained in the Directives. In other words, its decisions influence the shape of EU regulation through the interpretation of the treaties and secondary EU legislation and it fulfils a crucial role in the enforcement of the Directives. Last but not least, the Court through its decisions forces the Member States to deal with issues they have tried to avoid.

[37] So far, the bid protest system has not exerted an effective monitoring function at European level: complaints addressed directly to the Commission from January 1981 to 1994, amount to a total number of 269.

[38] A public procurement questionnaire with all the details of contracts awarded must be submitted (either with a grant application or with request for payment, as appropriate). If questionnaires are not submitted payments will be suspended and, if failure to comply is established, the commission will take steps to recover the funds allocated.

[39] The rationale for regional policies lies in the disparities in income and employment levels existing among different regions in the Union.

REFERENCES

Commssion of the European Communities, 1998, *Public Procurement in the European Union*, Com (98) 143, Brussels.

Commssion of the European Communities, 1997, *Special Sectorial Report N 1: Public Procurement*, Brussels.

Commission of the European Communities, 1996a, *Public Procurement in the European Union: Exploring the Way Forward*, Brussels.

Commission of the European Communities, 1996b, *Impact and Efficiency of the Single Market*, Com (96) 520, Brussels.

Commission of the European Communities, 1991, *The Large Market of 1993 and the Opening-up of Public Procurement*, Brussels.

Diggins, L., 1991, *Competitive tendering and the European Communities*, London, Association of Metropolitan Authorities.

Fernandez Martin, J.M., 1996, *The EC Public Procurement Rules - A Critical Analysis*, Oxford, Clarendon Press.

Finger, J.M., Hall, H.K. and D. R. Nelson, 1982, 'The Political Economy of Administered Protection', *American Economic Review*, 452-466.

Forte, F., 1985, 'The Theory of Social Contract and EEC', in Greenway, D. and K. Shaw (eds.), *Public Choice, Public Finance and Public Policy*, Oxford, Blackwell, 148-166.

Helms, D., 1993, 'The Assessment: the European Internal Market: The Next Steps', *Oxford Review on Economic Policy*, 9, 1.

Hillman, A.L., 1989, *The Political Economy of Protection*, Hardwood Academic Publishers.

Kelman, S., 1990, *Procurement and Public Management: the Fear of Discretion and the quality of Government Performance*, American Enterprise Institute.

Laffont, J.J. and J. Tirole, 1993, *A Theory of Incentives in Regulation and Procurement*, Cambridge, MIT Press.

Mcafee, R.P. and J. Mcmillan, 1988, *Incentives in Government Contracting*, University of Toronto Press.

Meade, J.E., 1991, *The Building of the New Europe: National Diversity versus Continental Uniformity*, The David Hume Institute, Occasional Paper n.28.

Peacock, A., 1992, *Public Choice Analysis in Historical Perspective* Cambridge University Press.

Peacock, A. and M. Ricketts, 1991, *Government and Industry*, London Putnam Publishing.

Rizzo, I., 1998, 'Alcune considerazioni sui contratti pubblici nell'Unione Europea', in Amirante, C., and S. Cattaneo (eds.), *Efficienza, trasparenza e modernizzazione della pubblica amministrazione in Europa*, Roma, Università di Roma "La Sapienza".

Rizzo, I., 1994, 'I contratti nella pubblica amministrazione: considerazioni metodologiche per una verifica empirica', *Economia pubblica*, 1-2, 7-16.

Rizzo, I., 1992, 'Government Purchasing: Some Policy Implications', *Il Politico*, 1, 109-126.

Schuknecht, L., 1991, 'The Political Economy of EU Protectionism: National Protectionism based on Article 115, Treaty of Rome', *Public Choice*, 72, 37-50.

Siedentopf, H., and C. Hauschild, 1988, 'L'application des Derectives communautaires par les administrations nationales', *Revue francaise d'administration public*, 48, 31-39.

Teutemann, M., 1990, 'Completion of the Internal Market: an Application of Public Choice Theory', *Economic Papers*, 83.

Turpin, C., 1989, *Government Procurement and Contracts*, Harlow, Longman.

Williamson, O.E., 1985, *The Economic Institutions of Capitalism*, New York, The Free Press.

Woolcock, S., Hedges, M. and K. Screwier, 1991, *Britain, Germany and 1992. The Limits of Delegation*, London,The Royal Institute of International Affairs.

Chapter 7

AGENCY AND HEALTH CARE

Andrew Jones[1] and Roberto Zanola[2]

[1]University of York, UK; [2]University of Torino, Italy

1. INTRODUCTION

What is the nature of the agency relationships that arise in health care? To explore this issue Figure 1 presents a stylised model of a health care system which involves six economic actors:

(1) the state, which encompasses politicians and administrators;

(2) the general public in their roles as both citizens and patients;

(3) providers of insurance, such as sickness funds or private insurance companies;

(4) purchasing agencies, such as GP fundholders and District Health Authorities in the U.K.;

(5) providers of health services, including organisations such as hospitals, along with doctors and other health care professionals.

In Figure 1 the nature of possible agency relationships between the groups is indicated by the direction of the arrows; the uninformed principal is identified by the starting point of the arrow, while the informed agent is the arrival point.

Figure 1. Agency relationships and health care.

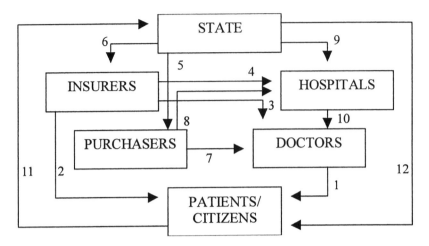

The introduction of third party payers, whether they be public or private insurers, brings about an agency relationship between insurers and insurees; consumers may not reveal their risk status (adverse selection) and they do not have an incentive to minimise medical costs (consumer moral hazard) (2). In most systems the purchasing of health care is in the hands of third-parties such as private insurers, sickness funds or District Health Authorities and GP fund holders. Here there is any agency problem when the government, as regulator, attempts to ensure that purchasers behave in the public interest (5,6). Another set of agency relationships involve the third party payer or purchaser as principal and the providers as agents (3,4,7,8); this raises the issue of optimal reimbursement mechanisms and the design of purchaser-provider contracts.   The government also engages in direct regulation of the hospital sector, for example in setting pricing rules for NHS Trusts. This creates an agency relationship between the regulator and provider organisations (9). Agency relationships also occur within the internal organisation of hospitals with hospital managers, who have incomplete information about effort and outcomes, as principals and doctors and other providers as agents (10).

The relationship between government and citizens can be seen in two different ways.   In the first (11) government is the agent who must be induced to operate according to the citizens' preferences in financing and organising health care.   In the second (12), the roles are inverted. The government must induce the citizen-agents to reveal their preferences for publicly funded health care in order to maximise social welfare.   In this case a classic free-rider problem arises.

2. THE DOCTOR-PATIENT AGENCY RELATIONSHIP

Individuals face uncertainty about the incidence of disease and the appropriate diagnosis for symptoms they experience. In addition potential patients are uncertain about their chances of recovery (in other words about the clinical effectiveness of care). Part of this uncertainty is related to the infrequency of use. For conditions that occur regularly and for which they receive regular treatment (eg. hay fever), patients may be fairly sure of the outcome and be as well-informed as their doctors (although clinical epidemiology tells us that individual experience is a poor substitute for population based studies, when it comes to evaluating the effectiveness of a treatment). However, the role of infrequency of personal use of medical care should not be exaggerated and may be mitigated by pooling of information. Pauly (1988) argues that medical care that is frequently used by an individual can be viewed as a private good; medical care that is infrequently used by the individual but that is in common use by the public can be viewed as a "perfect reputation" good; and that only care that is infrequently used by the individual and by the general public should be viewed as an "imperfect reputation good" [see also Pauly and Satterwaite (1981)]. But in many cases there is a special quality of uncertainty about medical care. Doctors have more information about the consequences of medical care for an individual's health (not just the production methods); creating an information asymmetry between doctor and patient.

Evans (1974) argues that there is a significant information differential between doctor and patient which permits the doctor to exert direct, non-price influence on the demand for his own services. The doctor can directly influence the demand function of the consumer by altering the patient's perceptions of his needs and of the capacity of medical care to satisfy them. This creates strong incentives for the doctor to overemphasise the supply of his own services rather than alternatives.

What is the source of the information differential between doctors and patients? According to Mooney (1994) there are three possible kinds of information that patients have difficulty in obtaining. The first is information about their own health. If the patient knows what is wrong because of his previous experiences, there is a minimal agency problem between the doctor and the patient. Otherwise, if symptoms are unfamiliar, agency applies both to the process of giving information to the patient and reducing patient anxiety. The second kind of information is about the availability of treatment and the third is about the effectiveness of that treatment.

2.1   Perfect and Imperfect Agency

The nature of the agency relationship between doctor and patient and, in particular the concept of a perfect agent who acts purely in the interest of the principal, has pre-occupied health economists for some time. The perfect agent is contrasted with an imperfect agent who exploits the relative ignorance of the principal/patient to achieve their own objectives. For example Rice (1983) defines the nature of the agency relationship by the extent to which a doctor "provides or recommends the provision of medical services that differ from what the patient would choose if he or she had available the same information and knowledge as the physician". The definition of perfect agency is developed further by Labelle, Rice and Stoddart (1994) who ask, "whether the physician adopts a role that is congruent with the patient's wishes". In a sense, this definition captures the main concern of the principal-agent literature; designing incentive mechanisms so that the self-interested agent behaves in a way that is congruent with the objectives of the principal.

However, an important feature of agency in health care is that the doctor's and patient's utility functions are, to a certain extent, interdependent. Evans (1974) writes:

"What distinguishes the professional agency relationship is that the professional includes part at least of the patient's/client's interests in her own objectives".

The importance of caring and altruism on the part of the agent is not a feature of the standard principal-agent framework which typically assumes independent objective functions.

Evans (1984) argues that three factors lead to an imperfect agency relationship.   The first is the possibility that the doctor may respond incompletely, the second is that the doctor has imperfect information about the effectiveness of the treatment, and the third is the tendency for the doctor to overstate its effectiveness. In the principal-agent framework the response to the imperfect agency is to consider the nature of incentives and the design of contracts. This is reflected in the health economics literature which stresses analysis of both reimbursement mechanisms and the licensing of medical practitioners. The agency relationship is often used to explain the element of trust in doctor-patient relationship, the strong ethical restrictions on doctors, and the legal role of medical certification. Much of the economics literature has concentrated on the way in which reimbursement mechanisms, for example capitation versus fee for service, affect doctors' behaviour.

Mooney and Ryan (1993) review the implications of the principal-agent literature for reimbursement mechanisms. In standard principal-agent models, with a risk neutral agent, the solution is straightforward and involves designing contracts in which all the risk is shifted on to the agent (for example where the principal receives a fixed payment, allowing the agent to claim the residual). If both principal and agent are risk averse the optimal contract involves risk-sharing. However Arrow (1963) pointed out the problem with using risk-sharing contracts in the context of medical care. He suggested that an "ideal insurance" contract to deal with the uncertainty of treatment effects would relate doctors' pay to the medical benefits of their treatment, so that the doctor bears the risk. In explaining why this kind of "payment by results" has not been adopted in the market for health care Arrow emphasises the incomplete coverage of risks facing the patient. It may be possible to arrange for a refund on the doctor's bill, but it is less likely that the contract could compensate for the indirect costs such as lost earnings, or the direct loss of "life and limb". A further problem is ex-post monitoring of the effectiveness of a particular treatment for an individual patient. Although, when doctors are operating as multiple agents, there is scope for monitoring of relative performance. This may be institutionalised, for example through peer review, which brings us back to Arrow's (1963) emphasis on trust and delegation and on the institutional protection provided by licensing and educational standards.

Perfect agency as a normative concept has lead to another strand of thought in health economics. This aims to move towards perfect agency by providing both doctors and, to some extent their patients, with more information [Mooney and Ryan (1993) Mooney (1994)]. This approach stresses the need to find out "what goes in doctors' and patients' utility functions" [Vick and Scott (1995)], and implies that if more can be learnt about patients' priorities this information can be passed on to doctors through, for example, better medical education in communication skills.

2.2   Supplier Induced Demand

Asymmetry of information can give doctors the power to create demand for their own services. In the health economics literature this is known as Supplier-Induced- Demand (S.I.D.) [see eg. Phelps (1986), Reinhardt (1985), Rice (1987)]. The definition of S.I.D. is controversial but, building on Rice's (1983) concept of agency, demand inducement is usually said to occur when the supplier recommends treatment in excess of that which would be chosen by a fully informed consumer.

Since Evans (1974) the question of whether supplier-induced demand exists has been a preoccupation in the health economics literature. One of the important implications of S.I.D. is that demand and supply are no longer independent, and this could have important effects for a policy (such as increased user charges) designed to reduce the demand for health care.

An important distinction in analyses of S.I.D. is whether the patient is able to evaluate the behaviour of doctors. Some authors assume that patients are not able to evaluate the physician's behaviour within the agency relationship. Others assume that the patient can monitor the doctor's behaviour. An example of the latter approach is Rochaix (1989) who introduces an *ex ante* technique used by patients to monitor their doctors' behaviour; "voting with their feet". She applies a search model to the doctor-patient relationship in which patients are "willing to seek a second opinion if the gap between these prior expectations and their physician's message about severity is too wide". The information asymmetry between the doctor and patient is defined in terms of a differential in uncertainty about the patient's health status. Doctors recommend a treatment and its intensity, and patients have to accept or refuse it. The model is characterised by multiple agents and principals, and it is shown that a small number of well informed patients are sufficient to make doctors behave in patients' interests.

The model defines medical conditions according to a level of severity, s, and the patient's preferences over the level of treatment. The patient's response to uncertainty about the appropriate level of treatment is formulated as a search model. The optimal stopping rule is defined in terms of the minimum (maximum) acceptable level of treatment. On the basis of prior expectations about severity and of information about treatment available elsewhere, the solution to the patient's optimisation problem defines a reservation level of treatment. Comparative static analysis shows how key parameters affect this reservation level. In particular the effect of an increase in the mean of severity, the effect of a change of the patient's ignorance about the range of acceptable treatment, the effect of a change in the mean of the distribution of treatment and, finally, the effect of an increase in the riskiness of the distribution of treatment.

The second part of the model analyses the doctor-patient relationship. The doctor maximises utility by choosing an intensity of treatment, taking account of the probability that a randomly selected patient will accept the treatment. The doctor does not know his patient's specific knowledge and experience, represented by a risk parameter, but he knows its distribution across the patients' population. Analysis of the first order condition shows how overtreatment depends on the doctor's preferences and on the remuneration system. A fee for service system encourages the doctor to maximise the number of procedures while a salary/capitation system encourages effort minimisation. Rochaix uses discrete simulation exercises to investigate the existence of non-degenerate equilibrium. The results are that patients' search induces physicians to reduce moral hazard and, that a small number of informed patients is enough to establish this result.

2.3 Evidence of Inducement: Variations in Medical Practice

The evidence of wide variations in utilisation rates between areas in the same country and between countries is well-established [see eg. Wennberg (1984), McPherson (1990)]. There are numerous possible explanations for the source of these variations: these include differences in morbidity and demographic structure; randomness; statistical artefacts (incomplete coverage, different terminology); clinical judgement; prevailing customs (medical and public); consumer demand; and the supply and availability of resources (eg. reimbursement mechanisms, the distribution of specialists) [see eg. McPherson (1990), Mooney (1994)]. Mooney (1994) makes a distinction between the "professional uncertainty hypothesis", which associates these variations with clinical uncertainty about the effectiveness of care, and the "professional disagreement hypothesis", which captures Evans's (1990) view that individual doctors are "certain", but they disagree over objectives and over the best method of treatment due to access to different information and to different interpretations of information.

The distinction between these two hypotheses is important because they have different policy implications. The professional uncertainty hypothesis is associated with the need to get more information on effectiveness (and efficiency) and disseminate it to doctors; on the assumption that they will change their behaviour accordingly. This perspective is associated with initiatives such as standards of care, medical audit, and clinical guidelines. In contrast, the professional disagreement hypothesis suggests the need to look at the way in which incentives and reimbursement mechanisms influence doctors' behaviour. In a study that is likely to stimulate considerable future research, Phelps and Mooney (1993) propose a framework to evaluate the social costs associated with variations in medical practice.

The relationship between variations and differences in supply conditions could indicate the effects of S.I.D.. But some have argued that a common pattern in many studies is the fact that the extent of variation is (at least partly) correlated with the degree of agreement about diagnosis, about the consequences of inappropriate action, and about the proper mode of treatment. The greater the extent of clinical agreement, the lower the extent of variation. However, clinical uncertainty about appropriate diagnosis and treatment does not appear to be enough to refute the inducement hypothesis. The conditions in which variations are lowest are also conditions in which the extent of inducement would be expected to be less because inducement is easier to detect. Variations also exist between countries as well as within countries, and this is more difficult to explain as differences in clinical judgement would be unlikely to produce such a systematic difference.

2.4   Econometric Evidence of Inducement.

The standard approach to testing the S.I.D. hypothesis in the economics literature has relied on evidence of a (positive) correlation between physician/population density and utilisation rates per capita. Labelle et.al. (1994) summarise the common criticisms of the econometric evidence. They argue that there is a lack of rigorous theoretical models of the agency relationship and that those that have been used often lead to ambiguous predictions, are incomplete (eg. the target income model), or lead to untestable microeconomic specifications. Many of the empirical analyses, particularly those based on the physician density approach, have suffered from econometric specification error such as omitted variables (e.g. health status, insurance coverage), endogeneity (e.g. physician density), and identification problems. Empirical studies have also suffered from measurement errors such as aggregation bias and unrepresentative sampling.

In response to the identification problems associated with the physician density approach a range of studies have exploited quasi-experimental data. Rochaix (1993) uses a panel of 677 Quebec GP's collected between 1977 and 1983 to investigate the impact of fee rigidities and price controls. Her results show evidence of quantity adjustments and drifts to more complex activities during a fifteen month tariff freeze. Expenditure caps (on GPs income) are effective in curbing high activity rates. Mooney and Ryan (1993) argue that studies of S.I.D. have failed to provide direct tests against the benchmark of "fully informed patients", but Hay and Leahy (1982) found that (after controlling for health and socioeconomic status) medical professionals and their families are at least as likely to visit doctors as others. Rossiter and Wilensky (1984) distinguish between the impact of physician availability on patient-initiated and doctor-initiated visits. They find evidence of a small S.I.D. effect.

3.   HEALTH CARE FINANCE AND INSURANCE

An idealised model of complete insurance markets would offer insurance policies for all conceivable risks and their associated costs. These would include both the risk of becoming ill and the risk of incomplete or delayed recovery from medical care. The costs would include expenditure on medical care itself but also loss of earnings and the loss of quality of life and risk of death. As Arrow (1963) points out "the nonexistence of suitable insurance policies for either risk implies a loss of welfare". He argues that market failure will lead to the existence of non-market social institutions:

> ".....the special structural characteristics of the medical care market are largely attempts to overcome the lack of optimality due to the nonmarketability of the bearing of suitable risks and the imperfect marketability of information".

The problems associated with health insurance markets are well known. These include adverse selection of risks, consumer and provider moral hazard, interdependent risks, increasing returns, and transactions costs [see eg. Besley (1991), Culyer (1993), Pauly (1968, 1974, 1986), Rothschild and Stiglitz (1976)].

3.1   Adverse Selection and Incomplete Coverage

Asymmetry of information between insurers (the principals) and insurees (the agents) leads to the problem of adverse selection. If insurance is compulsory and the supplier of insurance is a monopolist, insurance is viable at a pooled premium.   The community rate will cover costs, and implies a subsidy from low to high risk groups. In this sense community rated insurance becomes a redistributive policy. If insurance is voluntary, with competitive suppliers, community rating is unlikely to be viable. It will be vulnerable to cream-skimming by insurers offering contracts with low premia and partial coverage, designed to attract low risks. Adverse selection will result in a situation in which the community rated insurance is attractive predominately to high risk groups. In these circumstances, the insurance company will not cover costs. If the insurance company cannot separately identify the two groups, the market may fail to provide adequate cover for low risk groups. If insurers can identify the two groups they may offer contracts based on experience rating in which the premium set is different for the two groups.

Even where the informational asymmetry inherent in adverse selection can be overcome by experience rating, some groups will find it difficult to buy insurance in a competitive market. Low income groups may not be able to afford a fair premium. If these individuals have low incomes and high risk, this problem is exacerbated.   For those suffering from permanent disabilities and chronic conditions (eg. Alzheimers, HIV/AIDS) the probability of health care expenditure approaches 1. No cover is available as insurance premia simply correspond to direct payments.

Besley and Gouveia (1994) highlight the role of the long-term sick in the problem of the uninsured. They argue that under imperfect information (about the incidence of chronic illness) insurance will work but that it becomes a "redistribution scheme ex post", with redistribution from the healthy to the long-term sick, rather than an insurance scheme. If heterogeneity is observable the premiums converge on direct payments and become prohibitive for the high risks. So, "the market failure problem here can be viewed as a problem of writing long-term binding contracts" [Besley and Gouveia (1994, p.24)]

Social concern over incomplete coverage leads to government intervention in the financing of health care. There are two broad approaches to this issue. The first is a private market system plus a selective subsidy for particular groups (e.g. the elderly, low-income and chronic sick). The subsidy could be in cash, or in-kind (in the form of public insurance cover such as Medicare and Medicaid in the U.S.). The second, which is typical of most developed countries other than the United States, is based on compulsory community rated public insurance. This may take the form of social insurance with premia paid by employers and employees plus public subsidies for those not in employment, or a national health service financed by general taxation.

3.2   Consumer Moral Hazard

In a system with third party payers and full coverage, whether it be a private insurance system or a tax funded NHS, the consumer faces a zero price at the point of use. This creates a potential problem of consumer moral hazard and the incentive to over use medical care. Consumer moral hazard creates a cost containment problem. In an insurance-based system this will lead to higher premiums, and in a tax-financed system it will lead to higher taxes. The result will be reduced coverage, and/or reduced levels of benefit. Hence, there will be a trade-off between reductions in utilisation and cost inflation, and increases in coverage. Responses to consumer moral hazard include the use of co-payments or user charges; pre-payment schemes such as health maintenance organisations (HMOs); incentives to select from a restricted set of providers (preferred provider organisations - PPOs); limited indemnity (eg. "no frills" policies); non-price rationing (eg. waiting lists); and medical assessment of need [Donaldson and Gerard (1993)].

The rationale for the use of user charges and copayments depends on both the price elasticity of demand, which determines the consumer's response to the charge, and on the inefficiency of medical consumption at the margin. Evidence on the price elasticity of medical care is fairly clear. Results for the U.S. from the RAND Health Insurance Experiment find a negative price elasticity, with the greatest effect on utilisation among low-income groups and children [Manning et.al (1987)]. Analysis of prescription charges in the UK [eg. Hughes and McGuire (1995)] also show evidence of a negative price elasticity. Evidence on the inefficiency of consumption at the margin is more problematic. The role of information asymmetry and the agency relationship is crucial, and it is important to make a distinction between reductions in consultation (patient-initiated), and in treatment (doctor-initiated). Evidence from the RAND experiment casts doubt on whether user charges are discouraging inappropriate medical care at the margin [Lohr et. al. (1986)]. Many would argue that, due to the relative ignorance of consumers, user charges do not address the key incentives affecting the efficiency of health care delivery. Attention therefore turns to budget mechanisms, regulation of providers and the importance of supplier incentives.

4. THE REIMBURSEMENT AND REGULATION OF PROVIDERS

4.1 Objectives of Regulation

The health care market is characterised by overlapping principal-agent relationships. It follows that opportunities for co-operation and collusion between different agents against the principal exist, creating a role for regulation [Laffont and Tirole (1993)]. McGuire et al. (1988) describe three categories of regulation. The first, *self-regulation*, concerns the use of ethical codes of conduct. It is argued that the introduction of standards and control over conduct in the health care market may let the providers compete between themselves in a transparent way. However, these codes give the power of monitoring, policing and enforcement to the producers themselves. It is also possible, however, that

"...the profession's own imposition of standards of entry, of competence and of behaviour can be interpreted as a means of developing an agency relationship with inadequately informed consumers, in an attempt to mitigate the imperfections of decision-making that would otherwise result from this and other market failures" [McGuire et.al. (1988)].

Civil litigation is the second category of regulation. This mechanism provides patients with a financial incentive to bring information about inferior quality into the public domain, but it does so at a high cost. Finally, the third category is *statutory regulation*. This represents the classic way for the government to regulate relations and performance in health care. In discussing direct regulation it is important to distinguish between competition policy and the regulation of fees and reimbursement mechanisms.

4.2   Competition Policy

Encouraging competition in the health care market could help to reduce the problems associated with asymmetric information by constraining the abuse of local monopolies. More specifically, Chalkley and Macolmson (1995c) suggest four potential advantages of competition;

> "... reducing the economic inefficiencies that arise from monopoly power; reducing the influence providers have over purchasers' decisions; ensuring customers receive the type of products and services they want; and providing information to purchasers about the prices at which suppliers can provide products and services..."

Possible mechanisms for reducing monopoly power and increasing competition include franchising, competitive tendering, and tournaments. For example, Propper (1995b) discusses franchising of the purchasing role in the NHS; with payments for franchises determined by competitive bidding. This suggests that it is possible to apply Sappington and Stiglitz's (1987) "privatisation theorem" to health care market in order to increase utility of the government, but not, unfortunately, "automatically increase the responsiveness of purchasing agents to the demands of end-users"[Propper (1995b)].

It is important to proceed with caution in drawing general conclusions about the desirability of competition in the health care market. First, the presence of third-party payers makes competitive firms compete for patients on the basis of non-price factors rather than on the basis of prices. The implication of this is that non-price competition leads to "excess capacity, duplication of services, increased levels of amenity and higher costs" [Ferguson and Posnett (1991)]. Also, contrary to competitive markets where providers are motivated by the search for profits, in the health care market the lack of profit-maximising objectives and the control of bureaucracy over enterprises reduces the "strength" of the competitive process.

Consider the effect of competition in a health care system that combines full-cost reimbursement and third-party payment. With third party payment patients do not bear the costs of health care directly, and they are likely to choose between competing providers on the basis of non-price factors. Patients, or primary care doctors referring their patients, will demand the highest available quality of care, taking account of waiting time, location, clinical and non-clinical amenity. With full-cost reimbursement, doctors (acting as agents for the consumer) face the same incentives. They will seek access to the best and most up-to-date diagnostic and therapeutic facilities available. This suggests that if patients have unrestricted choice between providers, and if providers compete for patient affiliation, the effects of competition are perverse. Instead of competing on the basis of price, as would be the case if price was an important choice variable for patients, providers engage in non-price competition. Under these conditions the predicted effect of competition is to promote technical efficiency but also to increase costs [Culyer and Posnett (1990)]. Propper (1995a) argues that the crucial factor determining whether the "medical arms race" scenario described above occurs is whether consumers and/or their insurers face a hard budget constraint. She argues that non-price competition is less likely when purchasers face a hard budget constraint.

4.3   Rate Regulation and Reimbursement

In a fee-for service (FFS) system payers may regulate fee schedules. However providers can compensate their total reimbursement by adjusting their workload (the number of cases treated) or the intensity of services provided per case. An alternative is to regulate cost per case rates (eg. diagnostic related group (DRG) pricing in the U.S.). This removes the ability of providers to compensate for lower fees by increasing resource use. However, total reimbursement can still be increased by increasing workload. The incentive to increase workload can be addressed directly by regulated capitation rates. Then reimbursement depends only on patient affiliation (eg. HMOs, GP fundholders). The incentive for providers is to control not only cost per case, but also total expenditure. It is important to note that the nature of the reimbursement contract affects the allocation of risks between provider and payer. For example, in a prospective capitation contract most of the risk falls on the provider.

Third party regulation will only be sustainable if patient choice is constrained, otherwise consumers are likely to opt for unregulated providers. The ability to constrain patient choice is most likely to be the case with employer based or publicly provided insurance schemes (eg. Medicare and Medicaid, the NHS). Then third-party payers can impose regulation in return for preferred provider (PPO) status. The ability of a payer to behave in this way depends on the extent of its local market power.

Reimbursement by fee schedule, cost per case or capitation rate may be set directly by the purchaser (eg. Medicare DRG pricing), or it may be determined by a process of competitive contracting designed to enhance technical efficiency (as in the NHS internal market). Competitive contracting is not expected to have any substantial effect in constraining costs in a monopoly market. The NHS internal market in the UK is characterised by substantial elements of local monopoly, and the operation of a system of selective contracting is moderated by the imposition of an average cost pricing rule designed to restrict the abuse of monopoly power [Ferguson and Posnett (1991), Dawson (1994)].

4.4   The Agency Approach and Regulation

Conflicting objectives and asymmetry of information between purchasers and providers of health creates a moral hazard problem. Two alternative solutions that have been developed by the agency theory: firstly defining contracts such that the agent is obliged to meet a target, or, second, the provision of supply incentives. Laffont and Tirole (1993) model represents a datum point in the development of this latter method.

Pellisé (1994) applies Laffont and Tirole's (1993) framework to analyse MUFACE, an experimental health care system for Spanish civil servants and their dependants. The MUFACE system uses an internal market system in which insurance carriers compete for clients in exchange of a fixed capitation fee. Pellisé makes the same assumptions as Laffont and Tirole's theory of incentives and procurement in the presence of incomplete information. The regulator pays the firm's cost C and a net transfer t, which has a linear form, $t = a-bC$, where a represents a fixed fee and b is the portion of costs reimbursed by the regulators. The agency problems arises because the regulator cannot observe both the agent's effort (moral hazard), and that part of systematic variation in cost that is exogenous to the agent (adverse selection). The firm is only interested in its utility function $U=t-\psi(e)$ which depends on its effort e. While MUFACE tries to maximise social net surplus, defined as,

$$NS = S - (1+\lambda)(t+c) + U$$

where S is the utility of the beneficiaries and $(1+\lambda)$ is the tax cost.

There are two solutions for the benevolent regulator's optimisation problem. With complete information the firm does not obtain any surplus and effort reaches an optimum level. With incomplete information a problem of incentive compatibility arises and the low cost firm lowers its unobservable effort. Laffont and Tirole's solution to this problem is to pay firms facing low specific costs prospectively and firms facing high specific costs retrospectively. Pellisé evaluates the insurance companies' response to MUFACE's contract under different scenarios according to the form of the firm's specific costs. The case of homogeneous costs across insurance carriers and, on the other hand, the case in which the private insurers leave bad risks to the public insurers (heterogeneous costs), are analysed. Apart from the analytic exposition - for which we refer to the paper - an interesting result is the following:

> "...pre-contractual selection (of insurances dealing with MUFACE) is bound to occur if risks vary exogenously across insurances (and) post-contractual risk selection (of enrollees) might be observed if insurers are unable to "skim the cream" and the reimbursement scheme is prospective".

Although Pellisé's model is applied to the insurance market, it is straightforward to see the analogy between it and the government-hospital relationship. For example, the possibility that insurers may optimise their own pool of risks by "attracting" good risks and "avoiding" bad risks is analogous to the possibility of hospitals skimming the cream in order to improve their performances.

Laffont and Tirole's model is only the latest economic paradigm used to analyse the introduction of incentive contracts in hospital sector in order to encourage efficiency. In particular, there has been a considerable amount of research about the importance that different reimbursement mechanisms have in countering moral hazard [see eg. Donaldson and Gerard (1993)]. As far as this literature is concerned, renewed interest has been stimulated by the 1991 NHS reforms; which introduced an internal market, by separating the responsibility for purchasing from the responsibility for providing services. On the demand side the District Health Authorities (DHAs) and the General Practice Fund-Holders (GPFHs) are given the role to assess the population's needs for health care and to purchase services to meet them, while, on the supply side, the NHS Trusts become responsible for provision of them. As a result the previous system, in which the local district health authority acted as the agent for the government in a single geographical area, has been replaced by a new set of agency relationships, and a new set of problems;

> "... the agency relationship between government and purchaser is characterised by monitoring arrangements which appear likely to limit gains in efficiency and consumer responsiveness, while the agency relationship between government and Trust management is characterised

by poorly defined property rights, which also give limited incentives for efficiency improvements" [Propper (1995b)].

4.5   Purchaser-Provider Contracts

An important issue in contracting for health care is the lack of verifiability, that is, the lack of information needed to enforce a contract. This occurs when the quantity or the quality of output is not easily verifiable by the purchaser. As far as health services are concerned the most important aspect of contracting is to ensure the quality of service while keeping costs under control. Thus, underlying each health care contract is an incentive problem caused by asymmetric information.

Levaggi (1994) highlights some of the difficulties that the creation of internal markets for health care can cause. She develops her analysis in the context of the NHS reforms. The internal market created by the reforms is represented in the model by a contract through which the purchaser hires a provider to produce a state-contingent output for a unit price. More specifically, the relationship between purchaser and provider can be illustrated by a model in which the principal maximises a social expected benefit function subject to two constraints: a participation constraint and a binding budget-constraint on the purchaser's side. The benchmark model assumes symmetry of information between purchasers and providers. Two kinds of contract are defined; a cost per case agreement in which the price paid by the principal depends on the state of nature that prevails and a block contract agreement in which the purchaser is fully insured against uncertainty.

Asymmetry of information introduces a third constraint, the incentive compatibility constraint, through which the principal encourages the agent to reveal the true state of the world and to set his effort accordingly. In this way comparisons are possible with the previous two kinds of contracts, used now as a benchmark. The presence of both uncertainty and asymmetry of information makes it difficult to meet the conditions for market efficiency. In this context, the block contract can represent a solution to asymmetry, because it shifts risk to the agent. But, in the long-run it can have negative effects, because the purchaser is never able to observe the state of the world even ex-post.

Finally Levaggi analyses the role of competition, as introduced by the internal market, in reducing inefficiency created by asymmetry of information. Following Demski and Sappington (1984) she introduces competition by using tournaments, through which the principal reduces the information rent by offering each agent a pair of lotteries. "By basing each agent's final compensation upon his prediction about the performances of his counterparts, the principal is able to extract the agent's private information at least cost".

Starting from a similar basic model, two papers by Chalkley and Malcomson (1995a and 1995b) highlight two different, but related issues. The first concerns what can be done to maintain appropriate levels of quality and the effort required to reduce costs when patient demand is not entirely effective in maintaining quality. The second concerns the type of contracts that can be chosen to induce the hospital to supply the first best outcome when quality has a single dimension, and how these conclusions are modified when multi-dimensional quality effects are introduced.

The basic model is organised as follows. A purchaser contracts with a provider to treat x patients with a specific diagnosis q. Its purpose is to define a contract with the hospital to maximise social welfare, defined as the sum of its assessment of the benefit of treatment and the hospital's utility net of costs, subject to two constraints. The capacity constraint states that the hospital cannot treat more patients than its capacity. The hospital's individual rationality constraint sets the reservation utility to make the hospital agree to the contract. Like Levaggi's paper, first order conditions are used as a benchmark for the analysis.

Because of the asymmetry of information, the quality, q, and the effort the hospital puts into keeping costs down, e, are not all enforceable by contract. Thus, it is necessary to define an optimisation programme in which the hospital maximises its direct utility function subject to the capacity and the budget constraints. It is here that the two papers differ in their analysis.

The first paper, Chalkley and Malcomson (1995a), analyses contracts used to maintain quality and keep down costs when the quality of health services is not fully reflected in patient demand. In this case the budget paid to the hospital is a function of the verifiable variables; the number of cases treated x, the maximum number that could be treated X, and the total cost of treatment $C=c(x,q,e)$; and it is denoted by $B(x,X,C)$. Starting from this definition of the budget, three different kinds of contract are defined; the simple block contract, $B(x,X,C)=B^*$; cost per case $B(x,X,C)=px$; and cost reimbursement, $B(x,X,C)=C$.

Once x is known, the hospital maximises its utility function subject to the budget constraint. Because the number of instruments derived from the optimisation programme - $B_x(.)$ and $B_c(.)$ - are less than the number of margins - x,q and e - the result depends on the form of the hospital utility function.

In the case of *a purely self-interested hospital* there exists a trade-off between quality and cost-reducing effort. In fact, the hospital is ready to reduce costs only if it is not reimbursed for all its costs. But, in doing so, it does not increase quality, since that represents a cost.   However, the purchasing agency can still achieve a second best outcome. In particular, if it aims to maximise the hospital's effort the solution is a cost per case contract (if the hospital has limited capacity to borrow to cover financial shortfalls, a cost and volume contract is less expensive).   Otherwise, if it aims to maximise quality, a fixed price per case with cost reimbursement in relation to the number of treated cases is the solution.   As far as a *fully benevolent hospital* is regarded, the first best solution can be achieved with a block contract. In fact, the hospital will choose to do what the purchaser would want it to do. However when the number of patients is not known in advance, and the hospital has difficulties in borrowing to cover financial shortfalls, a cost and volume contract can prevent possible inefficiencies. Finally, with a *partially benevolent hospital* some cost reimbursement element, along with monitoring the actual costs incurred, is the best solution.

The second paper, Chalkley and Malcolmson (1995b), analyses the characteristics of contracts that can achieve a first best solution with both single and multi-dimensional quality. In this second model the budget paid to the hospital is a function of the number of patients treated x, the total cost of treatment $C=c(x,q,e)$ and the number of patients demanding treatment $N=n(q)$, and it is denoted by $B(x,N,C)$. Starting from this definition of budget, different kinds of contract are defined: a   prospective payment system $B(x,N,C)=px$; aggregate cost reimbursement $B(x,N,C)=C$; partial cost sharing $B(x,N,C)=px + \zeta C$, where ζ is the share of cost paid by the purchaser; and a block contract $B(x,N,C)=B^*$.

The hospital maximises its utility subject to the capacity and budget constraints.   Because the number of instruments derived from the optimisation programme, $B_x(.)$, $B_n(.)$ and $B_c(.)$, are less than «the number of margins - $I+2$ - achieving a first best solution may be problematic on a number of dimensions of quality and the relationship between demand, $n(q)$ and benefit, $b(x,q)$». Two different cases are illustrated;   one quality dimension and many quality dimensions. In the first case, the authors prove that "a demand constrained first best can be implemented by a prospective payment (cost per case) contract in which payment consists only of a lump sum transfer T and a fixed price per patient treated". However, if the first best is not demand constrained, this kind of contract is ineffective in achieving the first best outcome. The possible solution to this question is to introduce a contract for the hospital «conditional on the number of patients waiting for treatment N as well as the number actually treated x».

With many dimensions of quality, additional restrictions are introduced. In fact it is still possible to achieve a first best outcome through a contract, but in this case the payment consists of a lump sum transfer T, a fixed price per patient treated and, also, a fixed amount per patient wanting to be treated which differs between unconstrained, or capacity constrained and demand constrained. In reality this kind of contract achieves a first best solution only if the purchaser values quality in the same way as patients. When this is not the case, a more complex contract is required in order to attain an efficient outcome.

While the papers described above analyse the question of incentive contracts by using a standard maximisation approach, Glazer and McGuire (1994) use a game theoretic approach, by searching for Nash equilibria. They compare two kinds of contract, fully prospective and full cost reimbursement contracts. The purpose of the paper is to analyse "whether in equilibrium hospital input decisions are distorted by the payers' incentives to engage in cost shifting". A common agency problem is implemented through a three stage game: in stage 1 two purchasers choose different contracts, in stage 2 the hospital accepts or rejects the first and/or second contract, and in stage 3 the hospital chooses the level of inputs used to treat patients. The presence of non-contractible inputs means that competition will not lead to an efficient level of hospital activity, as purchasers attempt to use the cost allocation rules to shift costs to their rivals. The effect of these rules is not clear. The two possible cost-shifting incentives for purchasers can lead to under-provision or over-provision of the input, "depending on the relative importance of the non-contractible input and the weight given to patient benefit in hospital input decisions"[Glazer and McGuire (1994)].

5. PROSPECTS FOR FUTURE RESEARCH

Democratic electoral systems are characterised by some level of asymmetry of information: candidates have incomplete information about voters' preferences and voters are uncertain about the candidate's policy promises. The agency relationship may operate in both directions. In the first case "the ill-informed citizen faced with uncertainty has to rely to some extent on a better informed politician or policy maker (the agent) to help in making choices" [Mooney (1994)]. Thus, the question becomes how politicians can be constrained by voting behaviour, or by other parties and constitutional structures, to put their policy promises into action. In fact politicians have a representative, not mandated, role and are not irrevocably bound to their electoral manifestos. Political parties do not define their programmes precisely and tend to be elusive about the way they intend to finance them. This creates a problem of information asymmetry between the elected government and the public.

As far as health care is concerned, it may be possible to introduce some «direct voter instruments», such as referenda and/or earmarked taxes, in order to reflect voters' preferences.   Earmarking provides a mean for compartmentalising fiscal decisions: the median-voter can vote separately about the quantity of each service to be supplied at a fixed «tax price». With earmarking citizens can vote independently on specific budget allocations, such as on health care.   However earmarking raises important practical problems [Jones and Duncan (1995)].

In the second case, the state may be a benevolent principal who must elicit citizens' preferences in order to maximise social welfare.   In the second view of the citizen-government relationship the government becomes the principal, which must estimate the public's preferences in order to maximise a welfare function.   But, how can the government know citizens' preferences, and how can it be sure that citizens do not behave as free-riders?   The problem of revelation of preferences has been extensively analysed in the economics literature: from Clarke-Groves mechanisms to contingent valuation, many models have been developed, the analysis of which goes beyond the scope of this paper.

In health economics it is often stressed that doctor's and patient's utilities are not independent.   This may also be true in the political arena, "where a realistic specification of the politician's decision-making process would include elements of both public interest and self-interest" [Marmor and Christianson (1992)].   This means that the separation we have made by considering the government as either an agent or a principal is too restrictive and only the simultaneous consideration of multiple agency relationships can lead to a full model of public health care expenditure.   The health care system is characterised by multi-level agency models. However the models described above tend to analyse incentive contracting between government and hospitals and doctors and patients in isolation. What are the implications for the analysis of health care markets when more than two subjects are considered? For example Laffont and Tirole (1993, ch.11) consider a three-level hierarchy: firm/agency/Congress. The model is used to explain the role of interest groups in the formation of public policy. Some modifications would be required to apply the model to health care, but it provides a framework for analysing multi-level agency relationships based on a hierarchy of providers/purchasing agencies/government.

A related way of describing health care systems is offered by common agency models. These define the case in which an agent may serve several principals. In this context one principal's attempts to influence the agent affect other principal's utility. This allows the agent to deceive both principals, possibly in different ways. In health care doctors may be agents of both patients and government. However patients' and the government's utility functions are different. An attempt to analyse the implications of this trade-off on doctors' output is given in Blomquist (1991).

In the previous pages we have described proposals for improving competition through tournaments or franchising mechanisms. The underlying idea is to achieve contestability in the health care market. Tournaments and auctions have been proposed as mechanisms to improve the competition between parties in order to increase information. In health care the use of these mechanisms is complicated by the fact that there will often be post-contractual asymmetry of information associated with the problems of monitoring the quality of health outcomes.

With regard to public health care expenditure, is it possible to define forms of "incentive contracts" to induce politicians to implement their promises? This issue is part of the more general question of commitment, analysed by Laffont and Tirole (1993, Ch.16). They investigate both the case in which the government is short-lived and the case in which politicians have longer-term career concerns. For the latter a rational re-election model is analysed in which "voters update their belief about the current government's integrity on the basis of its policy record".

The prospects outlined here represent just some of the avenues for future research that could combine the analytical insights of the agency literature with the particular characteristics of health care. In developing this research it is important to recognise the importance of altruism and inter-dependent objective functions in health care decisions, as in the work of Chalkley and Malcolmson (1995a); the problems associated with evaluating the effectiveness and efficiency of medical technology; the problems of monitoring outcomes, particularly with respect to the quality of care and its impact on patients' quality of life; and the importance of equity objectives in the design of health care systems.

ACKNOWLEDGEMENTS

This paper was presented at a meeting on «Public decision-making processes and asymmetry of information» organised by the University of Catania, 29-30 September 1995. We are grateful for comments from the participants at the meeting and from John Posnett and Carol Propper.

REFERENCES

Arrow, K. J., 1963, 'Uncertainty and the welfare economics of medical care', *American Economic Review*, 53, 941-973.

Besley, T., 1991, 'The demand for health care and health insurance', in McGuire, A., Fenn, P. and K. Mayhew (eds), *Providing Health Care*, Oxford University Press.

Besley, T. and M.Gouveia, 1994, *Alternative systems of health care provision*, mimeo, Princeton University.

Blomquist, A., 1991, 'The doctor as double agent: information asymmetry, health insurance and medical care', *Journal of Health Economics*, 10, 411-432

Chalkley, M. and J.M.Malcolmson, 1995a, 'Contracting for health services when patient demand does not reflect quality', Discussion Paper No.9514, Department of Economics, University of Southampton.

Chalkley, M. and J.M.Malcolmson, 1995b, 'Contracting for health services with unmonitored quality', Discussion Paper No.9510, Department of Economics, University of Southampton.

Chalkley, M. and J.M.Malcolmson, 1995c, 'Contracts and competition in the NHS', Discussion Paper No.9513, Department of Economics, University of Southampton.

Culyer, A. J., 1993, 'Health care insurance and provision', in Barr, N. and D. Whynes (eds), *Current Issues in the Economics of Welfare*, London, MacMillan.

Culyer, A. J. and J. Posnett, 1990, 'Hospital behaviour and competition', in Culyer, A., Maynard, A. and J Posnett (eds), *Competiton in Health Care*, London, MacMillan.

Dawson, D., 1994, 'Costs and prices in the Internal Market: market vs the NHS Executive guidelines', *CHE Discussion Paper*, 115.

Dawson, D., 1995, 'Regulating competition in the NHS. The Department of Health guide on mergers and anti-competitive behaviour', *CHE Discussion Paper*, 131.

Demski, J. and D. Sappington, 1984, 'On optimal incentive contracts with multiple agents', *Journal of Economic Theory*, 17-152-171.

Donaldson, C. and K. Gerard, 1993, *Economics of health care financing, the visible hand*, London, MacMillan.

Evans, R. G., 1974, 'Supplier induced demand; some empirical evidence and implications', in Perlman, M. (ed) *The Economic of Health and Medical Care*, London, McMillan.

Evans, R.G., 1984 *Strained mercy. The economics of Canadian health care*, Butterworths.

Evans, R.G., 1990, 'The dog in the night time: medical practice variations and health policy', in Anderson, T.F. and G.Mooney (eds.) *The Challenges of Medical Practice Variations*, London, MacMillan.

Ferguson, B. and J. Posnett, 1991, 'Pricing and openness in contracts for health care services', *Health Services Management Research*, 4, 46-52.

Glazer, J. and T.G.McGuire, 1994, 'Payer competition and cost shifting in health care', *Journal of Economics and Management Strategy*, 3, 71-92.

Hay, J. W. and M. J. Leahy, 1982, 'Physician-induced demand: an empirical analysis of the consumer information gap', *Journal of Health Economics*, 1, 231-244.

Hughes, D. and A. McGuire, 1995, 'Patient charges and the utilisation of NHS prescription medicines: some estimates using a cointegration procedure', *Health Economics*, 4, 213-220.

Jones, A.M. and A.S.Duncan, 1995, *Hypothecated health taxes: an evaluation of recent proposals*, Office of Health Economics.

Labelle, R., Stoddart, G. and T. Rice, 1994, 'A re-examination of the meaning and importance of supplier -induced demand', *Journal of Health Economics*, 13, 347-368.

Laffont, J. J. and J. Tirole, 1993, *A theory of procurement and regulation*, The MIT Press.

Levaggi, R., 1994, *NHS contracts: an agency approach*, mimeo, University of Genoa.

Lohr, K. N., et al, 1986, 'Effect of cost-sharing on use of medically effective and less effective care', *Medical Care*, 24 (Supplement), 31-38.

McGuire, A., Henderson, J. and G. Mooney, 1988, *The Economics of Health Care*, Routledge Keegan Paul.

McPherson, K., 1990, 'International differences in medical practices', in *Health Care Systems in Transition*, OECD.

Manning, W., et al.,, 1987, 'Health insurance and the demand for medical care: evidence from a randomised experiment', *American Economic Review*, 77, 251-277.

Marmor, T. R. and J.B. Christianson, 1992, *Health Care Policy*, Sage Publications.

Mooney, G. and M. Ryan, 1993, 'Agency in health care: getting beyond first principles', *Journal of Health Economics*, 12, 125-135.

Mooney, G., 1994, *Key issues in health economics*, Harvester Wheatsheaf.

Pauly, M., 1968, 'The Economics of Moral Hazard', *American Economic Review*, 58, 531-557.

Pauly, M. V., 1974, 'Overinsurance and public provision of insurance: the roles of moral hazard and adverse selection', *Quarterly Journal of Economics*, 88, 44-62.

Pauly, M. V., 1986, 'Taxation, health insurance and market failure in the medical economy', *Journal of Economic Literature*, 24, 629-75

Pauly, M. V., 1988, 'Is medical care different? Old questions, new answers', *Journal of Health Politics, Policy and Law*, 13, 227-232.

Pauly, M. V. and M. A. Satterwaite, 1981, 'The pricing of primary case physicians' service: a test of the role of consumer information', *Bell Journal of Economics*, 12, 88-506.

Pellisé, L., 1994 'Reimbursing insurance carriers: The case of "Muface" in the spanish health care system', *Health Economics*, 3, 243-253.

Phelps, C., 1986, 'Induced demand - can we ever know its extent?' *Journal of Health Economics*, 5, 355-365.

Phelps, C. and C. Mooney, 1993, 'Variations in medical practices', in Arnould, R. J., Rich, R. and W. White (eds), *Competitive Approaches to Health Care Reform*, The Urban Institute Press.

Propper, C., 1995a, 'Market structure and prices: the responses of hospitals in the U.K. National Health Service to competition', Discussion Paper No.95/390, Department of Economics, University of Bristol.

Propper, C., 1995b, 'Agency and incentives in the NHS internal market', *Social Science and Medicine*, 40, 1683-1690.

Reinhardt, U., 1985, 'The theory of physician-induced demand: reflections after a decade', *Journal of Health Economics*, 4, 187-193.

Rice, T. H., 1983, 'The impact of changing Medicare reimbursement rates on physician-induced demand', *Medical care*, 21, 803-815.

Rice, T. H., 1987, 'Comment on Phelps', *Journal of Health Economics*, 6, 375-376.

Rochaix, L., 1989, 'Information Asymmetry and Search in the Market of Physicians' Services', *Journal of Health Economics*, 8, 53-84.

Rochaix, L., 1993, 'Financial incentives for physicians : the Quebec experience', *Health Economics*, 2, 163-176.

Rossiter, L. F. and G. R. Wilensky, 1984, 'Identification of physician-induced demand', *Journal of Economic Perspectives*, 4, 135-148.

Rothschild, M. and J. Stiglitz, 1976, 'Equilibrium in competitive insurance markets: an essay in the economics of imperfect information', *Quarterly Journal of Economics*, 90, 629-650

Sappington, D. and J. Stiglitz, 1987, 'Privatisation, Information and incentives', *Journal of Policy Analysis and Management*, 6, 567-582.

Vick, S. and A. Scott, 1995, 'What makes a perfect agent? A pilot study of patients' preferences in the doctor-patient relationship', mimeo, HERU, University of Aberdeen.

Wennberg, J.E., 1984, 'Dealing with medical practice variations: a proposal for action', *Health Affairs*, 3, 6-32.

Chapter 8

INCENTIVE FAILURE AND THE MARKET FOR INFORMATION GOODS

Michele Trimarchi[*]
University of Catanzaro, Italy

1.   INTRODUCTION

The debate about the scope and limits of public intervention in the economy has often focused upon sectors strongly financed by the state like education or the arts, in which public support is often seen as the source of wasteful decisions, economic inefficiency, managerial rent-seeking and overproduction.

On the contrary, the advocates of private intervention in these sectors have emphasised that competition among the different producers, and the stronger interest of private sponsors in effectively monitoring the recipients of their support, would likely introduce powerful incentives to efficient production.

In such a view, private education would widen the choice of families, and private support of the arts would operate the desired selection among theatres; furthermore, this would give the state an opportunity to reduce the amount of resources devoted to these sectors, even if private intervention should be encouraged by some tax exemption scheme.

A question arising from such an argument concerns the likely modifications in the nature and composition of supply in the sectors in which private financing is introduced in order to reduce the financial burden of the state. Is a private firm giving contributions to a school, a university or a theatre inclined to accept the present composition of supply, or would it rather tend to prefer some units over others? Is there a risk of reduction and concentration of each sector's supply to the units more appealing for the private sponsor? How does such an outcome influence social welfare?

This paper tries to address these issues, applying the common agency framework to the sectors of education, and the arts; in these sectors a number of non-profit institutions sell goods characterised by a strong informational content, and by the presence of different components between which a trade-off is also recorded in consumers' evaluation. The next section will attempt a description of such characteristics, emphasising the preferences of each sponsor. Section three will describe the relationships among public and private sponsors and non-profit producers of such goods within a common agency framework, describing the likely types of each agent and arguing that each type is strictly dependent upon each agent's organisational structure. Section four will examine the possible outcomes of such relationships, showing that the principals do not manage to extract the agent's informational rents. Each principal will induce the agent to lie to the other, finding himself in a dilemma, since on one hand he wants the agent to sell products characterised by his like aspect, but on the other he prefers not to be the sole sponsor. Section five will sketch some conclusive remarks, suggesting that a non-paternalistic selection of activities can be obtained through specialisation of support on the part of principals, with the private sector giving financial contributions, and the public sector giving in-kind subsidies.

2.   INFORMATION GOODS

Information is very often the object of exchange; many economic agents purchase information in order to adopt their decisions, to sign contracts, to verify whether a contract is implemented, to evaluate the likely profitability of some activity. There are also cases in which information is the main characteristic of some goods, which are made the object of exchange because of their content of information; higher education and the performed arts are among the sectors producing and selling goods that consumers buy in order to increase their own stock of knowledge.

The value of such goods is strongly dependent upon subjective evaluations, since the utility derived from their consumption is increasing with the amount of the information stock already possessed, and also to the intrinsic heterogeneity of the different units forming the stock. A further characteristic of such goods is the impossibility to consider them strictly private goods, on one hand because of their imperfect divisibility and excludability, on the other because the externalities they produce are not easily internalisable. For the sake of simplicity we can therefore distinguish between a private component, divisible and measurable, and a public one, less easily identifiable and evaluable, but clearly (although generically) perceived by consumers.

In higher education, it is possible to identify such components respectively in technical and scientific knowledge on one hand and in classical studies on the other. Pupils of a technical school can manage quite precisely to identify the amount of learning supplied, and above all they can eventually evaluate the causal link between such learning and the increase in their future earnings; such a relationship is almost impossible to evaluate when it comes to classical learning, in which it appears very difficult to establish the effective amount of notions necessary to form a teacher, a philosopher, a literary critic or a creative artist.

As far as the arts are concerned, we can identify the two components in what we could define "culture" and "entertainment", the former being an increase in consumers' stock of knowledge and in social cultural wealth, the latter being on the contrary a source of individual utility; consumers purchase units of the arts, searching for unknown units - whose value is not easily determined - if their aim is an increase in their stock of knowledge (see Trimarchi, 1993), or looking for "popular"[1] units of which any consumer can identify the utility he will derive.

The composition of supply in the sectors we are dealing with, associated with the low willingness to pay on the part of consumers who cannot properly test the quality of their purchases before consumption, justifies the low level of admission fees or prices for the goods exchanged in these sectors, such as a school year or a theatrical season: the revenues accruing to producers from consumer expenditure are never sufficient to cover the production costs of such sectors, a wide proportion of which is represented by fixed costs; as a consequence, the public sector is called to support financially these sectors, as long as taxpayers are not willing to record their progressive contraction and eventual extinction (see for all Baumol and Baumol, 1985).

Of course, in the light of our description of the different components of the information goods sold in the education and the arts sectors, it could be possible to enucleate, within each sector's supply, those units which, being more easily measurable, imply less uncertain evaluations and give to their sponsors the possibility to verify the worthiness of their support in terms of the results obtained (i.e. of the utility derived by the direct consumers).

In such a respect a major problem for the public sector supporting the non-profit producers is given by the strong relevance of adverse selection; this is mainly due to the heterogeneity of the different units sold in each of the sectors examined, together with the need to possess adequate technical tools in order to evaluate their quality; monitoring also appears to be costly and, above all, technically difficult, giving only controversial results due to the subjectivity of evaluations typical of such sectors. The producers can use their private information about the proportion of the different components of their own supply in order to obtain a higher financial support than what they would obtain if their sponsors could evaluate the actual composition and quality of their supply.

Therefore, it is easy to observe that the problem is not correctly addressed when the suggestion is made of leaving such sectors to the rules of the marketplace, and to the sole financial support coming from private sources. A major objection is that private sponsors are not interested in units of supply for which it is difficult - if not impossible - to formulate any uncontroversial evaluation, since this does not allow them to effectively compare effort and outcome.

This could induce the producers of information goods to specialise in the provision of units in which the "private" component is prevailing, therefore limiting their supply to technical education, or popular live performances; accountants and physicians would crowd out archaeologists (and economists?), and the surviving opera companies would perform "The Happy Widow" much more often than "Semiramide"[2].

Although we have pointed at the trade-off existing between the two different components of the information goods, we must acknowledge that within their supply there is often a grey area in which both components can coexist (e.g. the case of a live performance providing a strong increase in consumer's cultural stock and entertaining at the same time); in any case, even if the trade-off is not always perfect, there is evidence that the sole public or private support for the arts ends up influencing the composition of supply, making culture and, respectively, entertainment prevail in either case (Di Maggio, 1984).

The problem is then to let both the public sector and private corporations give their contributions to support the sectors we are dealing with, in order to avoid the loss of important parts of their total supply and to overcome the threat of extinction that an insufficient level of financing would imply. Moreover, while each sponsor will likely prefer its "like" components, this does not mean that the "opposite" component is absolutely ignored: there are some private schools teaching the humanities, and some private art companies supporting experimental or innovative live performances.

3.   ORGANISATION AND EXCHANGE

The description made above does not necessarily imply a rigid distinction between objectives of the public and the private sectors. In fact, quite often the state gives support to "private" education, or to entertaining live performances; this appears to be consistent with constitutional aims, since objectives like technical specialisation, or the quantitative diffusion of the arts appear to be quite relevant in order to increase social welfare.

On the other hand, it must be noted that even private corporations are not as rigid as it might seem at first sight in pursuing typically "public" objectives, providing classical studies, or high culture. This is generally made for reputational aims, and it appears not negligible within the wider set of the financial interactions between firms and nonprofits operating in the sectors we are dealing with.

The following discussion is explicitly based upon the production and exchange mechanisms of the performed arts sector; of course, such a framework can be easily adapted to higher education and to the other sectors producing and selling information goods.

The exchange network among the public sector, private corporations and the non-profit institutions producing live performances can be examined as a complex principal / agent framework in which heterogeneous objectives can be pursued by each of the parties involved. It is possible to attempt an explanation of such a multiplicity, starting from the observation that the choice of objectives is strongly dependent upon the decisional processes and therefore upon the organisational structure of each institution.

In such a respect, the analysis of the internal structure of each institution can lead us to identify the prevailing objective-functions and therefore the possible types of each agent involved in the process in which public and private financing are exchanged for a certain kind and level of activity on the part of non-profit institutions operating in the sector of the performed arts.

In fact, the objective of each institution is likely to be determined by the prevailing arguments in the utility function of its managers; we can simply identify the possible extremes of a smooth, continuous set of types: at one extreme, each institution producing and exchanging live performances tends to consider cultural activity as a sort of mission, at the other the production and sale of live performances is considered a commercial activity which gives material advantages to its producers and sponsors.

Cultural institutions can be "mission orientated" if they appear to offer units of the performed arts characterised by experimental or innovative aspects, able to generate substantial increases in consumers' cultural stock, and indifferent towards the success they will obtain at the box office: it is typical of nonprofits' managers to derive utility from their activity *per se*. At the other extreme, cultural institutions can be described as "revenue orientated", also taking into account that the non-profit constraint concerns the eventual distribution and not the mere existence of net revenues; in such a case, they will likely set a programme characterised by popular shows in the attempt to attract the largest possible audience, also employing superstars in order to set the price at quite high levels. We can presume that each cultural institution will appear to be closer to the "mission orientated" type as long as the proportion of artistic personnel involved in its organisation is higher.

The public sector can appear, in the same way, "culture orientated" and therefore tends to support those units of the performed arts which are likely to contribute to the development of social cultural wealth (these are "novel" units of culture, characterised by an innovative mix of artistic or technical factors). At the opposite extreme the public sector can be defined "consensus orientated", favouring popular units of culture in order to exchange "bread and circuses" for votes.

We can hypothesise a stronger preference for the culture orientated type on the part of agencies *ad hoc* such as the Arts Council of Great Britain, in which the bureaucratic structure is not deriving utility from the amount and distribution of the subsidies channelled to cultural institutions, and whose managers or consultants very often come from the performed arts sector showing a strong preference for "cultural" units of culture (see Peacock and Ricketts, 1990).

On the other hand, state departments appear to be more inclined to favour popular units of culture, since these appear to widen the scope for bargaining with the performed arts institutions; local governments, whose bureaus are managed by elected politicians, tend to support those units of culture for which their financial effort is visible to the widest possible proportion of their constituency.

Finally, private firms can also be either "reputation orientated" (and therefore prefer a higher level of culture, in order to associate their brand-name to live events of performed arts institutions characterised by a strong cultural content), or "publicity orientated", in order to convey their brand-name to a wide audience attracted by the popular live shows these firms decide to support. In such a case, rather than the internal organisation of private firms, a relevant influence upon the choice to support activities of either kind is exerted by the kind of sector they operate in, although the borderline cannot be precisely defined[3].

The exchange occurring between the two principals and the agent is made up of different stages, in which each party reveals his type, a contract is set, the exchange operated and the eventual monitoring exerted. In the sectors considered, we must take into account some specific aspects: *a)* the contract is normally repeated, its time horizon normally covers a year (normally a theatrical season); *b)* there is no tournament among the potential recipients of financial support given from both the public and the private sectors; rather, they appear to enjoy a certain degree of monopoly within a certain area or subsector, and this implies that there is seldom actual competition between potential recipients for the event of public and/or private support; *c)* only a tighter budget constraint could increase the competition to a certain extent; *d)* the level of price is not relevant for the clauses of the contract; this is because there are units of supply (in our example, the units with a high experimental or innovative component) for which the consumers show a low propensity to pay, since their consumption can expand their stock of knowledge but it does not necessarily imply a high level of entertainment; these units cannot be successfully sold even at zero price, since those who do not want to consume them are not induced by a low price to change their mind. On the other hand, for some units (in the arts sector, an example can be given by popular operas such as "Traviata") consumer's surplus appears to be quite high, allowing considerable increases in the price level, since the potential consumers are confident that they will derive a very high satisfaction from the attendance at such performances (see Blaug, 1978). In both cases, setting a threshold for the price level is not the first objective of regulators, and the determination of price levels (corresponding to the different units of the total supply) is left to the knowledge each producer has of the demand he faces.

4. COMMON AGENCY

A further characteristic of the market for information goods is that the agent does not sell his output to the principals, as normally happens in many regulated sectors, but offers it to consumers. The producing institutions can then be considered common input suppliers for a more complex production organised by the public sector and some private corporations. It enjoys the advantages of private information both upon its own characteristics and the structure of its costs and upon the contents of its supply (i.e. the proportion of the different components of such supply).

The programme of activity the agent is committed to undertake after having contracted with the principals can record the prevalence of either component of the information good; in the performed arts sector, the programme of live performances covering a whole season can be either culture-intensive or entertainment-intensive, according to the mix of these components in the various performances; the evaluation about the actual proportion of either component remains strongly linked to subjective arguments, therefore each principal has to rely on the agent's report in order to adopt his decision about the level of support.

The exchange process among the principals and the agent can be viewed as a sequential game, in which the sequence of moves develops along the following lines: *a)* each principal reveals his type, setting the criteria according to which the level of support will be identified; *b)* the agent, having known such criteria, sets his programme (the performances in a season, the mix of subjects, the research project) and thus reports his type to each principal; at this stage, the principals have no way of making inferences upon the agent's true type, therefore they must rely upon the agent's report; *c)* a contract is signed between each principal and the agent; the coexistence of both principals is not necessary, therefore the relationship we are describing can be considered a kind of "delegated" common agency (see Bernheim and Whinston, 1986); in such a contract a certain level of activity characterised by an unobservable proportion of the different components of supply is exchanged for a certain level of financial support; d) the agent produces and sells the good; the outcome is observed by the principals who try to infer the agent's true type from the outcome of his activity.

As far as the payoffs are concerned, we must consider that both principals and the agent derive from the game mostly immaterial payoffs: even if the goods are sold to individual consumers in exchange for a price, the payoff obtained by each agent is often nonpecuniary: *a)* the institutions producing information goods tend to pursue a complex reward, in which revenues are just one of the arguments, since activity *per se*, reputation, the position occupied in the sector, ideological relevance (either in the arts or in the intellectual club) appear to have quite a strong importance in the utility function of managers and workers of such institutions; *b)* public sector contracts with cultural, research or educational institutions in order to obtain the provision of goods and services which are among its constitutional aims; *c)* the private firms supporting such institutions either to keep or widen their market share (and in such a case, the indirect reward is pecuniary), or to strengthen their own reputation: in the latter hypothesis, things are quite complex, and the aim can be for example the access to qualified shares of the market (certain consumer classes).

A further remark must be made about the payoff obtained by private firms supporting an institution producing information goods; in many advanced countries, support given by private firms (and often also by individuals) is encouraged through tax exemptions; in any case, such a rule normally determines the tax exemption as a proportion of the total amount of support given; such process is automatic, therefore the managers of private firms willing to give their financial support to any institution producing information goods discounts *ex ante* the value of such exemption when the decision is adopted; there is no scope for any bargaining between the public sector and the firm.

Some observations are necessary: first of all, the kind of exchange is often peculiar, since in the hypothesis of private support of the arts there can be cases in which the agent sells his audience to a private firm selling information upon its own brand-name or, more specifically, upon a product. In a different respect, even if the outcome is observable by each principal, the subjectivity of quality and the eventual difficulty in evaluating the actual ability to increase one's cultural stock does not allow the principals to correctly infer the agent's true type. It is then quite difficult to extract the agent's informational rents, in order to evaluate whether and how a contract for the next period must be written.

The agent's type θ, belonging to a compact set $\Theta \equiv [\underline{\theta}, \overline{\theta}]$, is distributed according to the differentiable density function $f(\theta) > 0$ with cumulative distribution function $F(\theta)$; it is known by each principal simply through the report directly received by the agent; the joint perception of the agent's report does not eliminate the problem, since there may be a certain amount of cheap talk and side negotiations between the agent and each single principal.

The contract $y_i(\cdot)$ chosen by each principal[4] includes a decision $x_i(\cdot)$ and a monetary transfer $t_i(\cdot)$ paid to the agent: $y_i(\hat{\theta}) = [x_i(\hat{\theta}), t_i(\hat{\theta})]$. The principals' utility functions are given by $V^i(x_i, \theta) - t_i$, $i = 1,2$; we assume that the level of activity provided by the agent to principal j does not affect principal's i utility. The agent's utility function is $U(x_1, x_2, \theta) + t_1 + t_2$. Since the components of the goods sold are considered as substitutes, contracting with one principal affects the agent's marginal utility, and therefore affects the costs of contracting with the other principal. Given a contract pair, the agent's indirect utility is a function of reports and type,

$$U(\hat{\theta}_1, \hat{\theta}_2, \theta) = U(x_1(\hat{\theta}_1), x_2(\hat{\theta}_2), \theta) + t_1(\hat{\theta}_1) + t_2(\hat{\theta}_2).$$

Of course, the possible combinations of types make different outcomes possible; there are cases in which the principals and the agent appear to pursue the same objective; for example, they can be equally culture orientated in the arts sector: this happens when the public sector is interested in the increase in society's cultural stock, private firms want to enhance their own reputation, and arts institutions are mission orientated, since their managers are more inclined to produce high culture rather than to earn high revenues.

In such a case, the contract which maximises the principals' utility must have decisional functions which satisfy

$$V_{x_i}^i(x_i) + U_{x_i}(x_1, x_2, \theta) = \left[1 - F(\theta) / f(\theta)\right] U_{x,\theta}(x_1, x_2, \theta)$$

and optimal transfers which satisfy

$$t(\theta) = \int_{\underline{\theta}}^{\theta} U_{\theta}(x_1(s), x_2(s), s) ds - U(x_1(\underline{\theta}), x_2(\underline{\theta}), \underline{\theta}).$$

5.   INCENTIVE FAILURE

The contracted levels of activity to be undertaken by the agent are below the efficient level for all $\theta < \theta$. In fact, for each θ the principals maximise their virtual surplus, i.e. the real contractual gains less the expected information rents of the agent. The result is not optimal if the principals do not care about their joint surplus and therefore act noncooperatively[5].

In fact, there are many cases in which, due also to the different time horizon in which the public and the private sectors take their decisions, the principals pursue reciprocally conflicting objectives, and the contract appears to depend on the agent's report meant specifically for each principal. Therefore the transfer is independent of the level of activity provided to the other principal, while it depends upon the agent's type as it has been reported to each principal.

The pair of contracts is implementable if the transfer function satisfies the common incentive compatibility constraint:

$$U(\theta, \theta, \theta) > U(\hat{\theta}_1, \hat{\theta}_2, \theta), \quad \forall (\hat{\theta}_1, \hat{\theta}_2, \theta) \in \Theta^3$$

It is commonly feasible if the decision functions are implementable, and the transfer can satisfy the participation constraint:

$$U(\theta, \theta, \theta) > 0, \quad \forall \theta \in \Theta.$$

Since the components of the goods we are dealing with appear to be substitutes, i.e. $U_{x_1 x_2} < 0$, then common implementability is obtained if

$$t_i' = -U_{x_i}(x_1, x_2, \theta)x_i', \quad i = 1,2$$

$$U_{x_1 x_2}(x_1, x_2, \theta)x_1'x_2' + U_{x,\theta}(x_1, x_2, \theta)x_i' > 0, \quad i = 1,2$$

$$U_{x_1\theta}U_{x_2\theta}x_1'x_2' + U_{x_1 x_2}x_1'x_2'[U_{x_1\theta}x_1' + U_{x_2\theta}x_2'] > 0.$$

Each principal finds it convenient to induce the agent to report falsely to his rival, extracting in such a way a larger share of the agent's information rents: each principal's contract can be changed in such a way so as to induce the agent to choose a contract pair from the other principal which he had not originally intended. This can allow the agent to obtain additional rents from the contract with principal 2, and principal 1 can manage to extract part of these additional rents in his new contract. Since the components of information goods are taken here as substitutes, in our hypothesis, an increase in the level of activity contracted with one principal results in a decrease in the activity contracted with the other principal through the revelation of a different type on the part of the agent.

This can be considered a sort of principal's dilemma, since each principal (and mainly the public one) is certainly interested in an increase of support coming from the other principal, for reasons linked with the budget constraint and the arising opportunity to increase the level of support given to other recipients. On the other hand, each principal knows that a wider support of the agent's activity can produce a stronger influence upon his choices, and can therefore make the composition of supply shift to the advantage of the other principal. In fact, if the components of output are substitutes, then the agent prefers to contract in a common agency environment which allows him to take advantage from his private information and from the potential conflict between the principals.

In the performed arts sector, the principals will likely offer the agent a more powerful incentive structure rather than accepting that in the agent's activity the component pursued by the rival principal prevails. This is often because of the ideological characteristics of the goods provided by the agent, and because the possibility of both components indicated above being not actual substitutes is not predictable and it is in any case perceivable *ex post*, once the consumption has been made. Therefore, the agent prefers common agency while the principals prefer cooperative equilibrium.

6. POLICY IMPLICATIONS

The description of the interactions among the public and private sponsors and the producers of information goods suggests that, as long as the mechanisms of public support of the arts are essentially based upon quantitative indexes, the recipients of public monetary transfers can easily manage to exploit their own private information through falsely reporting to their public principal about characteristics which appear to be impossible or controversial to monitor.

In such a respect, risk is shifted towards the public sector, and adverse selection operates encouraging entry for those producers who appear to be revenue orientated, ignoring the cultural value of their supply. A possible way to overcome many of the problems generated by adverse selection is to introduce a mechanism of vertical specialisation in financial support of producers; given the high fixed costs recorded in the sectors examined, the principal orientated towards the public component of the information goods can find it convenient to give in-kind input subsidies rather than untied monetary transfers.

This could bring to a virtuous selection among the different potential recipients of public support: only the mission orientated non-profit institutions can derive substantial advantages thanks to the opportunity to use public resources without paying any price or fee for their utilisation; on the other hand, the provision of in-kind subsidies discourages the institutions mainly interested in obtaining financial contribution: they can either attempt to convince a private firm to support their activity, or they can alter the composition of their supply increasing the proportion of entertainment.

Producers orientated towards the public component of the information goods will derive great advantage from the free provision of productive factors on the part of the public sector, only when their activity proves to be financially sound, able to attract new consumers (whose contribution would cover for example the artists' salaries) and less sensitive to the need to earn a high revenue (see Throsby, 1994). On the contrary, the revenue orientated producers would find little advantage in the provision of in-kind input subsidies, whose proportion of the total financial need would be negligible: a company producing musical shows could hardly consider the opportunity to perform in a small publicly owned theatre.

To sum up, specialisation of support on the part of public and private principals of a common agent producing information goods can imply several advantages: *a)* it avoids or limits the retention of rents on the part of the common agent, since in-kind input subsidies make any interest in reporting falsely the agent's type fade; *b)* it eliminates waste and double subsidisation in the cases in which there are many sources of support, each of which is not informed about the amount of transfers given by the others; *c)* it eliminates or reduces the possibility of widening the gap between strong and weak (established and young) institutions; *d)* it induces the agent to select among the different sources of support in order to contract with the principals who appear to be closer to his own type; *e)* it encourages the heterogeneity and diversification of supply, without restricting its composition to the more easily measurable units (see Trimarchi, 1996) and hence reducing social welfare. With the necessary adaptations, such conclusions appear to apply also to the higher education sector.

In-kind subsidies can therefore be an effective screening device, when adverse selection is relevant within an exchange network involving two or more principals and a common agent producing information goods. It can be interesting to observe that such a mechanism brings us to the conclusion that when a sector is supported by both public and private sponsors, increases in social welfare can be obtained through more advanced interactions between them rather than through the mere quantitative reduction of public intervention; specialisation of support appears to respond quite effectively to some unresolved questions regarding the desired role of both the public and the private sectors in a complex economy.

NOTES

* The Author wishes to thank Jean-Jacques Laffont, Malcolm Rees, Martin Ricketts and Keith Shaw for the comments at an earlier version of this paper. The usual caveat applies.

[1] "Lowbrow" according to the definition provided by Austen-Smith (1984).
[2] The examples provided represent a strong simplification, in order to show that the greater proportion of supply would be represented by units characterised by a prevailing private component; of course, such examples do not carry any ethical judgement about this hypothesis.
[3] Even petrol or cigarette companies give financial support to live performances of a very high quality, not necessarily characterised by a strong popular appeal.
[4] The description of the contract and of its implications is based upon the analysis made by Stole (1992).
[5] See Stole (1992).

REFERENCES

Austen-Smith, D., 1984, "Subsidies to the Arts with Multiple Public Donors", *Economic Record*, 60 : 381-89.

Baumol, W., 1985, "On the Cost Disease and its True Policy Implications for the Arts", in Greenaway, D. and G.K. Shaw (eds.), *Public Choice, Public Finance and Public Policy. Essays in Honour of Alan Peacock*, Oxford, Blackwell : 67-77.

Bernheim, D. and M. Whinston, 1986, "Common Agency", *Econometrica*, 54 : 923-42.

Blaug, M.,1978, "Why Are Covent Garden Seat Prices so High?", *Journal of Cultural Economics*, 2: 1-20.

Di Maggio, P.J.,1984, "The Nonprofit Instrument and the Influence of the Marketplace on Policies in the Arts", in McNeil Lowry, W. (ed.), *The Arts and Public Policy in the United States*, Englewood Cliffs, N.J., Prentice-Hall: 57-99.

Fudenberg, D. and J. Tirole, 1991, *Game Theory*, Boston, Mass., The M.I.T. Press.

Laffont, J.-J. and J. Tirole, 1993, *A Theory of Invcentives in Procurement and Regulation*, Boston, Mass., The M.I.T. Press.

Peacock, A.T. and M.J. Ricketts, 1990, "Government and Industry", mimeo.

Stole, L.A., 1992, "Mechanism Design under Common Agency", mimeo.

Throsby, C.D., 1994, "A Work-Preference Model of Artist Behaviour", in Peacock, A. and I. Rizzo (eds.), *Cultural Economics and Cultural Policies*, Dordrechts, Kluwer: 69-80.

Trimarchi, M., 1993, *Economia e Cultura. Organizzazione e Finanziamento delle Istituzioni Culturali*, Milano, Angeli.

Trimarchi, M., 1996, "The Economics of Cultural Institutions. Information and Incentives in the Performed Arts Sector", forthcoming.

Index